DEMYSTIFYING SHAMANS AND THEIR WORLD

DEMYSTIFYING
SHAMANS
AND THEIR WORLD

A MULTIDISCIPLINARY STUDY

Adam J. Rock &
Stanley Krippner

imprint-academic.com

Published in the UK by Imprint Academic
PO Box 200, Exeter EX5 5YX, UK

Published in the USA by Imprint Academic
Philosophy Documentation Center
PO Box 7147, Charlottesville, VA 22906-7147, USA

ISBN 9 781845 402228

A CIP catalogue record for this book is available from the
British Library and US Library of Congress

Contents

Preface: Why Attention Must Be Paid to Shamanism ix

Introduction: An Overview of the Chapters. 1

1. Shamanism and Shamans: Points and Counterpoints 7

2. Epistemology and Technologies of Shamanic Knowledge 41

3. The Confusion of Consciousness with Phenomenological
   Content in Shamanic Studies. 77

4. Two Cross-Cultural Models for Studying Shamanic
   Healing Systems 91

5. Applying a 10-Facet Model to North and South American
   Shamanic Dream Systems. 113

6. The Construction of an Ontology and Epistemology of
   Shamanic Journeying Imagery 141

7. Necessary Conditions for Shamanic Journeying Imagery 153

8. The Issue of Realism and Shamanic Journeying Imagery 165

9. Methods for Studying Shamanic Reports of Psychic Phenomena 179

10. Shamanism and the Demystification Journey. 195

References. 215

Indexes 249

ACKNOWLEDGEMENTS

The authors express their gratitude to Jürgen Kremer, Stephen Brown, Rosemary Coffey, Steve Hart, and Cheryl Fracasso for their editorial assistance, and the Saybrook University Chair for the Study of Consciousness for its support in the preparation of this book.

PERMISSIONS

Portions of this book were originally published as articles in *American Psychologist* (2002, vol. 57, pp. 962-977), *International Journal of Transpersonal Studies* (2008, vol. 27, pp. 12-19), *Journal of Consciousness Studies* (2000, vol. 7, pp. 93-118), *Journal of Shamanic Practice* (2009, vol. 2, 33-40), *Transpersonal Psychology Review* (2008, vol. 12, pp. 23-31), *North American Journal of Psychology* (2007, vol. 9, pp. 485-500), *Psi Research* (1984, vol. 3, pp. 4-16), and *Journal of Scientific Exploration* (2008, vol. 22, pp. 215-226).

Permission to reprint has been granted by the publishers.

This book is dedicated to
Michael and Sandra Harner
and to shamans past, present and future

Michael Harner, Ph.D. is an anthropologist and founder of the Foundation for Shamanic Studies, an international nonprofit organisation dedicated to preserving shamanic knowledge.

Sandra Harner, Ph.D. served as co-founder and Vice President of the Foundation for Shamanic Studies and also serves on its international teaching faculty.

Both of these visionaries recognised the importance of preserving shamanic traditions and adapting them to help contemporary people face the ecological and existential crises of the 21st century.

Why Attention Must Be Paid To Shamanism

Albert Einstein once wrote, "The most beautiful thing we can experience is the mysterious. It is the source of all true art and all science. He to whom this emotion is a stranger, who can no longer pause to wonder and stand rapt in awe, is as good as dead: his eyes are closed." Einstein's comments certainly apply to scholarly studies of shamanism, a composite of spiritual practices and rituals found worldwide. After reviewing the literature on this topic, Narby and Huxley (2001) concluded, "Even after five hundred years of reports on shamanism, its core remains a mystery. One thing that has changed..., however, is the gaze of the observers. It has opened up. And understanding is starting to flower" (p. 8).

Much of the mystery surrounding the phenomenon of shamanism is perhaps attributable to the fact that it emerged during a time of preliteracy. Thus little is known about its origins. Although the term "shaman" is of uncertain derivation, it is often traced to the language of the Tungus reindeer herders of Siberia, where the word *šaman* translates into "one who is excited, moved, or raised" (Casanowicz, 1924; Lewis, 1990, pp. 10–12). An alternative translation for the Tungus word is "inner heat," and an alternative etymology is the Sanskrit word *saman* or "song" (Hoppal, 1987). Each of these terms applies to the activities of shamans, past and present, who enter what is sometimes described as "an ecstatic state" in order to engage in spiritual rituals and psychological practices for the benefit of their community (Hoppal, 1987, pp. 91–92; Krippner, 1992).

When Eliade (1989) called shamans "technicians of ecstasy", he used the term *ecstasy* to describe "a trance during which his soul is believed to leave his body and ascend to the sky or descend to the underworld" (p. 5). However, not all shamans undertake this type of "ecstatic journey"; in many cases, the shaman might incorporate a spirit, an animal ally, or some other discarnate entity in order to obtain information of value to his or her social group (Peters & Price-Williams, 1980). Voluntary incorporation is not to be confused with involuntary possession. A member of the shaman's community might be "possessed" by a demon or malicious spirit, and this condition might require shamanic intervention of one type of another. However, shamans are in control of whatever agency they incorporate, even if it is a demon they have tricked into leaving the body of its victim in favour of that of the shaman, who eventually disposes of it in one way or another. This process usually involves a struggle that is far from "ecstatic". Neither is the "dark night of the soul" experienced as being "ecstatic", even though it is part of many shamanic initiations. Hence, "technicians of ecstasy" is far from inclusive as a term that describes shamans.

The adaptive character of shamanism is confirmed by its appearance around the world, not only in hunter-gatherer and fishing societies, but in more centralised societies as well. A hallmark of shamanism is its ubiquity, even though its cultural diversity is obvious to anyone who makes a serious study of the topic. Shamans are labelled differently in different cultures, and their roles have evolved in tandem with the needs of those cultures. Eliade provided a list of what he considered universal functions of shamans, but Heinze (1991) found many exceptions. Contrary to Eliade, she identified shamans who did not claim to control animals, to have immunity to fire, to have experienced "dismemberment", or to have had a near-fatal illness that constituted a shamanic "call". Heinze did find a universal response to community needs among the shamans she interviewed, and these needs often required mediation between the living and the dead, between the sacred and the profane, between the "upper world" and the "lower world", and even between shamans' own masculine and feminine attributes. Wearing clothes of the opposite gender is a common practice in many shamanic traditions; indeed, it was a custom that alarmed European visitors to Siberia and the Americas because it violated their conventional gender boundaries. Furthermore, shamans often play the role of "tricksters" who violate borders and cross limits in order to challenge a person, a family, or a community for a variety of reasons, among them to force their onlookers to conceptualise problems in novel ways. Indeed, it is noteworthy that shamanism is currently attracting increasing interest as an alternative or complementary therapeutic technique in the disciplines of psychotherapy and medicine (Bittman et al., 2001).

Winkelman (2010) maintained that shamanism has emerged worldwide and has survived because it involves adaptive potentials derived from the structure of the brain and the evolution of consciousness (p. 4). Nonetheless, Hubbard (2003) pointed out that mainstream science has tended to dismiss shamanism as manifesting psychopathology, charlatanism, or both. Indeed, the present book was born of the conviction that attention must be paid to shamanism because it is a worthwhile academic study. Consequently, this in no sense is a book that belittles shamans or their contributions. In addition, it is our contention that, in order for academics to grasp the nature of shamanic phenomena, there are useful research strategies, such as those exemplified by this book. Each chapter in this book whittles away at one or more shamanic "mysteries" by placing shamanic imagery, shamanic journeying, shamanic incorporation, shamanic healing, and so on into terms more understandable from a multidisciplinary perspective. However, we must emphasise that our aim is not to reduce the authority and utility of these phenomena; we are merely recasting them.

Although so-called *neo-shamanism* is becoming faddish in the West (Taylor & Piedilato, 2002), indigenous shamans are becoming increasingly endangered (Walsh, 1990a, p. 267). It is crucial to learn what shamanism has to offer the social and behavioural sciences before archival research in libraries replaces field research as the best available method for investigating these prototypical psychologists.

An Overview of the Chapters

In Chapter 1 we attempt to demonstrate that Western perspectives on shamanism have changed and clashed over the centuries. This chapter presents points and counterpoints regarding what might be termed the demonic model, the charlatan model, the mental illness model, the *soul flight* model, the decadent and crude technology model, and the deconstructionist model of shamanism. Indeed, Western interpretations of shamanism often reveal more about the observer than they do about the observed. In addressing this challenge, we note that the study of shamanism could make contributions to cognitive neuroscience, social psychology, psychological therapy, and ecological psychology.

In Chapter 2 we contend that the shamans' epistemology, or ways of knowing, depended on deliberately altering their awareness and/or heightening their perception to contact "spiritual entities" in "upper worlds", "lower worlds", and "middle earth" (i.e., ordinary reality). For the shaman, the totality of inner and outer reality is fundamentally an immense *signal system*, and the shaman's entries into so-called "shamanic states of consciousness" were the first steps toward deciphering this signal system. We point out that *Homo sapiens* was probably unique among early humans in the ability to symbolise, mythologize, and, eventually, to shamanize. This species' eventual domination may have been due to its ability to take sensorimotor activity and use it as a bridge to produce narratives that facilitated human survival. Shamanic technologies, essential for the dramatic production and ritual performance of myths and other narratives, interacted with shamanic epistemology, reinforcing its basic assumptions about reality.

Chapter 3 features a critical examination of the term "shamanic states of consciousness". We argue that affixing the qualifier "shamanic states" to the noun "consciousness" results in a theoretical confusion of consciousness and its content; that is, consciousness is mistaken for the content of consciousness. We refer to this fallacy as the "consciousness/content fallacy". We argue that this fallacy can be avoided if one replaces "shamanic states of consciousness" with "shamanic patterns of phenomenal properties", an extrapolation of the term "phenomenal field". Implications of the consciousness/content fallacy for "states of consciousness" studies are also considered. Thus it would follow that shamans could be defined as socially designated practitioners who are capable of shifting their patterns of phenomenal properties to obtain information not ordinarily available to other members of their community, using that information to help and to heal community members as well as the community as a whole. We consider this definition operational because it describes shamans in terms that can be observed and, to some extent, measured. One can identify the social group that selected its shamanic practitioners, one can describe the shaman's phenomenal shifts (preferably using the shaman as informant), one can record the information provided by the shaman, and one can observe and measure the effects it appears to have on the well-being of both an individual and a group.

Chapter 4 presents two contemporary templates that can be used for cross-cultural comparisons of healing systems. We have chosen one North American and one Asian system, comparing them with each other as well as with Western biomedicine. The differences in theory and practice are obvious, but, at a more subtle level, one can see some commonalities, especially in terms of how the outcome depends, in part, upon the effectiveness of the placebo response and the dynamics of the client-practitioner relationship. As was the case with the dream model, these two healing models allow for a full description of indigenous healing systems, with no compromise being necessary to force native beliefs and customs into a Western conceptual box.

Chapter 5 describes a 10-facet model that has been, and can be, applied for the cross-cultural study of shamanic dream systems. While this model was originally used to compare Western systems such as those used by Freudians and Jungians, its application to indigenous North and South American dream systems yielded instances of complexity and sophistication that are helpful in comprehending why dream reports play a vital role in many of these cultures.

In Chapter 6 we argue that attempts to elucidate the kinds of "thing" or "things" to which the term "shamanic journeying image" is referentially linked must grapple with two related questions: What is the fundamental nature of shamanic journeying images? And how might the origin of a shamanic journeying image be found? The first question is ontological, concerned with the nature and essence of shamanic journeying images. In contrast, the second is epistemological and methodological, concerned with how to acquire knowledge of shamanic journeying images. We demonstrate how inductive and deductive reasoning, the private language argument, and reification render problematic the resolution of both questions.

In Chapter 7 we propose criteria pertaining to four necessary conditions for a visual mental image to qualify as a shamanic journeying image. Subsequently, we demonstrate how these necessary conditions may be used to extrapolate a scoring system that allows one to test empirically, via falsification, a visual mental image's ostensible shamanic status. If this approach is found useful for identifying the status of shamanic imagery, it could be applied to other shamanic experiences and behaviours.

The aim of Chapter 8 is to examine the relationship between the shaman's conscious experiences and the *spirit world*. We point out that numerous scholars have suggested that shamans are "realists" in the sense that they conceptualise their multi-layered universe (e.g., upper, middle, and lower worlds) as real, objective, and independent of the perceiver. We contend, however, that previous research has neglected to analyse the logical coherence of a realist interpretation of these shamanic "nonphysical" worlds (NPWs). We address this lacuna first by determining which variant of realism is most consistent with the shaman's purported views concerning the ontological status of the aforementioned NPWs. Subsequently, we consider shamanic journeying imagery with regards to the key definitional elements of the term "mental image". Finally, we formulate three premises pertaining to shamanic journeying imagery and NPWs with the aim of assessing the logical coherence of the shaman's realist ontology. We conclude that, if shamanic journeying images constitute mental images, then this does not necessarily preclude shamanic NPWs from existing independently of the percipient's mind-body configuration(s).

The shaman often plays a trickster role, and there are numerous accounts of shamanism that are filled with alleged phenomena that cross the boundaries of what mainstream science knows about time, space, and energy. Are these phenomena the trickster's sleight-of-hand at play? Or could at least some of them resemble the reported anomalies studied by parapsychologists? Chapter 9 describes various research methods that can be used to verify or falsify claims that at first glance appear to be impossible manifestations but that deserve serious consideration because they are so frequently cited.

Chapter 10 surveys the Western encounter with shamanism, allowing us to revisit each of the preceding nine chapters, pointing out their points of congruence with those of other investigators. As psychologists, we have emphasised psychological writings, but we do not deny the importance of other scholars who have attempted to demystify shamanism. Walsh (2007) has pointed out that "most scientific studies of shamanism have been by anthropologists ... who have braved everything from arctic winters to tropical jungles to observe native shamans at work". However, Walsh continues, "several other disciplines, and especially psychology, can complement and enrich anthropological contributions. And of course, the study of shamanism also has much to contribute to psychology" (p. 7). In the spirit of Walsh's assessment, we invite scholars from scores of disciplines to join this quest; there are enough mysteries to intrigue us all!

Chapter One

Shamanism and Shamans: Points and Counterpoints

Recent developments in qualitative research and the innovative use of conventional investigative methods have provided the tools to bring both rigour and creativity to the disciplined examination of shamans, their behaviour, and their experiences. However, a review of Western psychological perspectives on shamans reveals several conflicting perspectives. This chapter focuses on these controversies.

The term *shaman* is a social construct, one that has been described, not unfairly, as "a made-up, modern, Western category" (Taussig, 1989, p. 57). Kremer (1996) also commented on the historical happenstance that led to the generalised use of what was originally a Tungus term. This appellation describes a particular type of practitioner who attends to the psychological and spiritual needs of a community that has granted that practitioner privileged status. Shamans claim to engage in specialised activities that enable them to access valuable information that is not ordinarily available to other members of their community (Krippner, 2000). Hence, *shamanism* can be described as a body of techniques and activities that supposedly enable its practitioners to access information that is not ordinarily attainable by members of the social group that gave them privileged status. These practitioners use this information in attempts to meet the needs of this group and its members.

Contemporary shamanic practitioners exist at the nomadic-pastoral, horticultural-agricultural, and state levels of societies. There are many types of shamans. For example, among the Cuna Indians of Panama, the *abisua* shaman heals by singing, the *inaduledi* specialises in herbal cures, and the *nele* focuses on diagnosis. The Rarimuri Indians of northern Mexico are nominally Roman Catholic, but continue to per-form their traditional shamanic rituals, especially in times of sickness and social emergency. The most revered practitioners are the *si'paaame* or "raspers", who conduct nightlong rituals in which they ingest pey-ote and play a percussion instrument that is "rasped" back and forth with another stick atop an inverted gourd that serves as a resonator. The *ouiruame,* or "medicine makers", are thought to travel to distant parts of the universe in their dreams; they track lost souls and attempt to maintain "balance" in their community. The *waniame* are called upon when a man or woman is the victim of a *sukuruame* or sorcerer, and proceed to suck out the rock, maggot, or other intrusive object from the victim's body. The *saweame* may or may not be a shaman, but he is the master chanter and is called upon when a ritual requires him to chant and use his sacred rattles (Levi, 2004).

Shamanic Roles

Winkelman's (1992) seminal cross-cultural study focused on 47 societies' *magico-religious practitioners* who claim to interact with non-ordinary dimensions of human existence. This interaction involves special knowledge of purported *spirit entities* and how to relate to them, as well as special powers that supposedly allow these practitio-ners to influence the course of nature or human affairs. Winkelman coded each type of practitioner separately on such characteristics as the type of magical or religious activity performed; the technology used; the mind-altering procedures used (if any); the practitioner's cosmology and worldview; and each practitioner's perceived power, psychological characteristics, socioeconomic status, and political role.

Winkelman's (1992) statistical analysis yielded four practitioner groups: (a) the shaman complex (shamans, shaman-healers, and healers); (b) priests and priestesses; (c) diviners, seers, and mediums; (d) malevolent practitioners (witches and sorcerers). Shamans were most often present at the hunter-gatherer level. Priests and priestesses were most present in horticultural/agricultural communities, and diviners and malevolent practitioners were observed in state-level societies.

Most diviners report that they are conduits for a spirit's power and claim not to exercise personal volition once they have *incorporated* these spirit entities. When shamans interact with spirits, the shamans are almost always dominant; if the shamans suspend volition, it is only temporary. For example, shamans surrender volition during some Native American ritual dances when there is an intense *perceptual flooding*. Nonetheless, shamans purportedly know how to enter and exit this type of intense experience (Winkelman, 2010). The distinction between voluntary shamanic (or mediumistic) incorporation and involuntary "possession" is a common one; Bourguignon (1976) added "trance" without possession or incorporation to describe other shamanic modifications of consciousness.

Shamanic Selection and Training

Shamans enter their profession in a number of ways, depending on the traditions of their community. Some shamans inherit the role (Larsen, 1976, p. 59). Others may display particular bodily signs, behaviours, or experiences that might constitute a *call to shamanize* (Heinze, 1991, pp. 146–156). In some cases, the call arrives late in life, giving meritorious individuals opportunities to continue their civil service; conversely, an individual's training may begin at birth. The training mentor may be an experienced shaman or a "spirit entity". The skills to be learned vary, but they usually include diagnosing and treating illness, contacting and working with benevolent spirit entities, appeasing or fighting malevolent spirit entities, supervising sacred rituals, interpreting dreams, assimilating herbal knowledge, predicting the weather, and mastering their self-regulation of bodily functions and attentional states.

The Demonic Model

Point

The European states that sent explorers to the Western hemisphere were, for the most part, the same states that were executing tens of thousands of putative witches and sorcerers. The practice of shamanism was already historically remote (except for inaccessible regions and remnants carried on in secret). The torture of the accused yielded confessions that they had made pacts with the devil, had desecrated sacred Christian ceremonies, or had consorted with spirits. Many chroniclers were Christian clergy who, therefore, described shamans as devil worshippers (Narby & Huxley, 2001).

A 16th century account by the Spanish navigator and historian, Gonzalo Fernández de Oviedo (1535/2001), described "revered" old men, held in "high esteem", who used tobacco in order to "worship the Devil" (pp. 11–12). The first person to introduce tobacco to France was a French priest, Andre Thevet (1557/2001). He described a group of "venerable" Brazilian practitioners called the *pajé*, portraying them as "witches" who "adore the Devil" (pp. 13, 15). The *pajé*, he wrote, "use certain ceremonies and diabolical invocations" and "invoke the evil spirit" in order to "cure fevers", determine the answers to "very important" community problems, and learn "the most secret things of nature" (pp. 13–15).

Another French priest, Antoine Biet (1664/2001), observed the rigorous training program undergone by indigenous practitioners, or *piayes*. To Biet, the rigors of a ten-year apprenticeship provided the *piayes* the "power of curing illness", but only by becoming "true penitents of the Demon" (pp. 16–17). Avvakum Petrovich (1672/2001), a 17th century Russian clergyman, was the first person to use the word "shaman" in a published text, describing one Siberian shaman as "a villain" (p. 18) who called upon demons to assist his nefarious work.

Counterpoint

Shamans engage in shamanic rivalries, wars, and duplicity (e.g., Hugh-Jones, 1996, pp. 32–37). The perception of the shaman's power also lends itself to fear and projection. Even so, ethical training is a key element of the shaman's education; according to M. Harner (1980), shamanism at its best has an ethical core (but see M.F. Brown, 1989, for a discussion of shamanism's dark side). Walsh's (1990a) study of various shamanic traditions revealed a rigorous system of ethics: "The best of shamanism has long been based on an ethic of compassion and service" (p. 249). Dow (1986) conducted field work with Don Antonio, an Otomi Indian shaman in central Mexico, who described his fellow shamans as warriors who must "firmly declare forever an alliance with the forces of good, with God, and then fight to uphold those forces" (p. 8). In addition, shamans must dedicate themselves to ending suffering, even it if requires them to forgo their own comfort (p. 39).

In Retrospect

Modern social scientists do not accuse shamans of consorting with demons. These accusations, however, are still being made by some missionaries as well as by shamans themselves, who may accuse rival shamans of using their powers for malevolent purposes (Hugh-Jones, 1996, p. 38). The Mexican Raramuri shamans have incorporated the Devil into their list of forces that threaten the "balance" of a person or a community, as have many other syncretic traditions.

The Charlatan Model

Point

Most writers in Western Europe's Enlightenment belittled the notion that shamans communed with otherworldly entities, much less the Devil. Instead, shamans were described as "charlatans", "imposters", and "magicians". These appellations undercut the Inquisition's justification for torturing shamans, but also kept Western science and philosophy from taking shamanism seriously.

Flaherty (1992), however, noted that Europe in the 18th century was not totally preoccupied with rationalism, humanism, and scientific determinism; manifestations of romanticism and the occult were present as well (p. 7). An example of this ambiguity appears in the writings of Denis Diderot (1765/2001), the first writer to define "shaman" and the chief editor of the *Encyclopédie* (Diderot and associates, 1784/1965), one of the key works of the French Enlightenment. In his definition, Diderot referred to shamans as Siberian "imposters" who function as magicians performing "tricks that seem supernatural to an ignorant and superstitious people" (p. 32).

According to Diderot, shamans lock themselves "into steamrooms to make themselves sweat" (p. 33), often after drinking a "special beverage [that they say] is very important to receiving the celestial impressions" (p. 35). He remarked that shamans "persuade the majority of people that they have ecstatic transports, in which the genies reveal the future and hidden things to them" (p. 37). Despite their trickery, Diderot concluded, "The supernatural occasionally enters into their operations.... They do not always guess by chance" (p. 34).

The French Jesuit missionary Joseph Lafitau (1724/2001) spent five years living among the Iroquois and Hurons in Canada. He reported that the tribe's people discriminated between those who communicated with spirits for the good of the community and those who did the same for harmful purposes. Lafitau argued that the latter might be in consort with the Devil, but that demonic agencies played no part in the work of the former, to whom he referred as "jugglers" or "diviners" (p. 25). On the other hand, Lafitau admitted that oftentimes there was something more to these magicians' practices than trickery, especially when shamans exposed "the secret desires of the soul" (p. 24).

According to Johann Gmelin (1751/2001), an 18th century German explorer of Siberia, the shamanic ceremonies he observed were marked by "humbug", "hocus-pocus", "conjuring tricks", and "infernal racket" (pp. 27–28). A Russian botanist of the same era, Stepan Krasheninnikov (1755/2001), reported to the imperial government that the natives of eastern Siberia harboured beliefs that were "absurd" and "ridiculous" (p. 29). Krasheninnikov wrote that shamans were "considered doctors" and admitted that they were "cleverer, more adroit and shrewder than the rest of the people" (p. 30). He described one shaman who "plunged a knife in his belly" but performed the trick "so crudely" that "one could see him slide the knife along his stomach and pretend to stab himself, then squeeze a bladder to make blood come out" (p. 30).

Counterpoint

Not all Enlightenment scholars were hostile to shamanism; for example, the German philosopher Johann Herder (1785/2001) noted wryly that "one thinks that one has explained everything by calling them imposters" (p. 36). Herder continued, "In most places, this is the case," but "let us never forget that they belong to the people as well and … were conceived and brought up with the imaginary representations of their tribe" (p. 36). Indeed, "among all the forces of the human soul, imagination is perhaps the least explored" (p. 37). Imagination seems to be "the knot of the relationships between mind and body" and "relates to the construction of the entire body, and in particular of the brain and nerves — as numerous and astonishing illnesses demonstrate" (p. 37).

   The small body of parapsychological research conducted with shamans suggests that on irregular occasions some practitioners may be capable of demonstrating unusual abilities (Rogo, 1987; Van de Castle, 1977). These data were collected not only by means of controlled observations, such as having shamans locate hidden objects (Boshier, 1974), but also through experimental procedures such as asking shamans to guess the symbols on standardised card decks (Rose, 1956) or requesting that they influence randomly generated electronic activity (Giesler,

1986). (We will discuss these investigations in more detail in Chapter 9, but need to note that these purported shamanic capacities appear to be effective on some occasions, but not on others, lending fuel to a well-deserved scepticism as to their existence.)

As for the use of sleight-of-hand, Hansen (2001) has compiled dozens of examples of shamanic trickery from the anthropological literature, but adds that deception may promote healing by triggering the placebo response (pp. 89–90). Unusual abilities, if they exist, are likely to be unpredictable; trickery may accompany their use, as shamans are prototypical "tricksters" and, as do some contemporary psychotherapists, believe that they must often "trick" their clients into becoming well (e.g., Warner, 1980).

In Retrospect

Shamans operate on the *limens*, or borders, of both society and consciousness, eluding structures and crossing established boundaries. They are in some aspects related to the trickster figure described in the literature (e.g., Hansen, 2001, p. 27). As liminal practitioners, they often use deception and sleight-of-hand when they feel that such practices are needed. Thus, shamans can be both cultural heroes and social hoaxsters, alternating between gallant support of those in distress and crass manipulation. Like other tricksters, however, they are capable of reconciling opposites; they justify their adroit manoeuvring and use of legerdemain in the cause of promoting individual and community health and well-being (pp. 30–31).

The Mental Illness Model

Point

When mental health professionals first commented on shamanic behaviour, it was customary for them to use psychopathological descriptors. The French ethnopsychiatrist George Devereux (1961) concluded that shamans were mentally "deranged" (p. 1089) and should be considered severely neurotic or even psychotic. The American psychiatrist Julian Silverman (1967) postulated that shamanism is a form of acute schizophrenia, because the two conditions have in common "grossly non-reality-oriented ideation, abnormal perceptual experiences, profound emotional upheavals, and bizarre mannerisms" (p. 22). According to Silverman, the only difference between shamanic states and contemporary schizophrenia in Western industrialised societies is "the degree of cultural acceptance of the individual's psychological resolution of a life crisis" (p. 23).

Taking a psychohistorical perspective, DeMause (2002) proposed that all tribal people "since the Paleolithic ... regularly felt themselves breaking into fragmented pieces, switching into dissociated states and going into shamanistic trances to try to put themselves together" (p. 251). According to DeMause, shamans were "schizoids" (p. 250) who spent much of their lives in fantasy worlds where they were starved, burned, beaten, raped, lacerated, and dismembered, yet were able to recover their bones and flesh and experience ecstatic rebirth. This account by DeMause is reminiscent of the portrayal of shamans as "wounded healers" who have worked their way "through many painful emotional trials to find the basis for their calling" (Sandner, 1997, p. 6) and who have taken an "inner journey ... during a life crisis" (Halifax, 1982, p. 5).

The notion of "shamanic illness" or initiatory crisis lends itself to misunderstandings, since some of the behaviour observed appears to fit psychiatric diagnostic categories when taken outside of its cultural context. Vajnstein (1968) describes a person experiencing the Tuvan *albystar* (special shamanic disease) as follows: "The person in question 'goes off his head', utters inarticulate sounds, breaks dishes, leaves the house and roams about the taiga, twitches in hysterical convulsions, is seized with nausea and rends his garments, etc." (p. 331). Mandelstam Balzer (1996) describes a contemporary individual in a Sakha (Yakut) village who "had had all the signs of a shamanic sickness— *etteten yald'ar*—a torturing and testing by the spirits" (p. 305). As a result of the Soviet repression, he was twice taken to psychiatric prisons and served lengthy terms.

Znamenski (2007) has traced the development of the mental illness model beginning with descriptions of "arctic hysteria" in the general population of the Siberian Kolyma River region at the end of the 19th century and the common assumption of Russian ethnographers that such hysteria is the root of the shamanic call. Hysteria, depression, irritability, moodiness, neurosis, epilepsy, and schizophrenia were popular diagnoses (together with ascriptions of cunning and deceit). Shamanism was often seen as an ailment akin to female hysteria.

The most recent contribution to the mental illness model by Whitley (2009) sees "manic-depression as the shaman's disease" (p. 228). Whitley, an archaeologist by training, makes probably the most detailed case that shamans are suffering from mood disorders; his argument includes the discussion of the heritability of mood disorders and shamanic family lines. "Shamanism ran in family lines primarily because its defining characteristic is a hereditary spectrum of mental illness" (p. 232). He concludes that "shamans were mad, as the ethnographic accounts describe with reasonable certainty. But shamans were also capable of functioning in society" (p. 237). The main reason for this is that "mood disorders are diseases that you can live with" (p. 235). Whitley continues the long tradition of ascribing mental illness to shamans that originated with Russian ethnographers, and provides the most elaborate argument to date.

Counterpoint

Znamenski (2007) details the problems with the early Russian ethnographic diagnostic descriptions, observing that they were clearly given by scholars without psychological or psychiatric training. Thus they are deficient in understanding the complexities of cultural behaviour and fail to take into account the impact of colonialism and impoverishment. It is notable that the indigenous Siberians themselves had no difficulty distinguishing between individuals suffering from mental illness and a shaman's initiatory illness.

Shirokogoroff's classic *Psychomental Complex of the Tungus* (1935) represents an early dissent from the notion that shamans were skilled but mentally ill individuals. He concluded that arctic hysteria was always performed collectively, a culturally endorsed behaviour, and thus had nothing to do with mental illness. He understood the initiation via "shamanic illness" as culturally endorsed behaviour that was understood by the members of the surrounding community as a set of specific signals pointing to an emerging shaman. Shirokogoroff pointedly noted that many of the scholars suffered from a "superior civilisation" complex, blinding their understanding of cultural behaviour (see Znamenski, 2007). It is clear that early ethnographic descriptions have to be seen as very unreliable, limited in scope, and biased, as the diagnoses of mental illness were provided by non-specialists. The Soviet repression of emerging shamans by way of psychiatric imprisonment and the long history of ascribing mental illness to shamans have resulted in the persistent image of the shaman as mentally ill.

Roger Walsh (2007), an American psychiatrist, provides probably the most detailed analysis of the various diagnoses given to shamans. He specifically discusses grand mal epilepsy, temporal lobe epilepsy, "hysterical" epilepsy or conversion disorder, brief psychotic disorder, schizophrenia, schizophreniform disorder, and psychotic disorder not otherwise specified. He identifies possible potentials and problems with each of these diagnoses and notes that "native peoples often make sharp distinctions between shamanic crises and mental illness.... Shamans often seem to end up not only psychologically healthy, but even exceptionally so" (p. 277). Previously, Walsh (2001) provided a penetrating analysis of shamanic phenomenology in which he concluded that it is "clearly distinct from schizophrenic ... states" (p. 34), especially on such important dimensions as awareness of the environment, concentration, control, sense of identity, arousal, affect, and mental imagery.

The descriptions of "spiritual emergence or emergency" can be considered a Western psychiatric concept equivalent to notions of shamanic illness. In the United States, the American Psychiatric Association's *Diagnostic and Statistical Manual* is commonly used to diagnose mental disorders. The inclusion of "religious or spiritual problem" in the fourth edition of the manual (referred to as *DSM*) allows for a non-pathologising understanding of spiritual emergences in Western cultures that are by all appearances analogous to shamanic illness. Spiritual emergencies can be defined as:

> Crises when the process of growth and change becomes chaotic and overwhelming. Individuals experiencing such episodes may feel that their sense of identity is breaking down, that their old values no longer hold true, and that the very ground beneath their personal realities is radically shifting. In many cases, new realms of mystical and spiritual experience enter their lives suddenly and dramatically resulting in fear and confusion. They may feel tremendous anxiety, have difficulty coping with their daily lives, jobs, and relationships, and may even fear for their own sanity. (Grof & Grof, 1989, back cover)

It is important to note that Western societies do not have a culturally endorsed form of spiritual emergence (while shamanic societies have a clear cultural reading of symptoms of shamanic illness), thus easily leading to a misinterpretation of a possible spiritual emergence as psychiatric illness. The work of Lukoff and his co-authors (Lukoff, Lu, & Turner, 1998) as well as the inclusion of the "religious or spiritual problem" category in the *DSM-IV* have begun to facilitate a more differentiated understanding of these profound experiences in Western and non-Western cultures.

Critics of the schizophrenia model claim that shamans have been men and women of great talent; thus Basilov's (1997) case studies of Turkic shamans in Siberia demonstrate their ability to master a complex vocabulary as well as extensive knowledge concerning herbs, rituals, healing procedures, and the purported spirit world. Sandner

(1979) described the remarkable abilities of the Navajo *hataalii*: to attain their status, they must memorise at least ten ceremonial chants, each of which contains hundreds of individual songs.

Noll (1983) compared verbal reports from both schizophrenics and shamans with criteria described in the third edition of the *Diagnostic and Statistical Manual of Mental Disorders*. He reported that important phenomenological differences exist between the two groups and that the "schizophrenic metaphor" (p. 455) of shamanism is therefore untenable. This assertion is supported by personality test data; for example, Boyer, Klopfer, Brawer, and Kawai (1964) administered Rorschach Inkblots to 12 male Apache shamans, 52 non-shamans, and 7 pseudo-shamans (practitioners who considered themselves shamans, but had been denied that status by their community). Rorschach analysis demonstrated that the shamans showed as high a degree of reality-testing potential as did non-shamans. Boyer et al. concluded, "In their mental approach, the shamans appear less hysterical than the other groups" (p. 176) and were "healthier than their societal co-members…. This finding argues against [the] stand that the shaman is severely neurotic or psychotic, at least insofar as the Apaches are concerned" (p. 179). Fabrega and Silver's (1973) study used a different projective technique with 20 Zinacanteco shamans and 23 of their non-shaman peers in Mexico and found few differences between the groups; however, they described the shamans as "freer" and "more creative".

The first epidemiological survey of psychiatric disorders among shamans was reported in 2002. A research team associated with the Transcultural Psychosocial Organisation of Amsterdam (Van Ommeren et al., 2002) surveyed a community of 616 male Bhutanese refugees in Nepal, assessing *International Classification of Disease* disorders (World Health Organisation, 1992) with structured diagnostic interviews. Of the refugees, 42 claimed to be shamans; after controlling for demographic differences, the shamans' general profile of disorders did not differ significantly from that of the non-shamans. Indeed, shamans had fewer of the general anxiety disorders that afflicted non-shamans.

Wilson and Barber (1981) identified *fantasy-prone personalities* among their hypnotic participants. This group was highly imaginative but, for the most part, neither neurotic nor psychotic. It is likely that many shamans would fall within this category, as shamans' visions and fantasies are thought to represent activities in the spirit world (Noel, 1997; Noll, 1985). Ripinsky-Naxon (1993) concluded, "The world of ... a mentally dysfunctional individual is disintegrated. On the other hand, just the opposite may be said about a shaman" (p. 104). Along these lines, Frank and Frank (1991) traced the roots of psychotherapy back to shamanism, and Torrey (1986) asserted that the cure rate of shamans and other indigenous practitioners compares favourably with that of Western psychologists and psychiatrists.

In Retrospect

Contemporary social scientists rarely pathologise shamans; when they describe them as "wounded healers" or "fantasy-prone", these attributions are usually combined with admiration, respect, or indifference. Of course, the variety of shamanic selection procedures undercuts these generalisations, especially when shamanism is hereditary and a novice assumes the role even without having experienced a "wounding" illness. A far greater commonality among shamanic practitioners is the consideration they give to resolving the psychological problems and challenges faced by individuals, families, and communities within their purview.

The Soul Flight Model

Point

The Romanian-American religion historian Mircea Eliade (1989) integrated the many tribal variations of shamanism into a unified concept, referring to its practitioners as "technicians of ecstasy" (p. 5).

Znamenski (2007) points out that Nora Chadwick was among the first to use the term "ecstasy" to describe trance states, in her book *Poetry and Prophecy* (1942) discussing Old Norse mythology, and noted that Eliade picked up on this usage. According to Eliade, "The shaman specialises in a trance during which his soul is believed to leave his body and ascend to the sky or descend to the underworld" (p. 5). Many other writers have agreed, stating that *altered states of consciousness* (ASCs) are the sine qua non of shamanism, particularly those ASCs involving *ecstatic journeying*, (i.e., soul flight or *out-of-body experience*). Heinze (1991) wrote, "Only those individuals can be called shamans who can access alternative states of consciousness at will" (p. 13). Ripinsky-Naxon (1993) added, "Clearly, the shaman's technique of ecstasy is the main component in the shamanic state of consciousness" (p. 86).

Proponents of the soul flight/ecstatic journeying model point to the close association among rhythmic percussion (and other forms of perceptual flooding), journeying, and healing. Neher's (1961) investigations demonstrated that drumming could induce theta wave EEG frequency. Maxfield (1994) built on and extended Neher's work and found that theta brain waves were synchronised with monotonous drumbeats of 3 to 6 cycles per second, a rhythm associated with many shamanic rituals. S. Harner and Tryon (1996) studied students of shamanism during drumming sessions and observed trends toward enhanced positive mood states and an increase in positive immune response. Bittman et al. (2001) also reported that rhythmic drumming had a salubrious effect on immune systems.

The term *shamanic state of consciousness* (M. Harner, 1980) implies that there is a single "state" that characterises shamans, even though it can be induced in several different ways. Winkelman's (1992) cross-cultural survey of 47 societies yielded data demonstrating that at least one type of practitioner in each populace engaged in ASC induction by one or many vehicles. For Winkelman (2000), each vehicle to the ASC resulted in an *integrative mode* of consciousness. This mode reflects slow wave discharges, producing strongly coherent brainwave patterns that synchronise the frontal areas of the brain, integrating nonverbal information into the frontal cortex, and producing visionary experiences and insight.

Counterpoint

According to its critics, the soul flight model ignores the diversity of shamanic ASCs as well as activity that does not seem to involve dramatic shifts in consciousness. Peters and Price-Williams (1980), comparing 42 societies from four different cultural areas, identified three common elements in shamanic ASCs: voluntary control of the ASC, post-ASC memory of the experience, and the ability to communicate with others during the ASC. Peters and Price-Williams also reported that shamans in 18 out of the 42 societies they surveyed specialised in spirit incorporation: 10 were engaged in out-of-body journeying, 11 in both spirit incorporation and out-of-body journeying, and 3 in some different ASC. In other words, there are several shamanic states of consciousness, and not all of them use ecstatic soul flight (Walsh, 1990a). Eliade's statements are further constricted by his emphasis on flights to the shamanic *upperworld* rather than to the *underworld,* which is of equal importance (Noel, 1997).

Eliade's use of the term *ecstasy* is problematic in three regards: 1) it suggests positive affect, neglecting the tremendously challenging and hazardous encounters described by shamans (see Halifax, 1979; also Whitley, 2009, for a discussion of "the myth of ecstasy"). Shamans work on behalf of their clients and communities and frequently put themselves in peril—a process that can hardly be described as euphoric or blissful. 2) Eliade's emphasis on ecstatic soul flight does not cover shamans who incorporate (possession trance). Descriptions suggest that shamans may use soul flight or incorporation or both; the lines between so-called "shamanic trance" (soul flight) and possession trance (incorporation) are fluid and may shift during one single ceremony. 3) While alterations of consciousness can be seen as a hallmark of the shaman's work, the emotional states experienced cover a much wider range than ecstasy and include emotions such as fear, anger, and vengeance. In fact, positive emotions are much more easily observed *after* individuals have experienced integrative states of consciousness (Winkelman, 2010).

The soul flight model also has been criticised by those who deny that profound alterations of consciousness are the defining characteristic of shamanism. Berman (2000) has suggested that the term *heightened awareness* captures shamanic behaviour more accurately than altered states, because shamans describe their intense experience of the natural world with such statements as "things often seem to blaze" (p. 30). Shweder (1972) administered a number of perceptual tests to a group of Zinacanteco shamans and non-shamans, asking them, for example, to identify a series of blurred, out-of-focus photographs. Non-shamans were more likely than shamans to respond, "I don't know". Shamans were prone to describe the photographs, even when the pictures were completely blurred. When the examiner offered suggestions about what the image might be, the shamans were more likely than the non-shamans to ignore the suggestion and give their own interpretations.

Paradoxically, shamans in this study were characterised both by an acute perception of their environment and by imaginative fantasy. These traits include the potential for pretending and role playing and the capacity to experience the natural world vividly. During times of social stress, these traits may have given prehistoric shamans an edge over peers who had simply embraced life as it presented itself, without the filters of myth or ritual (Shweder, 1972, p. 81).

In Retrospect

It may be more appropriate to speak of *shamanic modification of attentional states* rather than of a single *shamanic state of consciousness* (such as soul flight). Attention determines what enters someone's awareness. When attention is selective, there is an aroused internal state that makes some stimuli more relevant than others, thus more likely to attract one's attention.

More basic to shamanism may be a unique attention that shamans give to the relations between human beings, their own bodies, and the natural world — and their willingness to share the resulting knowledge with others (Perrin, 1992, pp. 122–123). The suppression of séances, spirit dances, and drumming rituals by colonial governments and missionaries led to the decline of altered states induction in many parts of the world (e.g., Hugh-Jones, 1996, p. 70; Taussig, 1987, pp. 93–104). The function of these procedures had been to shift the shaman's attention to internal processes or external perceptions that could be used for the benefit of the community and its members. Outsiders' bans of these technologies diminished the social role played by shamans and increased tribal dependence upon the colonial administrators.

The Decadent and Crude Technology Model

Point

The American transpersonal philosopher Ken Wilber (1981) divided what he called *higher states of consciousness* into several categories. His hierarchy started with the *subtle* (with and without iconography); proceeded to the *causal* (experienced as pure consciousness or the void); and moved on to the *absolute* (the experience of the true nature of consciousness).

Wilber (1981) granted that shamans were the first practitioners to systematically access "higher states", but only at the "subtle states" level, because their technology was "crude" (p. 142). He speculated that an occasional shaman might have broken into the causal realm, but insists that causal and absolute states could not be attained systematically until the emergence of the meditative traditions. Wilber placed shamanism at the fifth level of an eight-level spectrum.

Wilber (1981) supported his position by using examples from Eliade's (1989) classic book, *Shamanism: Archaic Techniques of Ecstasy.*

Eliade's position was that "shamanism is found within a considerable number of religions, for shamanism always remains an ecstatic technique" (p. 8). Eliade constructed a hierarchy of his own, however, taking the position that the use of mind-altering plants was a degenerate way to obtain visionary experiences. According to Eliade, those states attained "with the help of narcotics" are not "real trances" but "semi-trances" (p. 24). Eliade continued, "The use of narcotics is, rather, indicative of the decadence of a technique of ecstasy or of its extension to 'lower' peoples or social groups" (p. 477).

Counterpoint

Walsh (1990a) accepted the validity of Wilber's (1981) categories, but retorted that shamanism is an oral tradition. If shamans have experienced states higher than those at the subtle level, their accounts may have been lost to subsequent generations (p. 240); there is also the possibility that scholars may not have correctly read the myths that refer to such higher states. In addition, unitive experiences, such as those described by Wilber, were not a priority of shamans, because their efforts were directed toward community service (Krippner, 2000, p. 111; Walsh, 1990a, p. 240).

When D. P. Brown and Engler (1986) administered Rorschach Inkblots to practitioners of mindfulness meditation, they discovered that their responses illustrated their stages of meditative development, reflecting "the perceptual changes that occur with intense meditation" (p. 193). One Rorschach protocol was unique in that it integrated all 10 inkblots into a single associative theme (p. 191). However, Klopfer and Boyer (1961) had obtained a similar protocol from an Apache shaman, who used the inkblots to teach the examiner about his worldview and his journeys through the universe. Brown and Engler suggested that this may have been a response that, regardless of the spiritual tradition, pointed "a way for others to 'see' reality more clearly in such a way that it alleviates their suffering" (p. 214). Shamans' attempts to alleviate the suffering of their communities and what Wilber called their "crude" technology might be exceptionally well suited for this task (Krippner, 2000, p. 111).

Wilber (1981) made sweeping generalisations about shamanism without recognising the many varieties of shamanic experience and the rich diversity of shamanic traditions. For example, he identified "the classic symbolism of shamanism" (p. 70) as the bird, although in some shamanic societies the deer or the bear is the central totem (Ripinsky-Naxon, 1993). He claimed that the "true" shamanic experience involves "a severe crisis" (p. 74), although there are numerous accounts of shamanic callings that do not involve catastrophes. Indeed, the shamanic "crisis" could be a political strategy that limits the number of contenders for the shamanic role (Krippner, 2000, p. 111).

As for Eliade's charge that the use of mind-altering drugs represents degenerate forms of shamanism, Ripinsky-Naxon (1993) responded that "Eliade failed to recognise the critical role of hallucinogens in [shamanic] techniques" (p. 103). The archaeological evidence indicates that mind-altering substances date back to pre-Neolithic times rather than being a later, degenerate addition to shamanic practices (p. 153).

In Retrospect

After surveying the cross-cultural research data, Coan (1987) warned, "It would be a mistake to assume that shamanism represents just one stage either in the evolution of human society or in the evolution of human consciousness" (p. 62). Wilber's (1981) relegation of shamans to the subtle level of his higher states hierarchy virtually ignores the role played by shamans in their community. Such descriptors as *crude* and *degenerate* disregard the "cultivation of wisdom" (Walsh, 1990a, p. 248) that has long been a hallmark of shamanism.

The Deconstructionist Model

Point

Deconstructivism is a central strand in the intellectual movement known as *postmodernism*, which challenges the "modern" notions of rationality and objective reality. Postmodern scholarship, according to Gergen (2001),

> ... poses significant challenges to pivotal assumptions of individual knowledge, objectivity, and truth. In their place, an emphasis is placed on the communal construction of knowledge, objectivity as a relational achievement, and language as a pragmatic medium through which local truths are constituted. (p. 803)

Deconstructionism has its roots in literary criticism, but its influence expanded as members of other disciplines attempted to show that words are ambiguous and cannot be trusted as straightforward, dependable representations of reality or of something outside oneself. George Hansen (2001), an American parapsychologist and magician, identified *deconstruction* as a key shamanic role. Shamans break down categories; confound boundaries, especially those between worlds; and specialise in ambiguity. Trickster tales are an example of how language can use double meanings and paradox to provide instruction to their listeners (Babcock-Abrahams, 1975).

Deconstructionists maintain that polarities and privileged positions are simply arbitrary human constructions, a position that calls into question the notion of objective reality (Hansen, 2001, p. 64). By consorting with spirits, shamans deconstruct the polarity of life and death. By breaking taboos to obtain magical power, shamans challenge authority. After returning from their journeys, shamans describe strange dimensions of reality, thus confounding their community's sense of what is real. Reichel-Dolmatoff (1975/2001) observed that shamans mediate "between superterrestrial forces and society" (p. 217).

Shamans' status depends on the complexity of their societies. Winkelman (1992) found that shamans hold high status in hunting-gathering societies but lower status in agricultural states. When Western rationality becomes the dominant paradigm, shamans are often denigrated as "psychotic", "epileptic", or "deviant" (Hansen, 2001, p. 101). Writing about Siberian shamans and their persecution by both church and state, Hamayon (1996) concluded that shamans are "simultaneously adaptive and vulnerable" (p. 76) and that "there is an absence of shamanistic clergy, doctrine, dogma, church, and so forth" (p. 77).

Deconstructionism, no longer limited to literary texts, is often used to describe the impact of politically and financially powerful groups on societies' priorities and worldviews. Hansen used deconstructionism to describe how power is applied both by shamans and against shamans. Shamans speak of *power places* and *power objects*, and their quest for power is carried out in service of the community, usually in public rituals (Langdon, 1992, p. 14). Once shamans are relegated to the fringes of society, they become the victims of people and institutions that operate under different paradigms. Shamans may find support in communities that also have been marginalised. These shamans, in the tradition of deconstructionism, then challenge "privileged" authority, hierarchies, and structures.

M. F. Brown (1989) provided an example of the shaman as deconstructionist in his description of "Yankush", a pseudonym for a prominent shaman among the Aguaruna of northeastern Peru. Yankush specialised in treating victims of sorcery. Brown noted, "Shaman and sorcerer might seem locked in a simple struggle of good against evil, order against chaos, but things are not so straightforward. Shamans and sorcerers gain their power from the same source" (p. 11).

M. F. Brown continued, "The ambiguities of the shaman's role were brought home to me during a healing session I attended in Yankush's house" (p. 253). The clients were two women, both apparent victims of sorcerers' darts. Yankush waited until evening (an example of blurring boundaries, in this case between night and day), and drank ayahuasca, an herbal concoction, just before sunset. "As Yankush's intoxication increased ... he sucked noisily on the patients' bodies in an effort to remove the darts" (p. 253). Suddenly, a woman called out, "If there are any darts there when she gets back home, they may say that Yankush put them there. So take them all out!" (p. 254). Brown wrote, this "statement was an unusually blunt rendering of an ambivalence implicit in all relations between Aguaruna shamans and their clients.... If ... results are not forthcoming, the shaman himself may be suspected of, and punished for, sorcery" (p. 254). Finally, the participants left Yankush's house, expressing their contentment with the results of his effort (p. 255). This account is marked by a dissolution of boundaries (drinking a mind-altering brew at sunset) and by ambivalence (doubts regarding the shaman's competence), both hallmarks of deconstructionism.

Another example is provided by Townsley (1993/2001), who explored the epistemology of the Yaminahua, a people living in the Peruvian Amazon, and decoded the secret language used by its shamans. In the spirit world referred to in the songs of this language, "everything ... is marked by an extreme ambiguity" (p. 264). This language "is made up of metaphoric circumlocutions or unusual words for common things which are either archaic or borrowed from neighboring [sic] languages.... They also create new songs and invent fresh metaphors" (p. 268). "The important thing, emphasised by all shamans, is that none of the things referred to in the song should be referred to by their proper names" (p. 269). Hence, this deconstructionist model returns to its original emphasis on language.

Counterpoint

As Hansen (2001) noted, there have been many "furious denunciations" and "frantic utterings" (p. 27) about deconstructionism and other aspects of postmodern thought. Gross and Levitt (1998) agreed with Hansen that postmodernists are imbued with non-Western modes of thought, but concluded that this posture leads to higher superstition instead of to insight. They admitted that Western science has been "culturally constructed" (p. 43); that its projects "reflect the interests, beliefs, and even the prejudices of the ambient culture" (p. 43); and that "no serious thinker about science, least of all scientists them- selves, doubt that personal and social factors influence ... the accep- tance of results by the scientific community" (p. 139). Nonetheless, Gross and Levitt used the term *shaman* derisively each time it was men- tioned in their 1998 book, *Higher Superstition: The Academic Left and Its Quarrels with Science*, as when they derided the "mentality of LSD mys- ticism, shamanistic revelation, and ecstatic nonsense" (p. 224).

Is shamanic thought incompatible with Western rationality? Hub- bard (2002a), after evaluating the issue from the perspective of cogni- tive psychology, concluded that "conceptual structures underlying shamanism may result from the same types of cognitive processes and the same cognitive constraints (e.g., properties of mental representa- tion) also experienced by non-shamans and by scientists" (p. 135). Hubbard continued, "Shamanic thought thus would not reflect regres- sive or psychotic tendencies, but would instead reflect normative cognitive functioning" (p. 136).

Physical deconstruction is evident in many of the dreams and visions in which some shamanic initiates report being torn apart and dismem- bered. For the prospective shaman, however, this deconstructive pro- cedure is eventually followed by a *reconstruction* of bones and flesh, during which there is an ecstatic rebirth. In a similar way, shamans often reconstruct a shattered psyche. Pansy Hawk Wing (1997), a Lakota medicine woman, described the Yuwipi ceremony in which a practitioner intercedes between community members and spirit enti- ties to "pull together all the various parts of the whole" (p. 199).

The American anthropologist Jean Langdon (1992) wrote that *power* is the key concept that links shamanic systems, enabling shamans to mediate between "the human and the extrahuman" (p. 13). Langdon granted that shamans have an "ambiguous position in society" (p. 14), because they may employ power in negative ways, especially against enemies outside their social group. Nevertheless, shamanic power is usually manifested "in public ritual for the benefit of the community or for individuals" (p. 14). In addition, power is obtained by cross-gender behaviour, such as wearing clothes of the opposite gender in rituals that demand extra clout to be effective.

In Retrospect

Conflicts between shamans and zealous administrators of organised religion can be seen as a struggle between deconstructionists and "privileged" authority. Those writers who call shamanism a "religion" ignore the fact that there are Buddhist shamans, Christian shamans, Muslim shamans, pagan shamans, and so forth. Shamans are of great interest for many postmodernist writers because they represent the "marginalised other". More often than not, shamans engage in trickery, improvise and engage in unpredictable behaviour, embrace the fluidity of different planes of human existence, and exhibit ambiguous sexuality. In their efforts to share esoteric knowledge with their community, it is essential for shamans to deconstruct order, especially if a person's or a community's rigidity and inflexibility have blocked adaptation and growth. Nevertheless, shamans must eventually assemble what has been disassembled and reconstruct what has been deconstructed, if they are to be of service to their community.

Discussion

Shamans appear to have been humankind's prototypical psychotherapists, physicians, magicians, performing artists, storytellers, and even the first timekeepers and weather forecasters. Dow (1986) proposed that shamans not only represent the oldest profession but are "the world's most versatile specialists" (p. 6). This review of controversies regarding shamans and shamanism indicates that Western interpretations typically reveal more about the observer than they do about the observed, and that the construction of a psychology of shamanism needs to address this challenge.

Referring to shamanism, Walsh (1990a) remarked, "People's interpretations of the phenomena will be largely determined by their personal beliefs, philosophy, and 'world hypothesis'" (pp. 257–258). This world hypothesis, or *personal mythology* (Feinstein & Krippner, 1988, 2008), consists of the fundamental beliefs about the nature of the world and reality that underlie one's life and work. Most people simply take the consensual assumptions of their culture and subculture unquestioningly and interpret the world accordingly (Walsh, 1990a, pp. 257–258).

Information concerning world hypotheses and personal mythologies could predict the stance that individuals and groups will take when confronted with shamans or shamanic phenomena, because these phenomena are multilayered and can be interpreted from various perspectives. Unfortunately, as Walsh (1990a) pointed out in his discussion of shamanism, "At the present time, psychological studies are almost non-existent" (p. 270). Nevertheless, the psychological study of shamanism would have something to offer to cognitive neuroscientists, social psychologists, psychological therapists, and ecological psychologists, among others.

Cognitive Neuroscience

Cognitive neuroscience studies the neural processes that underlie the mechanisms, potentials, and limitations of mental operations. Winkelman (2000) has proposed that a "neurophenomenological framework" (p. 75) is needed to explain the worldwide distribution of specific constellations of shamanic characteristics and the role played by ASCs in shamanic practice. Meanwhile, researchers in *neurotheology*, who have used brain imaging techniques to study spiritual contemplatives, observe that prayer and meditation trigger a shift in brain activity that is associated with such unitive experiences as "the presence of God" and "oneness with the universe" (Newberg, d'Aquili, & Rause,

2001, pp. 115–116). The Canadian neuroscientist Michael Persinger (1993) utilised electrical stimulation to produce reported unitive experiences from volunteer subjects, and Austin (1998) singled out the thalamus and the temporal lobe as structures that may be associated with these effects. The British cognitive psychologist John Taylor (2002) has proposed an attention-based model of consciousness that identifies parietal lobe neural structures as crucial for attentional control. Taylor's model subsumes what contemplatives often refer to as *pure consciousness*, i.e., prereflective consciousness, "as basic for attentional control rather than as being 'generated' by it" (p. 208).

Several psychologists (e.g., Farthing, 1992) have proposed that attention, memory, and awareness are the three major components of the consciousness construct. Because attention involves both neural processes and mental operations (Ornstein & Carstensen, 1991, p. 741), shamanic practices provide cognitive neuroscientists an exceptional opportunity to study the neurological foundations of a technology that maintains awareness, enhances perception, and facilitates recall, while the adept's attention moves between internal and external foci.

Some theorists have suggested that neural networks may be instrumental in making connections between the cognitive processes of the organism and its understanding of the natural world (e.g., Hardy, 1998). They view some tasks, such as hunting and navigation, as a single cognitive activity that is distributed among several individuals (Hutchins, 1995). Such theoretical perspectives mirror the Native American assumption that all living beings are related, a concept that is shared by shamans worldwide. Hubbard (2002b) proposed that this assumption could provide appropriate *web* and *network* models for cognitive psychology, since it relies less on *artificial intelligence* and *digital computer* metaphors for the architecture of the nervous system. Web and network metaphors not only resonate with shamanic worldviews, but also reflect the multidimensional nature of human cognition (Hubbard, 2002b).

These insights could be applied to the cognitive neuroscientific study of what Winkelman (2000) called the "ubiquitous nature" (p. 27) of shamanic constructs. Neurological research in combination with the investigation of shamanic verbal reports could yield clues as to whether the basis for these constructs is "hardwired" (p. 5), and may contribute to a deeper understanding of both cultural and personal human evolution. As a result, Winkelman (2010) has developed a "neurophenomenological" perspective to consciousness that integrates knowledge of brain architecture with phenomenal experiences, providing a basis for understanding the interaction of biological and mental mechanisms in shamanic practices (p. 9).

Social Psychology

Social psychology, the study of individual attitudes and behaviours in settings where other people are present (or imagined), bridges the foci of psychology, with its emphasis on the individual, and sociology, with its emphasis on social structures. The typical shamanic worldview defines individuals in terms of their clans and kinship systems and provides a framework that is well suited for study by social psychologists. The human species is an incredibly social animal; unlike other animals, humans are neither especially strong nor fast. Survival thus depends on abstract problem-solving and group formation. There is probably a genetic basis for forming groups, as it has been highly adaptive in human evolution; even so, the social world modulates gene expression.

In this regard, McClenon (1997) hypothesised that shamanism is a cultural adaptation to biologically based adaptive potentials, especially those that foster hypnotisability, which coincides with anomalous and spiritual experiences (p. 346). Based on these experiences, shamans developed rituals that promoted intragroup cohesion, fertility, and therapeutic outcomes. Thus McClenon cited Winkelman's (1992) findings that shamans were the only magico-religious practitioners found in hunting and gathering societies. McClenon has further proposed several testable features of his model (pp. 346–347).

Social modelling involves clear presentations of the behaviours to be learned in a training program (Sprafkin, 1994) such as those given by magico-religious practitioners. An interest in the role of social model-ling in non-pathological dissociation motivated Negro, Palladino-Negro, and Louza (2002) to test 110 mediumistic practitioners in São Paulo. They reported mediumship activity as well as "control of the religious-related dissociative experiences" (p. 52) to be associated with high scores on tests for dissociation, in spite of positive scores on socia-lisation and adaptation tests. The investigators "found evidence of social modelling of non-pathologic religious dissociative experience for a population with extensive formalised mediumship training," but not for "social modelling as a causation of pathological dissociation" (p. 70).

Since Aristotle recorded his impressions of argumentation in the *Rhetoric*, humans have attempted to refine the principles of *social influ-ence*, the study of persuasion, influence, and compliance. In any social group, people spend a considerable amount of time cajoling, exhort-ing, and even manipulating each other to attain their goals. Credibility is essential to persuasion; thus credible practitioners display a degree of competence in their field and are commonly viewed as knowledge-able (Winkler & Krippner, 1994, p. 482). After studying both Western and indigenous health care practitioners, Torrey (1986) concluded that the nature of an effective treatment reflects one or more of four funda-mental principles: a shared worldview between practitioner and client, personal qualities of the practitioner, positive client expectations, and procedures that engender a sense of mastery on the part of the client. Social influence and persuasion are apparent in each of these princi-ples. Much of the effectiveness of shamans rests on the fact that their concepts of sickness are the same as those of their clients (Rogers, 1982, p. 14). In addition, shamans burnish a positive image of themselves and their powers in order to impress their clients (p. 8). Emotional arousal, and the evocation of faith, hope, and trust, enhance client expectations. Group processes may implement a sense of mastery; Western African shamans may invite half a dozen clients into their homes, spending considerable time with them each day (Torrey, 1986, p. 39). The net effect of these and other social procedures is to equip the client with strategies to cope with problems in living.

Opler (1936) described the way in which Apache shamans maximised their reputation as effective practitioners, by selecting receptive clients and rejecting sceptics along with those with apparently incurable conditions. They demanded payment in advance, bringing additional pressure on their clients to get well. They explained to the clients' families how they had achieved shamanic status so as to enrol the family's support for the treatment. They enlisted the aid of the community in the healing ritual, which further motivated the client to recover. This appeal to a client's community enlists *social support*, or resources from the social environment that can be beneficial to the client's psychological and physical health (Lepore, 1994, p. 247). Psychological research has indicated that people who receive social support from their social network, particularly if it is from significant others, tend to have fewer psychological problems than people who do not receive support, but there is less evidence regarding physical health (Lepore, 1994, p. 251; Vaux, 1988). Indigenous communities provide an excellent arena for research on this topic because social support is a mainstay of shamanic intervention.

Psychological Therapy

Psychological therapy (or psychotherapy) is a deliberate attempt to modify attitudes, behaviours, and experiences that clients and their social groups deem to be dysfunctional, that is, factors that inhibit interpersonal relationships, stifle competent performance, or block the actualisation of the clients' talents and capacities. Like other types of psychological therapy, shamanic healing procedures attempt to modify dysfunctional attitudes, behaviours, and/or experiences through a structured series of contacts between a socially sanctioned practitioner and distressed, but compliant, clients who acknowledge the status of that practitioner. Failed relationships, flawed performance, and faulty personal development are problems common to the human condition. When distressed individuals decide that neither their own resources, nor those of their families and friends, are sufficient to alleviate the distress, they often look for assistance from culturally sanctioned practitioners such as shamans (Krippner, 2000). However, what is considered dysfunctional in one culture (for example, seeing ghosts, hearing voices when nobody is present, engaging in competitive behaviour) may not be considered problematic in another culture. Problems that are widespread in one part of the world (for example, demonic possession, suffering from the *evil eye*, anorexia nervosa) may be virtually unknown elsewhere. Cultural myths that one society classifies as valid (for example, sickness as the result of breaking social taboos, malevolent spirits as the major causal factor in accidents, imperfect child-rearing practices as a contributing factor in emotional problems) may be considered magical thinking or superstitions in another.

As developed countries become more multi-cultural, Western-oriented psychological therapists need to be well informed regarding the belief systems that might accompany their clients to the counselling session. Cultural competence is a relatively new concept for the helping professions, but it developed from a long tradition of providing services to people from a variety of ethnic and cultural backgrounds (Hurdle, 2002). The fourth edition of the *Diagnostic and Statistical Manual of Mental Disorders* (*DSM-IV*; American Psychiatric Association, 1994) has attempted to enhance its universal validity not only with a brief mention of *dissociative trance disorder* but with a supplemental category of *religious or spiritual problems* and a glossary of *culture-bound syndromes*. Lewis-Fernandez and Kleinman (1995) admitted that this aspect of *DSM-IV* is the "main clinical development in current cultural psychiatry in North America" (p. 437), even though they judged the overall attempt to have been less than successful (p. 439). For example, Hopi Indian shamans identify five distinct indigenous categories related to "depression" (Vitebsky, 1995) only one of which shares significant parameters with *DSM-IV*'s *depressive disorders*. In addition, *DSM-IV* categories rarely are contextual. For example, in 1996 a 70-year-old Native American woman was diagnosed as schizophrenic because she had answered affirmatively when a psychiatrist asked if she heard voices when she was alone. The psychiatrist had not inquired as to whether this was an aspect of her culture as a Native American, where her lifestyle involved listening to the earth's messages for signs sent by a higher power. This woman was hospitalised as a result of this diagnosis and remained in the hospital until her *inner voices* told her what measures to take in order to obtain a release (Breasure, 1996).

Lewis-Fernandez and Kleinman (1995) noted that such *DSM-IV* disorders as those involving eating behaviour and sexual behaviour "show such pervasive Western cultural determinants that they cannot, as presently formulated, be compared across different cultures" (p. 437). Many mental health practitioners (e.g., Garcia, 1990) feel that the *International Statistical Classification of Diseases and Related Health Problems*, which includes a category for trance and possession disorders, is more culturally sensitive (World Health Organisation, 1992).

Finally, shamanic healing procedures provide a challenge for psychologists in the designing of outcome studies. Should the outcomes be defined in shamanic terms (for example, successful *soul retrieval*, regaining one's *flow of chi energy*) or in Western terms (for example, cessation of symptoms, resumption of daily work patterns)? Should the outcome be based on the purported "recovery" of the individual, of the family, or of the entire community? Should the ritualistic aspects of treatment (such as chanting and sand paintings) be separated from the possible impact of interpretive methods (such as dream sharing and shell reading) and that of herbal medicines and psychotropic drugs (such as ayahuasca and peyote)? Kleinman (1980) wrestled with these issues while conducting an outcome study of *tang-ki* (Taiwanese shamanic) healing, as did Leon (1975) in his seven-year study of spirit possession in Colombia. Another confounding factor is the fact that many shamanic healing systems do not discriminate between so-called physical and mental disorders, but do discriminate on the basis of age, gender, or social position (Krippner, 1992; Roszak, 1992, p. 75). These perspectives from shamanism challenge psychologists to take advantage of cross-cultural research methods, if their services to the growing diversity of their clients are to become more effective.

Ecological Psychology

Ecological psychology (or ecopsychology) attempts to understand behavioural and experiential processes as they occur within the environmental constraints of animal-environment systems, focusing on perception, action, cognition, communication, learning, development, and evolution in all species. There are several variants of this field, but all of them criticise what they see as mainstream psychology's emphasis on the individual's separation from other people and the natural environment. To be psychologically healthy, one must acknowledge that the planet is endangered and make real-world efforts to save it. Writing from an ecopsychological perspective, Metzner (1999) proposed that "healing the planet" is basically a shamanic journey (pp. 165); if so, the psychological study of shamanism can play a vital role in this endeavour. Perhaps the prototypical shaman could serve as the "responsible person model" called for by Kaplan (2000) to exhibit behaviour that is "environmentally responsible" (p. 491).

Roszak (1992) has posited an *ecological unconscious* representing the "savage element" in humans "that rises up to meet the environmental need of the time" (p. 96). As a sense of "ethical and psychological continuity with the nonhuman world deepens, we have the chance to recapture ... some trace of the ancestral sensibility" (p. 97). Shamanic models play an important role in evoking this sensibility; shamanic healing "is embedded in a place and a history, in the rhythms of climate, in the contours of a landscape where the birds and beasts have been close companions for centuries" (p. 76). Shamans were the original "group therapists", with groups including animal spirits, ancestors, and the like (p. 89).

Ecopsychologists take the position that human beings are an integral part of a greater system, and that the health of this system requires sustainable and mutually nurturing relationships not only among its parts, but also between the parts and the whole. Healthy functioning needs to include the realisation of this interconnectedness and interdependence, an insight that has been an essential part of shamanic traditions for at least 30,000 years.

Conclusion

Shamanism is ubiquitous. A plethora of definitions may be found in the anthropological and psychological literature. The definition that we used at the beginning of this chapter referred to shamans as socially designated practitioners who are capable of shifting their patterns of phenomenal properties to obtain information not ordinarily available to other members of their community, using that information to help and to heal community members as well as the community as a whole. This definition begins to demystify shamanism, because the definition is operational; that is, each term it uses can be observed and, to some extent, measured. Hence, the definition does not use such terms as "upper world", "spirits", "power animals", or the like. In contrast, many other definitions are mystified because they use, for example, the term "spirits", which we would consider a "hypothetical construct", or perhaps a "social construct" (or both). We have further demystified shamanism by pointing out that Westerners have viewed the topic from their own lenses, whether they are religious, philosophical, psychoanalytical, or deconstructive. Indeed, these Western interpretations of shamanism themselves need to be deconstructed for shamanism to be fully appreciated.

Chapter Two

Epistemology & Technologies of Shamanic Knowledge

Much of the behaviour of other animals is instinctive; it is their experiences that modify these complex, inborn behavioural patterns. However, drives and biological propensities, not innate behaviour patterns, characterise humans. Non-human animals, especially gorillas and chimpanzees, probably compare environmental stimuli to the memory images from past interactions. Humans fall on this continuum as well, as the satisfaction of their vital needs was once highly dependent on their ability to use these images as signal systems in order to produce the tools and procedures appropriate for drive satisfaction. Eventually, these procedures included a variety of social interactions, including speech and ritual behaviour (Guryev, 1990, p. 124; V. Turner, 1968).

Ritual, a step-by-step social performance, afforded an opportunity to express the community's conceptions of reality in a social setting. Ritual, in fact, is the key to the structure of a group's mythology, or worldview. In shamanic societies especially, ritual is a stylised technology, one whose symbols and metaphors may well trigger healing, relieve suffering, and provide a link between the ordinary world and those realms purportedly traversed by the shaman (Krippner, 1993; E. Turner, 1992, p. 14; V. Turner, 1968).

Using a specific example, María Sabina's shamanic work, it is important to keep in mind several central issues for the understanding of shamanic traditions and their practitioners. First and foremost, it is always important to recall the cultural diversity or diversity of rituals in which shamanic states of consciousness occur (see Vitebsky, 1995, for an overview). Different traditions have different patterns of initiation, some of them based largely on heredity, others on a singular initiatory dream, others on initiatory shamanic illness, and more (Krippner & Welch, 1992). Soul flight (also called shamanic or religious trance; Goodman, 1992) is not universal, but we also find shamanic practitioners who incorporate (possession trance) or do both. María Sabina's *veladas* quoted below suggest fluid boundaries between them. These cultural differences should lead us to be cautious about making generalisations.

Secondly, we cannot assume that the personality structure of an indigenous practitioner (past and present) conforms to Western assumptions about individuality and the self. Kremer (2002, 2004) argued that the well-bounded masterful self of Western aspirations is notably different from communal indigenous selves located in and through place (ecology), stories (or myths), ritual and ceremony, seasonal and stellar cycles, ancestors, ancestral spirits, and spirits in general (see also Cushman, 1995, and Gergen, 1992, for history of self). Vitebsky (1995) provides a detailed description of the embeddedness of a Sora practitioner in the landscape and its spirits, a description that defies easy interpretations from the viewpoint of Western personality theories.

Thirdly, it is important to remember that alterations of consciousness occur in a complex, culturally conditioned, ritual context. Frequently, the focus is on particular means of induction, such as drumming-induced sonic driving. However, Kremer (2003) has argued that it is crucial to take a multi-sensory perspective on shamanic technologies. He lists general cultural context, sacred or mythic geography in which the ritual exists, storytelling, verbal instructions, singing or chanting, use of percussion and other musical instruments, ritual implements (feathers, crystals, etc.), olfactory stimulation (incense, etc.), gustatory stimulation (including ingestion of mind-altering plants) and dietary practices (fasting, feasting), cleansing (sweating, use of emetics), tactile stimulation (massaging, etc.), movement (dance), body painting, drama, and changes in waking-sleeping cycles (see also Krippner & Kremer, 2010). This multidimensionality can be found in Navajo ceremonies (Kremer, 2003), the spirit dances of the Pacific Northwest (Jilek, 1982), and innumerable other traditions. The above list shows that shamans do not leave the impact of their work to chance but use a rich repertory of techniques to increase the probability of a successful intervention.

As an example of the role played by rituals, we will use material from accounts of a renowned 20th century Mazatec shaman.

The Veladas of María Sabina

Shamanic rituals were essential to the career of the Mazatec Indian María Sabina, who lived in the state of Oaxaca, Mexico. Born about 1894, María Sabina led a life of severe hardship. Her father died when she was quite young, and her first husband abused her terribly. After his death, she married again, but her second husband died when she was in her 40s. Since childhood, María Sabina had been interested in herbs and worked for a period of time as a *curandera*, or herbalist. Later, she felt that she had been called to become a *sabía* (i.e., "one who knows") and ingested psilocybin mushrooms as a way of "knowing" the condition and treatment of her clients. During Krippner's interviews with her in 1980, Doña María told him that Jesus Christ and other spiritual entities came to her and her client during the *veladas* (evening mushroom ceremonies), bringing information about her client's problem and its resolution.

As a *sabía* or shamanic healer, María Sabina manifested considerable control during the *veladas*, chanting liturgies containing an overlay of Roman Catholic imagery that cloaked the odes used by the Indian priests who had been overthrown by the Spaniards in the 1520s. The Spanish Inquisition outlawed the *veladas*, but the Mazatecs took them underground for four centuries. One night, María Sabina dreamed that it was her mission to share this sacred knowledge with the world. Soon after this dream, on June 29, 1955, a group of U.S. investigators headed by R. Gordon Wasson, a Boston banker, arrived. Eventually, Doña María and the psilocybin mushrooms were featured in *Life* magazine, and the field of ethnomycology was born (Estrada, 1981; Wasson, 1981). Doña María's reported dream is unique for several reasons: it ran counter to the attempt of male elders to keep their practices secret, and its egalitarian and universal motive violated the political power of her society's male hierarchy. She paid dearly for this action; her grocery store was burned to the ground, and her son was murdered.

María Sabina's worldview is expressed in her chants; in one, she apparently alludes to her shamanic journeys:

> I am a woman who flies.
> I am the sacred eagle woman, [the mushroom] says;
> I am the Lord Eagle woman;
> I am the lady who swims;
> Because I can swim in the immense,
> Because I can swim in all forms.
> I am the shooting star woman,
> I am the shooting star woman beneath the water,
> I am the lady doll,
> I am the sacred clown,
> Because I can swim,
> Because I can fly. (Estrada, 1981, abridged, pp. 93–94, 96)

Doña María's feelings of unity with nature and with the spirit world are revealed by another set of chants; the lyrics also portray her active role in attaining knowledge:

> I have the heart of the Virgin,
> I have the heart of Christ,
> I have the heart of the Father,
> I have the heart of the Old One,
>
> It's that I have the same soul,
> The same heart as the saint, as the saintess;

> I am a spirit woman,
> A woman of good words, good breath, good saliva,
> I am the little woman of the great expanse of the waters,
> I am the little woman of the expanse of the divine sea.
> I am a woman who looks into the insides of things,
> A woman who investigates, Holy Father,
> I am a woman born, I am a child born,
> I am a woman fallen into the world. (pp. 107, 129–130)

In other words, María Sabina employed an investigatory way of knowing; she "looks into the insides of things". She, and other shamans, learn from "the spirits", "the waters", and "the divine sea". Tradition and holy writ might provide source material for the shaman, but it is his or her "heart" and "soul" that are the final arbiters of knowledge.

Shamanism as a Biologically Derived Specialisation

Winkelman (1997) proposed that María Sabina and other shamans represent a "biologically derived" human specialisation, and that these potentials are actualised through social adaptations. This proposition could be used to explain the worldwide presence of shamans as well as the fundamental role of attentional shifts and/or heightened perception in shamanic healing and divination practices. An example of divination has been given by Lerche (2000). In his quest for the lost tribes of the Peruvian Chachapoya (or "Cloud People"), he consulted a shaman who claimed that he drew on the power of ritual objects. The shaman had a vision that some of the tombs remained unharmed and, soon after the consultation, Lerche detected a mummy bundle in a tomb high on a cliff (p. 68).

These potentials can be described as "neurognostic", because they involve neural networks that provide the biological substrate for ways of knowing (Laughlin, McManus, & d'Aquili, 1990), i.e., epistemology. We would add that these neurognostic potentials are not the exclusive domain of shamans; primordial humans performed healing and divinatory functions themselves before specialisation established a hierarchy (see Berman, 2000). Evidence for this position can be found in fairly egalitarian tribal societies such as the !Kung of southwestern Africa, where about half the males and a sizable number of females shamanize, producing the "boiling energy" (i.e., sweat) used in their healing rituals (R. Katz, 1982).

Neurognostic potentials provide the basis for those forms of perception, cognition, and affect that are structured by the organism's neurological systems. They are probably reflected in what Jungians call "archetypes", which can be conceptualised as the predispositions that provide organising principles for the basic modes of consciousness and elementary behaviour patterns, including the intuitive capacity to initiate, control, and mediate everyday behaviour. Stevens (1982) suggested that "from the viewpoint of modern neurology, Jung's work stands as a brilliant vindication of ... the value of intuitive knowledge" (pp. 273–274). When ritualised shamanic performance is described as "archetypal", the activity reflects biologically based modes of consciousness, a replacement of the ordinary waking state through discharge patterns that produce interhemispheric synchronisation and coherence, limbic-cortex integration, and integral discharges that synthesise cognition, affect, and behaviour (Winkelman, 1992). Shweder (1979) found that Zinacanteco shamans in Mexico possess cognitive capacities that distinguish them from non-shamans, such as having available a number of constructive categories and imposing these forms onto ambiguous situations; these integrative capacities may have facilitated the development of shamanic epistemologies over the millennia.

A variety of procedures, agents, and other technologies are available to evoke limbic system slow-wave discharges that synchronise the frontal cortex (Mandell, 1980). In addition, many shamans probably could be characterised as "fantasy-prone" (Wilson & Barber, 1983), endowed with capacities, genetic to some degree, that facilitate their use of imaginative processes. Fantasy-proneness exists on a continuum; most humans engage in fantasy, imagination, and play (especially "pretending" and "role-playing") periodically, but shamans draw upon this trait for their specialisation.

Many of the early shamans may not have been dependent on transient consciousness modification, but manifested a heightened perceptual style that was part of their everyday state of consciousness. Paradoxically, shamans are characterised both by an acute perception of their environment and by imaginative fantasy (Berman, 2000, p. 81).

All of these traits may be related to the evolution of the human brain, namely, the development of specialised subsystems that are activated during shifts in consciousness. The hallmark of cortical evolution is not the ever-increasing sophistication of specialised cortical circuitry, but an increasing representational flexibility that allows environmental factors to shape the human brain's structure and function (Gazzaniga, 1994; Quartz & Sejnowski, 1997). Pinker (1997) suggested that the "mind" is made up of many modules, each honed by aeons of evolution, and shamans may have learned how to integrate these modules (Winkelman, 2000, p. 7). If so, shamanic technologies represent the initial institutionalised practices for this integration, both through shifts in consciousness and through community bonding rituals (Winkelman, 1997). These practices became codified in the form of myth, ritual, and ceremony, providing for social solidarity and specialisation.

McClenon (1997) hypothesised that the benefits of so-called "shamanic states of consciousness" elicited an evolutionary increase in genes that would expedite this condition. However, all cultural changes in the past 90,000 to 100,000 years of *Homo sapiens sapiens* (i.e., modern humans) have been environmental, not genetic (DeMause, 1998). Therefore, we take the position that, once *Homo sapiens sapiens* arrived on the scene, and once shamanism developed as a societal specialisation, the contributions of shamanism to the evolution of human consciousness took on socio-cultural roots that built upon humanity's biological (i.e., neurognostic) groundings.

The initiation and direction of thought and behaviour owe as much to social construction as they do to biology (Rychlak, 1997, p. 143). Furthermore, all human societies contain inventive people, but some of them provide more unusual materials and more favourable conditions for utilising new technologies than do other environments (Diamond, 1997, p. 408). It is likely that spiritual activities originally involved the entire clan, but changing social and economic conditions brought about shamanic specialisation and, later, a priesthood (Anisimov, 1963) and social inequality (Berman, 2000, p. 82).

Shamanic Technologies

The oral traditions that preserved the myths that structured a culture's identity and worldview may not have been originated by shamans, but eventually they were passed down by them as well as by other community elders (Wiercinski, 1989). For example, María Sabina and her fellow shamans preserved, in their chants and rituals, Mazatec mythologies for more than four centuries, maintaining their cultural identity in the face of Spanish oppression. To facilitate this societal function, many shamans developed techniques to assist the elicitation and movement of "inner heat" to enable their shamanic journeys, and to facilitate their contact with what they called the "upper" and "lower" worlds (although the nature of these worlds differed from culture to culture). This technology allowed them to encounter spirits, ancestors, animal totems, and other resources that had found their way into mythological songs and stories.

Epistemology is concerned with the nature, characteristics, and processes of knowledge, and in this chapter we are suggesting that shamanic epistemology drew upon perceptual, cognitive, affective, and somatic ways of knowing that assisted early humans to find their way through an often unpredictable, sometimes hostile, series of environmental challenges. Not only did early humans have to become aware of potentially dangerous environmental objects and activities, they needed to have explanatory stories (enacted as mythic rituals) at their disposal to navigate through the contingencies of daily encounters and challenges. The acute perceptual abilities of shamans, in combination with their intuition and imagination, attempted to meet their societies' needs.

Eliade (1989) wrote of the "technologies of the sacred"; for us, shamanism is most accurately defined as a collection of these technologies. Shamanism comprises a group of techniques by which practitioners deliberately modify their conscious awareness, accessing information that they use to help and to heal members of the social group that has acknowledged their shamanic status.[1] In psychological terms, shamans are socially designated magico-religious practitioners who claim to self-regulate their psychological functions to obtain information unavailable to other members of their social group, information adaptive for their group's survival.

Mythological worldviews arise from epistemologies which, in turn, are fuelled by the motives, needs, and traditions of a group in a specific time and place. Examples would be pre-classical worldviews that conceptualised people as an integral part of nature; knowledge was mediated through tribal shamans and their activities. For the ancient Greeks and other classical groups, knowledge was obtained through rationally constructed metaphysical systems; in Asia and other parts of the world, these systems were less individualistic and more communal. In medieval European societies, knowledge was scholastic and could be found in the correct interpretation of sacred scriptures. The modern approach to knowledge involves a proper application of the empirical scientific method, taking as axiomatic that there can only be one possible answer to any question—a position shared by the metaphysical and scholastic epistemologies that were based on very different

---

1   In this book, the term "consciousness" is used to describe an organism's pattern of perceiving, thinking, and feeling at a given point in time. "Awareness" is used to denote "conscious awareness", hence is a more limited and specific term than "consciousness". Some writers (e.g., Goldman, 2000, p. 3) use the terms "conscious" and "aware" interchangeably, but there are values in making a differentiation, especially when discussing epistemology and consciousness.

assumptions (Krippner, 1995c). Although we disagree with the anti-epistemological slant of many so-called "postmodernists", we are pleased that postmodernism points to the need for honouring multiple narratives and for becoming aware of the process by which narratives are constructed (see Berman, 2000, p. 323).

Tribal people did not necessarily insist that their mythic worldview was applicable to their neighbours; even when they were locked in battle, there often was a regard and respect for their opponents' courage. In much postmodern writing, there is also a respect for diversity, empathy for other human beings, and concern for other life forms; all are reminiscent of shamanic worldviews. Postmodernists hold that there can be many viable worldviews, depending on who is asking the question and the methodology used in answering it (Krippner, 1995c). Therefore, the case can be made that postmodernists have returned full circle to certain premodern shamanic perspectives, regaining valuable aspects of an epistemology that was denigrated as a result of colonisation and conquest.

Shamanic eclecticism and syncretisation were apparent in Krippner's interviews with María Sabina, who put her epistemology into concrete terms. At the time of his interviews, Doña María had retired from active shamanizing, but she told him, "When someone came to me for help, we would eat the mushrooms together. Jesus Christ is in the mushrooms and he revealed to us the solution to the problem." Wasson (1981) observed that the mythical origin of Doña María's *veladas* dates back to the time when Piltzintecuhtli, the "Noble Infant", received the sacred plants as a gift from Quetzalcoatl. Doña María's references to Jesus represent a synthesis of the Christian and the pre-Conquest religions (p. 17).

Categories of Spiritual Practitioners

In Winkelman's (1992) study of the records of religious and magical practices in 47 different societies, he found documentation that magico-religious practitioners claimed to have access to spiritual entities (e.g., deities, ghosts, spirits). They used this access to direct a society's spiritual activities (e.g., prayer, sacred ceremonies), employing special powers (e.g., casting spells, bestowing blessings, exorcising demons) that allowed them to influence the course of human affairs in ways not possible by other members of their social group.

Winkelman found remarkable similarities among these clusters of practitioners, especially regarding the manner in which their roles changed as societies became more complex. For example, he found shamans in those groups with no formal social classes; their presence was typical of hunting and gathering tribes and fishing societies. The Creek, Crow, and Kiman were among the Native American tribes that awarded considerable prestige to the shamans in their midst. Each society had a different word to describe what are now called "shamans", and the specific duties expected of these practitioners differed from group to group.

Once a society became sedentary and centralised and began to practice agriculture, social stratification took place; in addition to the division of labour, political and economic specialisation occurred. Priests or priestesses emerged, taking control of a society's religious rituals, while the shaman's political power and social status were reduced. According to Winkelman, the term "shaman-healer" (or "shamanic healer") is a more accurate description of these practitioners because healing became their major function.

The role of the shamanic healer became specialised and formal; official initiation ceremonies and training procedures became more common, leading to the emergence of priests. Political development beyond the level of the local community was observed in almost all the societies in which priests were present. The Jivaros in South America and the Ibo tribe in western Africa are among the few groups in which priests were assigned a healing function; priests also served healing purposes in Japanese Buddhist and Kurd Dervish groups. However, the shamanic healer typically engaged in more self-regulatory activities including the modification of consciousness than did priests and priestesses.

Political integration became even more complex when separate judicial, military, and legislative institutions appeared. Along with this complexity, the malevolent practitioner (i.e., sorcerer or witch) appeared. Originally, shamans cast hexes and spells on tribal enemies; these functions were taken over by the sorcerer and, for a price, were often directed against members of one's own social group. Potions and charms became the province of witches and their associates. The shamanic healer's scope of action was now reduced not only by priests, but by sorcerers and/or witches as well. There were, for example, sorcerers among the Aztecs.

Further political complexities and continued dependence on agriculture became associated with the development of another practitioner, the diviner or medium, such as those found among the Eurasian Kazakhs. At one time the shaman's repertoire had included divination and talking with spirits; later, mediums and diviners began to specialise in this exploit, also incorporating the spirits, allowing them to speak and act through their voices and bodies. At this point, the shaman's role was dispersed to the extent that its only remaining functions were specialised healing capacities as in the performance of healing songs and dances, dispensing herbal medicines, diagnosis, bone-setting, midwifery, and surgery. Winkelman referred to these practitioners as "healers" (or, one might say, "shamanistic healers"). Like shamanic healers, shamanistic healers held the healing of one's soul in high regard, but became more involved in individual work than in community work. Furthermore, modifying one's conscious awareness and journeying to the spirit world no longer were core elements of their work, as was the case with shamans and shamanic healers.

This classification system was found to be quite accurate when cross-societal comparisons were made (Winkelman, 1997). With only two exceptions, shamans were never found in tribal groups that displayed an administrative political organisation beyond the local level.

No shamans appeared in sedentary societies where the nomadic way of life was absent. When Winkelman traced the development of these four categories (i.e., the shaman complex, priests, diviners, and malevolent practitioners), he did not assign the terms "higher" and "lower" to the modifications of consciousness utilised while they engaged in their practices, thus avoiding a Eurocentric hierarchy.

The shaman's ways of knowing depended on accessing information from spiritual entities in upper worlds, lower worlds, and middle earth or consensual reality. In contrast, the priest's epistemology was dependent on a body of revealed knowledge, often preserved in the form of sacred scripture. Diviners used their own bodies as vehicles for obtaining the information that was transmitted through them, while malevolent practitioners depended upon traditional knowledge, either written or passed down verbally. It was not unusual for this material to resemble a "cook-book" that spelled out the technology which was to be used to inflict various hexes and spells.

In contrast, shamanic ways of knowing were dynamic and active. Shamanism demanded both flexibility and strength on the part of the practitioner who would bargain, negotiate, or plead with spiritual entities for the knowledge that would save his or her community from a plague or restore a lost soul to its owner.

Shamanic "States of Consciousness"

The word "consciousness" is used in various ways, but we define it as one's awareness of one's pattern of phenomenal properties (perceptual, cognitive, and/or affective) at any given moment in time. Customarily, an "altered state of consciousness" is a significant shift or deviation in an organism's customary pattern as experienced by that organism and/or observed by others. Some of these shifts have been considered to be "states" of consciousness because they are marked by behaviours and experiences that typically cluster together; each society has its own conception of what constitutes an "ordinary" state of consciousness and what may be considered "changed" or "altered" states of consciousness. (In Chapter 3 we will re-conceptualise the term "states of consciousness".) Winkelman (1992) noted that in each of the 47 societies he studied at least one type of practitioner demonstrated a shift in consciousness associated with his or her apprenticeship and role-training. Wade (1996) added that "virtually all shamanic experiences occur in an altered state, which cannot be regarded as a naturally-occurring developmental stage" (p. 277). Here Wade is referring to such phenomena as "imaginary playmates", quite common in childhood but rare among well-functioning adults, except for those categorised as "fantasy-prone".

Bourguignon (1976) studied 488 societies (57% of those represented in an ethnographic atlas), reporting that 437 of them (89%) had one or more institutionalised, culturally patterned changed state of consciousness, some of which were experienced only by the society's spiritual practitioners. What can we make of the other 11 percent? Berman (2000) proposed that "such beliefs and practices, even if wired into the brain in terms of capacity, get triggered only in certain cultural contexts" (p. 29). (We might suggest that colonisation led to the disappearance of these behaviours in at least some of the 11%.) There are shamanic groups, such as the Navajo *hataalii*, who deny entering altered states. The *hataalii* rely on knowledge, not trance phenomena or magical effects. Their chant work is "a restrained and dignified procedure", and they represent, for the client, "a stable dependable leader who is a helper and guide until the work is ended" (Sandner, 1979, p. 258). This seems more like a case of heightened perception than an altered state. On the other hand, the Navajo "hand tremblers" appear to operate in a dramatically different mode of consciousness than the *hataalii*, one that could be considered an altered state. As a result, it may be more accurate to consider hand tremblers as shamans and *hataalii* more akin to Winkelman's category of priests.

Those shamans who enter altered states employ various technologies, many of them multi-sensory in nature. These include ingesting mind-altering plants (e.g., María Sabina's use of psychoactive mushrooms), chanting (again, Doña María), concentrating, dancing, drumming, jumping, fasting, running, visualising, participating in sexual activity, refraining from sexual activity, engaging in lucid dreaming, and going without sleep. Rarely is one procedure used in isolation. For example, mind-altering plants are often ingested in the evening; sleep deprivation, restricted night-time vision, and accompanying music often enhance the experience's profundity. Song and dance are important elements in ritual and probably preceded it. Naturally occurring altered states, such as dreaming and daydreaming, may also be utilised (Harner, 1988; Rogers, 1982). Whitley (1998) suggested that one of the functions of rock and cave image-making may have been to record the images elicited in shamanic states of consciousness.

The Ojibwa Indians shocked Jesuit priests on their arrival in North America with their behaviour during their traditional healing procedures. It was customary for Ojibway *wabeno* (shamans) to heal by means of drumming, rattling, chanting, dancing erotically (while naked), and handling live coals. The *wabeno* then rubbed their heated hands over the client while chanting the songs previously learned in their vision quests (Grim, 1983, pp. 144-145). Among the Diegueno and Luiseno Indians of southern California, potential shamans were selected as early as nine years of age on the basis of their dreams. It was important that a prospective shaman in both of these tribes also have visionary experiences that resulted from ingesting such mind-altering plants as datura or jimson weed during their ceremonials. During these altered states, the novice received a guardian spirit in the form of an animal totem as well as healing songs and other knowledge about cures and dream interpretation (Rogers, 1982, p. 21). Each of these examples demonstrates the multi-sensory nature of shamanic rituals; sight, hearing, taste, smell, touch, rhythm, and imagination were combined in effective ways.

Symbolic manipulation is apparent in shamanic rituals, and altered states often help to access these symbols. Symbols are more than ritual markers that denote the beginning, middle, or end of the process; they serve as keys that unlock the door to a full participation in the ritual, taking participants into another order of reality where spirits come to life and healing dramas unfold (V. Turner, 1968). The drum often symbolises the "World Tree" the shaman needs to climb in order to reach the upper world (or descend to the lower world) during the altered state. What they find in these realms differs from society to society; in some, the upper world is the home of ancestors, but for others, deceased family members reside in the lower world.

The ritualistic blowing of smoke in four directions symbolises an appeal to spirits in the "four quarters" of the universe. Directionality is apparent in the elaborate Navajo sand paintings that the shamans destroy after they have served their purpose. Symbolism is also evident in the reports from those vision quests of the Plains Indians that helped future warriors contact their guardian spirits. Dobkin de Rios (1984) described these quests as attempts at "personal ecstatic learning" in the service of eliciting biochemical changes in the body that would enhance the altered state. Hence, tribal shamans played an important role in preparing, instructing, and guiding their initiates, as well as interpreting their visions (p. 57).

The Evolving Mind

As the study of the origin, nature, and limits of knowledge, epistemology is closely associated with Western concepts of consciousness (Winkelman, 2000, p. 177). For many years, Durkheim's (1912/1995) theories were especially influential. Taking Australian totemism as the prototype for all early spiritual experience, Durkheim focused on the feelings of security gained by life in a secure group. He conjectured that early tribes projected these feelings onto whatever object they were close to at the time they experienced them. In this way, plants, animals, rocks, and other objects were imbued with *power*, the capacity to instil strong feelings and to assist the person who befriended, ate, or wore them. According to Durkheim, ritual behaviour preceded language, which only became necessary when communication with imaginary beings was mandatory.[2]

More recently, neuropsychology has impacted explanations of these phenomena. A perspective that is especially useful in understanding shamanic epistemologies has been proposed by Newton (1996), who attempted to unravel certain entrenched philosophical puzzles concerning both consciousness and representational thought. Taking exception to purely linguistic theories of cognition, Newton took a parsimonious postmodern position on humanity's attempts to represent reality. For Newton, humanity's variegated experiences with reality demonstrate the vast range of specific sensorimotor images and sensations that constitute its direct, ongoing understanding of the environment. Newton believed that thinking makes use of the same neurological (i.e., neurognostic) structures involved in sensorimotor activity, structures that take the form of analogue models of reality; the resulting images ground humankind's concepts, constructs, and intentions.

To support this thesis Newton cited behavioural data, findings from neuroscience, and evolutionary evidence indicating that language was a tool for communication before it became the primary determinant of cognition. Taking issue with both the "reductionists" who explain sensory phenomena simply as brain properties and the "new mysterians" who see consciousness as something beyond the reach of physical theory, Newton constructed a sturdy framework that unifies not only body and mind but linguistic and non-linguistic human activities as well. Donald's (1991) model, compatible with that of Newton, gives mythmaking a key role in human evolution, describing "scenario-building" as the primary function of human mental complexity (see also Alexander, 1979). When mythic worldviews were performed

2   Durkheim's work has been unjustly ignored by many contemporary writers. His suggestion that language is associated with "displaced reference" (i.e., to communicate what is imagined or imaginary) is worthy of consideration when discussing shamanic states of consciousness.

ritually, participants were confronted with representations of objects and events in addition to those items themselves.

Corballis (1991) posited a hypothetical "generative assembling device" in the human brain, giving it credit for constructing these cognitive representations from "small vocabularies of primitive units" (p. 219). Jerison (1990) described language as a "sensory-perceptual development", stating that its role in communication first evolved as a side effect to its role in reality construction; thus, "we need language more to tell stories than to direct actions. In the telling we create mental images in our listeners that might normally be produced only by the memory of events as recorded and integrated by the sensory and perceptual systems of the brain" (pp. 15–16). This capacity required an enormous amount of neural tissue, and the convolutions of the human brain appear to have been associated with the development of language and related capacities for mental imagery (p. 16).

Some of these mental images have been termed "images of achievement" by Vandervert (1996), because they reflect a learned imaging process in the cerebral-motor cortex. This process extends into the extrapolated anticipatory future by means of fast time computations of the cerebellum. These images continually predict the outcomes of the next steps of human action or achievement and are often symbolic in nature, allowing for a condensation of considerable information and meaning.

Since the time of Goethe, many scholars have proposed that the epistemology of primordial people began with their sensorimotor experiences (Flaherty, 1992, p. 168). According to these scholars, mythmaking, a basic propensity of humankind, has its referents in both external and internal bodily functioning as well as in observable nature. Sansonese (1994) noted, "The more ancient the myth, the more often do parts of the human body play an explicit role in the myth" (p. 7), as in, for example, Adam's rib and the Egyptian myth of Set and Isis. It will be recalled that one of the possible derivations for the term "shaman" is "one who is excited, moved, or raised", while another is "inner heat"; both refer to bodily processes and appreciation of the sensory world. In addition, they are both examples of politicised talents (along with fire mastery, symbolic death, and entering "trance") that privatise shamanism and restrict its membership.

In his account of the evolution of the human mind, Mithen (1996) described the emergence of general intelligence as well as of four specialised *cognitive domains*, namely, technical intelligence, social intelligence, natural history intelligence, and language. It is likely that these domains share information in what Baars (1997) referred to as a "global workspace". Consistent with Newton's (1996) emphasis on language as a tool for communication (and contrary to Durkheim's position), Mithen (1996) held that language was originally social. Once the capacity for language was present, it was highly adaptive, eventually providing early humans with the ability to reflect on their own and other people's mental states (p. 140). In this way, it began to interact with social intelligence; still later, early humans were able to talk about tool-making (technical intelligence) as well as hunting and plant gathering (natural history intelligence). Such capacities were adaptive to survival because they could construct more accurate, hence more adaptable, models and descriptions of external events (Povinelli, 1993, p. 507).

Once these intelligences became connected across their respective domains, the resulting "linkage" enabled the production of symbolic artefacts and images as a means of communication. It also led to the essentially human tendency to attribute personality and social relationships to plants and animals, a result of the integration of social intelligence and natural history intelligence. Artefacts indicating human body decoration (e.g., pieces of ochre) date back 80,000 years or more (Gore, 1997, p. 98); other artefacts demonstrating the capacity for visual decoration (e.g., beads, pendants) date back 40,000 years (Mithen, 1996, p. 155) to the time after the Cro-Magnon people emerged. A human-shaped ivory statuette from Hohlenstein-Stadel in southern Germany is the earliest existing statuette and has been dated

at 30,000 to 33,000 years (Mithen, 1996, p. 162). The origins of shamanism are often traced back at least 30,000 years (Eliade, 1989, p. 503).

In Western Europe, the Upper Palaeolithic era began some 35,000
years ago; it is best known for its remarkable efflorescence of image-
making (Lewis-Williams, 1998). For example, the paintings in the
Lascaux caves of southern France date back 17,000 years. The prone
figure depicted on one of the walls is often regarded as a shaman
experiencing an alteration of consciousness (e.g., Eliade, 1989, p. 504),
but Berman (2000, p. 25) asked, if shamanism was so important in
Palaeolithic times why do such figures occur so rarely? One answer
might be that the paintings were done by shamans themselves (and
their assistants), so there was no need to portray the designer of the figure, only the focus of the artistic ritual. No matter what these images
represent, it is possible that symbolic image-making had been accomplished earlier but was executed on materials that did not survive.

During Krippner's visit to Lascaux in 1997, his group was allowed
only 35 minutes to tour the cave and appreciate its images; even so, it
would take the cave's atmosphere several hours to recuperate from
their intrusion. The group was overwhelmed by the raw power of the
colourful wild horses, antlered reindeer, and massive bison they
encountered. Negative space, a technique not used again in Europe
until the 16th century, was utilised to create perspective. The cave's
surface brings a three-dimensionality to the paintings—a naturally-
formed hole provides the eye for one animal, and a bulging rock
becomes the shoulder of a bison.

There are a plethora of geometric forms thought by some to be signa-
tures of the artists; if so, this convention was not revived until the
Renaissance. Some animals have been cleverly painted so that they
share body parts, while other figures are superimposed on each other
and are distinguished by colour shading (Société Préhistorique
Française, 1990; Vanaria, 1997). For some observers, the most exceptional feature of the drawings is their narrative form; they appear to
tell a story (Delluc, Delluc, & Delvert, 1990, p. 57). Tattersall (1998)

commented that, upon leaving Lascaux, one is awed by the magnificence of what these remote ancestors wrought many millennia ago. However, Hughes (2000) noted that the rock paintings in the sacred cave sites scattered across northwestern Australia "are as impressive as anything in the caves of Lascaux or Altamira, and tens of thousands of years older. As far as we know, the Australian Aborigines stood at the very dawn of human image-making" (pp. 110–111).

In the Lascaux, Altamira, and other European caves, "a small nodule becomes an animal's eye; sometimes a natural swell of the rock face was taken to delineate the chest or shoulder of an animal; sometimes the edge of a shelf became the back of an animal. To these natural features, the artists added lines, thereby transforming the given into the created. Frequently these images appear to be coming out of the rock wall. At Rouffignac, for instance, a horse's head is painted on the side of a protruding flint nodule. The rest of the horse is apparently behind the rock face" (Clottes & Lewis-Williams, 1998, p. 16). To some, these features suggest a search for spirit animals that could become "allies" if they could be drawn by shamans through a permeable "membrane" that separated the ordinary and the non-ordinary worlds (p. 16). In the Niaux cave, for example, the shadows cast across the rock can represent, to the expectant eye, the outline of a bison; then only a few deft strokes were needed to add the rest of the body. If the light is moved, the animal disappears back through the "membrane". The person has thus mastered the spirit animal; he or she can make it come and go at will (p. 17). Once more, Berman (2000) cautioned that there are other explanations for the profusion of animal images, one of them a simple desire to execute a naturalistic portrayal. Sometimes, grazing deer are simply grazing deer (p. 31).

Symbolic or not, Winkelman (2000) pointed out that neuropsychology provides a basis for these rock art motifs; hardwired, neurologically structured, perceptual constants are the structural basis of these motifs, reflecting perceptions obtained through shamanic states of consciousness. The animal images reflect "the importance of neurognostic perspectives in understanding shamanism" (p. 6). Clottes and Lewis-Williams (1998) went even further, stating that "all shamanic activity and experience necessarily take place within a particular kind of universe, or cosmos. [But] the ways in which this shamanic cosmos is conceived are generated by the human nervous system rather than by intellectual speculation or detached observation of the environment" (p. 19). We contend that neurognostic potentials and social construction operate in tandem with each other as well as the ecology of time and location. The ensuing dance produces a phenomenon that needs to be examined from the vantage point of both perspectives.

Commenting on the paintings themselves, Mithen (1996) deduced, "There is nothing gradual about the evolution of the capacity for art: the very first pieces that we find can be compared in quality with those produced by the great artists of the Renaissance.... All that was needed was a connection between these cognitive processes which had evolved for other tasks to create the wonderful paintings in Chauvet Cave," which date back at least 30,000 years (pp. 162–163). Also predating Lascaux was the extraction of decorative red and black pigment from Bomvu Ridge in South Africa, some 40,000 years ago (Boshier & Costello, 1975).

The magnificent distinctiveness of these works is noteworthy in view of Ludwig's (1992) proposition that "the visionary or magic function of these media ... was more important than esthetics [sic]" (p. 459). "The shaman artist ... employed carved masks, music and art for the purposes of healing, negotiation with unseen spirits, exerting magical influences on creatures, and depicting his [or her] adventures in the spirit world" (p. 459). Again, neurognostic structures can be hypothesised to have formed the basis for these creative products; Clottes (in Gore, 2000) asserts, "People can no longer say art evolved from crude beginnings" (p. 108).

The sepia, black, and red ochre Chauvet, Altamira, and Lascaux paintings might be symbolic. However, Berman (2000) offered an alternative: the experience of these early humans was direct and immediate (p. 81). This epistemology runs through many postmodern writings; for example, Globus (1995) remarked, "We do not know reality, according to postmodernism, by means of any representations of reality. We know reality directly and immediately; there is nothing that gets between us and the reality we always and already find ourselves in" (p. 127).

Modernity, in contrast, relies on representations of reality — mental and neural representations that mediate between humanity and the world. In other words, modern epistemologies assume that an investigator can provide a near-identical match between words and the phenomena they attempt to describe. Postmodern epistemologies assume that this type of representation is impossible, and that symbolism, metaphor, and allegory provide better descriptions of outer and inner experience. Several descriptions, some of them paradoxical, are frequently used to "deconstruct" a phenomenon in an attempt to fathom it creatively.

Shamanic Epistemology

For the shaman, everything provided knowledge about everything else, and the whole of being was "fundamentally an immense signal system" (Kalweit, 1992, p. 77). Shamanic states of consciousness were the first steps toward deciphering (or deconstructing) the signal system; this was made possible once humanity's symbolic capacity matured. At that point "language shifted from a social to a general-purpose function, consciousness from a means to predict other individuals' behaviour to managing a mental database of information relating to all domains of behaviour. A cognitive fluidity arose within the mind, reflecting new connections rather than new processing power" (Mithen, 1996, p. 209). To this discussion of signal systems, we would suggest that role-playing, as well as language, be considered a likely contender as the mechanism for cognitive fluidity. Pretending and role-playing enable people to represent the internal state of others, a skill that enables cognitive cross-referencing to take place.

Clottes and Lewis-Williams (1998) have proposed three stages of shamanic consciousness. In Stage One, people move from alert consciousness to a "light" alteration, beginning to experience geometric forms, meandering lines, and other "phosphenes" or "form constants", so named because they are wired into the nervous system. For example, the Tukano of South America use undulating lines of dots to represent the Milky Way, the goal of shamanic journeying.

In Stage Two, people begin to attribute complex meanings to these "constants", and in Stage Three, these constants are combined with images of people, animals, and mythical beings. Experients began to interact with these images, often feeling themselves to be transformed into animals, either completely or partially (e.g., the celebrated *Les Trois Frères* animal/human); shamanic journeys are generally felt to be more feasible in this form (p. 19). Various chambers of Upper Palaeolithic caves seem to have been restricted to advanced practitioners; some caves have spacious chambers embellished with large, imposing images, while elsewhere there are often small, sparsely decorated diverticules into which only a few people could congregate (p. 20).

From an epistemological perspective, shamans gained knowledge from their journeys into other realms of existence, and communicated the results to members of the community (Flaherty, 1992, p. 185). Shamans provided information from a database consisting of their dreams, visions, and intuitions, as well as their keen observations of the natural and social world. Sansonese (1994) suggested that there was "a degree of genetic predisposition for falling into trance" and that this ability made a significant contribution to social evolution (p. 30). For example, there was a succession of Indo-European shamans whose traditions included parent-to-child transmissions of shamanic lore that, in turn, institutionalised extended-family shamanic groups (p. 30).

The ability to manipulate symbols was essential in the interpretation of dreams and visions as well as in the creation of myths. For Sansonese (1994), "a myth is an esoteric description of a heightened proprioception" (p. 36). "Myth describes a systematic exploration of the human body by privileged members of archaic cultures. Myth springs from an age of universal narcissism, rooted, one must suppose, in the elemental struggle for survival" (p. 37). Explanations were needed for birth, death, illness, procreation, and other bodily phenomena, as well as for cyclones, forest fires, floods, sunsets, eclipses, and the changes of seasons. The human brain is wired for beliefs and myths, not for facts; cultural myths provide immediate survival mechanisms, while the search for factual knowledge, which might be adaptive in the long run, requires discipline and is time-consuming.

There were many contenders for survival millennia ago. However, Mithen (1996) proposed that *Homo sapiens*, who date from about 250,000 years ago (Jerison, 1990, p. 10), had many evolutionary advantages over other early humans, abstract thought and language among them. Eventually, *Homo sapiens sapiens* had the ability to use symbolism in image making and storytelling, both of which were adaptive because they helped to make sense of one's body, one's peers, and one's environment.

Neanderthals were powerfully built, large-brained people who seemed to display an equivalent sophistication to modern humans in their manufacture of stone tools, and who had the vocal mechanisms needed for rudimentary speech. But Neanderthals lived in inclement climates (Mithen, 1996, p. 125), were prone to degenerate diseases (p. 126), and lacked the technology to sew garments and—most curiously—the ability to produce elegant pictorial images. There are a few pieces of pierced bone attributed to Neanderthals, but even these artefacts are in doubt (p. 135). There is no conclusive evidence that ritual was a part of Neanderthal burials, or that human-made objects were placed within the graves (p. 136). In any event, the Neanderthals disappeared some 30,000 years ago (Tattersall, 1998). In the meantime, with specialised intelligences that could effectively communicate with each other, *Homo sapiens sapiens* were probably unique among early humans in their ability to symbolise, mythologize, and, eventually, to shamanize.

Taussig (1987) described the "inscription of a mythology in the Indian body" where "power is invested" (p. 27), while Sansonese (1994) remarked, "Something is being described in myth, something about the human body, something essential to its workings but also truly technical and beyond mere fetish" (p. 38). He also noted that "the development of myth parallels the esoteric impulse in storytelling" (p. 38). The domination of *Homo sapiens sapiens* may have been due to their ability to use sensory and motor activity as a bridge to produce stories that assured survival (Boaz, 1997; Cavalli-Sforza & Cavalli-Sforza, 1995; Fagan, 1990; Kingdon, 1993; Ruhlen, 1994; Stringer & McKie, 1996).

The way people come to report the feeling states that arise within their own bodies is incompletely understood (Lubinski & Thompson, 1993). Nevertheless, these private events have been a prime source for the creation of myths by the shaman and the community (Devereux, 1997). Lubinski and Thompson (1993) have underscored the role of psychotropic agents in bringing internal feeling states into awareness, citing animal research to buttress their argument. Merkur's (1998) description of "psychedelic ecstasies" includes categories in which internal dialogues reflect feeling states invoked by LSD-type drugs, while Nesse and Berridge (1997) have identified the associated neural mechanisms, noting their evolutionary origins.

To the impact of external psychotropic agents one might add the contribution of the body's own biochemistry, especially during rapid eye movement (REM) sleep, typically characterised by dreaming. Ullman (1987) suggested that REM sleep reflects a genetic imperative that often orients the dreamer's "felt connections to others" in the interest of species survival; research with other organisms suggests that REM sleep or a precursor may be the earliest form of mammalian sleep (Siegel, 1997).

Hobson (1988), operating from a different paradigm, added that dreaming is a "behavioural state" that reflects an evolutionary specialisation (pp. 112–113). He continued, "In dreams, problems are not only posed but sometimes even solved" (p. 16), and somatic stimuli are one source of the images that the brain converts into dream narratives (p. 46). We would suggest that shamans were especially adroit in using dream and psychedelic imagery to address and find solutions to the conundrums periodically faced by members of their community and the group as a whole.

Shamanism and "Higher" States

Wilber (1981) noted that shamans were the first practitioners to systematically access "higher" states of consciousness. He has categorised these "higher" states as the "subtle" (those leading to enhanced mental imagery both with form—e.g., angels, spirits—and without form—e.g., "white light", "music of the spheres"; the "causal" (those states in which there are no longer any forms in one's awareness, e.g., "pure awareness", "the void"); and the "absolute" (the state in which consciousness has experienced its "true nature" and in which a "ground of being" is experienced). As previously mentioned, according to Wilber the shamans' focus has been on "subtle" states because their technology was directed toward assisting other people with the images obtained in their shamanic journeys.

Wilber (1981) has taken the position that consciousness unfolds not only during the life-span of an individual, but during the evolution of humanity in general, with some individuals representing the "farthest reaches" of that development (p. 142). This evolution of consciousness, according to Wilber, was not part of a biological process but was due to the development of such elements of spiritual practice as "rigorous systems of ethics", "emotional transformation", the "training of attention and concentration", and the "cultivation of wisdom" (p. 142).

However, Eliade (1989) found comparative examples of the oldest types of Christian and Hindu mystical experience in Alaskan Eskimo shamanism. Walsh (1990a) recognised "rigorous systems of ethics" in those North American shamanic traditions emphasising compassion. He discovered "emotional transformation" among Australian aboriginal shamanic initiation programs, and "training of attention and concentration" among Eskimo initiates who were subjected to a 30-day period of isolation where they were directed to "think only of the Great Spirit". Furthermore, Walsh found "cultivation of wisdom" in Ainu, Cuna, and Zuni shamanic traditions, where entire mythologies, pharmacopoeia, and song cycles had to be memorised and understood. After surveying the cross-cultural research, Coan (1987) warned, "It would be a mistake to assume that shamanism represents just one stage either in the evolution of human society or in the evolution of human consciousness" (p. 62).

Moreover, a careful reading of Wilber (1993) suggests a limited familiarity with the literature on shamanism. He referred to Eliade's (1989) *Shamanism: Archaic Techniques of Ecstasy* as "the definitive study of the subject" (p. 70). Yet it takes nothing away from the importance of this pioneering work to suggest that Eliade "did not address the subject matter in the appropriate cultural context" (Ripinsky-Naxon, 1993, p. 11). For example, Eliade displayed "personal bias" in using the term "degenerate" to describe the use of mind-altering substances by shamans, failing to "recognise the critical role of hallucinogens" in many forms of shamanism (p. 103).

Wilber described shamanism as a "religion", albeit one that is "extremely crude, very unrefined, and not highly evolved" (p. 75). But most writers on shamanism focus on its technologies, its worldviews, and its ways of knowing rather than on its resemblance to institutionalised religions (Harner, 1980; Krippner & Welch, 1992). At most, shamanic practices have led to religious syncreticism (Ripinsky-Naxon, 1993, p. 207), e.g., Tibetan Buddhism and Taoism reflect earlier shamanic practices. By writing about "the true shaman" (p. 76) rather than of shamans and shamanic experiences (Heinze, 1991; Walsh, 1990a), Wilber focused on a hypothetical figure that has been socially constructed over the ages, along with his own perspective of this figure. He could have served his purposes better by spreading his net more widely, catching and evaluating an assortment of practitioners and social groups who have manifested so-called "subtle" states over the millennia (see also Kremer, 1996, and Winkelman, 1993, for more detailed critiques of Wilber's model and his interpretations of shamanism).

Wilber probably would consider María Sabina's *veladas* typical "subtle" state imagery, but what could María Sabina have chanted that would have been more meaningful to her clients and more descriptive of her work?

> These are my children,
> These are my babies,
> These are my offshoots,
> My buds,
> I am only asking, examining,
> About His business as well,
> I begin in the depth of the water,
> I begin where the primordial sounds forth,
> Where the sacred sounds forth.
> I am a little woman who goes through the water,
> I am a little woman who goes through the stream,
> I bring my light,
> Ah, Jesus Christ,
> Medicinal herbs and sacred herbs of Christ,
> I'm going to thunder,
> I'm going to play music,
> I'm going to shout,
> I'm going to whistle,
> It's a matter of tenderness, a matter of clarity,
> There is no resentment,
> There is no rancour,
> There is no argument,
> There is no anger,

It is life and well-being.
(Estrada, 1981, abridged, pp. 136, 150–151, 165, 175)

In these brief excerpts from María Sabina's *veladas*, we find a woman who goes into the primordial waters of oceanic consciousness. However, she does not stay there, because her orientation is toward service, toward healing, toward her community, and toward the children and babies to whom she strives to bring life and well-being.

Obviously, there is no way of knowing if María Sabina had reached the "causal" or "absolute" realm of Wilber's hierarchy. If so, what knowledge would she have obtained that would have been more useful to her in her mission than the symbolic images and metaphors that emanate in her *veladas*? Nor is Coan (1987) impressed by Wilber's "sharp dichotomy" (p. 143); the shaman can use many dimensions of consciousness at different times for different purposes. No shamanic performance is ever exactly the same.

These *veladas* demonstrate María Sabina's shamanic ways of knowing by means of the "sacred herbs" that facilitate her journey through the "heart" and through the "water", bringing her "light" and "tenderness" in the service of "life and well-being". Here we have an example of the shamanic images "that are directed at reestablishing and maintaining a balanced relationship between nature and the community and at caring for the spiritual and physical welfare of its members" (Ripinsky-Naxon, 1993, p. 207). The *veladas* also provide examples of ritual as social performance (V. Turner, 1968) and of symbols that seem to "trigger" healing (E. Turner, 1992). From a postmodern perspective, it is merely an intellectual exercise to arrange such manifestations of consciousness on a scale of "lower" to "higher" without considering the demands of a local situation at a particular moment in time.

Discussion

Western science is characterised by a search for satisfactory explanations of "reality". This search is achieved by statements of general principles, which can be tested experimentally or through repeated observations (Goldstein & Goldstein, 1978). Shamanic epistemology also attempts to explain "reality". Shamanic mythology is adaptive because it employs repeated observations and makes statements about general principles. However, credence is given to revelation and inspiration from the "spirit world", from plant and animal "allies", and from "journeys" associated with changed states of consciousness. A provocative example is the complex brew ayahuasca, which goes by many other names, depending on the part of the Amazon where it is used. Shamans have imbibed ayahuasca for hundreds of years, but its origin remains a mystery to Western investigators. Some tribes attribute this knowledge to spiritual beings from subaquatic realms, others to the intervention of giant serpents, and others to the intelligence of the plants themselves (Luna & White, 2000).

Narby (1998) commented, "Here are people ... who choose, among 80,000 Amazonian plant species, the leaves of a bush containing a ... brain hormone, which they combine with a vine containing substances that inactivate an enzyme of the digestive tract, which would otherwise block the effect. And they do this to modify their consciousness.... When one asks them how they knew these things, they say their knowledge comes directly from [the] plants" (p. 11). For several years, Krippner worked with an intertribal medicine man and shamanic healer, Rolling Thunder. When Krippner asked him how he was able to identify the curative power of plants he had never used previously, he remarked, "I ask the plant what it is good for. Some plants are only meant to be beautiful. Other plants are meant for food. Still others are to be used as medicine. Once a healing plant has spoken to me, I ask its permission to take it with me and add it to my medicine pouch." Rolling Thunder's epistemology was remarkably similar to that of the Amazonian shamans who work with ayahuasca.

In a world beset by quandaries and crises, survival no longer depends upon the process of natural selection or chance mutations, but rather on intentional deliberations and conscientious decision making. Western modernity has failed to build a universal human culture upon a foundation of abstract rational thought. Humanity cannot repeat the past, but postmodernity would do well to reconsider the personal, metaphorical language that the Royal Society of London deliberately scuttled in its attempt to produce a universal language of objective and unequivocal symbols (Mahoney & Albert, 1997, p. 23). The failure of this project was, in part, due to its ignorance of one of the points permeating this chapter, namely: language makes use of the same structures as those involved in sensorimotor activity; these structures take the form of analogue models of reality; and the resulting images ground humankind's concepts, constructs, and intentions.

Vandervert's model (1996) provides a "neuro-epistemological" framework for this proposition; he wrote that "the neuro-algorithmic organisation of the phylogenetic brain is that which evolved originally as the algorithms for perception, learning-memory, cognition, and emotion-motivation involved in the struggle for survival" (p. 82). These representations are reflected in shamanic technologies that, first and foremost, were devoted to finding game animals, locating and using medicinal plants, determining the best time to plant and harvest crops, and other matters of daily survival. Shamanic technologies also had spiritual uses, but contemporary Westerners often emphasise the transcendental side of shamanism to the neglect of its practical aspects.

Vandervert (1997) proposed that "image-schemas" (see Mandler, 1988) are not tantamount to the organism's storehouse of images, but the space-time representations that co-exist with perceptual processes, both of which precede mental imagery. These space-time simulation structures are genetic in origin and are responsible for the state-estimating functions that are connected to the cerebrum's mapping systems. The resulting image-schemas are whetted by experience as well as by developmental processes.

Vandervert's proposal that image-schemas represent "foundational meanings" (p. 111) is reminiscent of Jung's description of "archetypes", the structural predispositions that allegedly provide the organising principles for consciousness and behaviour. These image-schemas collectively represent what Vandervert considered to be a "calculus" of archetypal processing. Such image-schematic process- ing, although a process of natural selection, had the immanent poten- tial to lead to emergent future state estimates (i.e., nonlinear simulations) that extended beyond purely naturally selected states or the selective mechanism that evoked them. In this way, image-sche- matic simulations imparted a freedom beyond natural selection that provided a world of potentially new paths for human intention.

The nervous system evolved in ways that enabled it to foresee many future events; indeed, rapid simulation was the basic approach to sur- vival-conducive prediction (Fox, 1988, pp. 160–161). The nervous sys- tem's ability to produce such simulation structures as image-schemas permitted anticipatory, feedforward processing (see Pribram, 1991, chap. 6). For Vandervert, image-schemas represent the foundational structures needed "for modelling/mapping functions conducive for survival" (pp. 114–115). Without this ability to make estimates of future conditions, vertebrate organisms could not have survived to reproduce. According to Vandervert, these processes originated in the cerebellum but eventually involved "the entire mapping machinery of the brain" (p. 118); it was the auditory-vocal sharing of image-schemat- ics that eventually led to language (p. 120).

We would propose that the image-schemas of those men and women held by a community to be shamanic practitioners were especially adept when prediction was demanded. Game needed to be located, weather patterns needed to be forecast, enemy movements needed to be anticipated, and flight paths needed to be discovered. These tasks required feedforward processing, and the shamanic fine-tuning of image-schemas through heightened perception and/or changed states of consciousness may have assisted this assignment. Such neuro- gnostic frameworks are needed to unite human neurophysiology with human epistemology, and to explore what Chalmers (1996) referred to as "the hard problem": how consciousness arises from physical sys- tems. "While evolution can be very useful in explaining why particular physical systems have evolved, it is irrelevant to the explanation of the bridging principles in virtue of which some of these systems are conscious" (p. 121).

One final example from the life of María Sabina demonstrates these image-schemas. When she was first called to shamanize, Doña María claimed that she received the image of an open book that grew until it reached the size of a person. She was told, "This is the Book of Wisdom. It is the Book of Language. Everything that is written in it is for you. The Book is yours, take it so that you can work." In accepting this call, Doña María became a "woman of language" and what Rothenberg (1981) called a "great oral poet" (p. 10).

Now may be the time to reconsider the ways of knowing exemplified by Doña María, and their sources in imagination, intuition, visions, dreams, the senses, and the body.[3] Perhaps these ways of knowing can enter into tandem with intellect and reason to construct cooperative and collaborative lifestyles for the pluralistic world in which we live, a world which shamanic epistemology would appreciate and enjoy.

Conclusion

In this chapter we continued the demystifying process by elucidating the shamans' epistemology, which, we argued, depended on deliberately altering their consciousness and/or heightening their perception to contact "spiritual entities" in realms consistent with the shaman's cultural cosmology. In addition, we contended that shamanic technol-

---

[3] Reports reminiscent of shamanic epistemology and technologies appear from time to time in first-person accounts regarding technical and creative accomplishments. Robert Louis Stevenson wrote that ideas for some of his short stories came from the "little people" who influenced his dreams; Giuseppe Tartini dreamed that a devil composed a piece of violin music for him, which he later transcribed; Sriniwasa Ramanujan noted that the Hindu goddess Namakkal provided him with original mathematical insights while he dreamed; Herman Hilprecht attributed an archeological discovery to a Babylonian priest who visited him in a dream; Francisco Candido Xavier's prodigious literary output was supposedly made possible by discarnate "spirits" who dictated his poetry, plays, and best-selling novels; Johannes Brahms confided that his best symphonic work was divinely inspired (e.g., Krippner & Dillard, 1998).

ogies, essential for the production of myths, interacted with shamanic epistemology, reinforcing its basic assumptions about reality. The resulting mythologies gave rise to ritual performances; on one level, they are impressive spectacles that entertain as well as perform, but on another level they were essential for survival itself.

The Confusion of Consciousness with Phenomenological Content in Shamanic Studies

Over the past few decades, several psychologists (e.g., Noll, 1983, 1985; Peters, 1981, 1989; Peters & Price-Williams, 1980; Walsh, 1993b, 1995) have postulated various phenomenological (i.e., subjective) elements of "shamanic states of consciousness" (e.g., altered volitional control, altered body image) in an attempt to operationalise the term. However, it is arguable that the concept of "shamanic states of consciousness" is neither well defined nor sufficiently understood (Rock & Krippner, 2008). The psychological literature on shamanism is replete with terms such as "shamanic states of consciousness", as we have seen in the first two chapters of this book. In this chapter, we will attempt to demonstrate that a fallacy herein referred to as the "consciousness/content fallacy" occurs when one moves from the key definitional elements of the term "consciousness" to "shamanic states of consciousness". We therefore recommend that the latter term be supplanted with "shamanic patterns of phenomenal properties".

The purpose of this chapter is to elucidate the aforementioned fallacy and provide an attempt at resolution. We proceed by reviewing several definitions of consciousness, arguing that they all exemplify a commonality with regard to the implicit distinction between consciousness and the content of consciousness. Secondly, the consciousness/ content fallacy is explicated through an analysis of the concept of "states of consciousness". Finally, after the consciousness/content fallacy is examined with reference to the concept of shamanic states of consciousness, a solution to the fallacy is proposed.

It is noteworthy that there exist instances in which the key definitional elements of the term "consciousness" range from conscious awareness plus unconscious functioning (Krippner, 1972) to no more than awareness, attention, and memory (Farthing, 1992). This chapter, however, is concerned with the concept of consciousness as the "cognisor" of objects (e.g., internal and external events) and the fallacy that occurs when a shift from the term "consciousness" to that of "states of consciousness" is accompanied by a confusion of consciousness with its content. Consequently, for the purpose of this chapter, only the conscious awareness component of the concept of consciousness will be considered.

Consciousness and Phenomenological Content

Forman (1996) stated that the inherent difficulty associated with providing an adequate definition of consciousness is due in part to the multiplicity of meanings ascribed to the term. Block (2002) suggested that this multiplicity of meanings derives from the erroneous treatment as a single concept of very different concepts. For example, in an influential series of articles, Block (e.g., 1995, 2002) distinguished a number of notions of consciousness: phenomenal, access, self, and monitoring consciousness.

Block (2002) stated that phenomenal consciousness (p-consciousness) refers to one being aware of "experiential properties of sensations, feelings and perceptions ... thoughts, wants and emotions" (p. 206). In contrast, access-consciousness (a-consciousness) is a non-phenomenal notion of consciousness. An entity exemplifying a-consciousness is one that is aware of information "poised for direct rational control of action" (Silby, 1998, p. 3). Block suggested that self-consciousness (s-consciousness) is illustrated by "me-ishness". An s-conscious entity is one that is aware of the concept of the self; one's usage of this concept (explicitly or implicitly) in thinking about oneself also reveals s-consciousness. Consciousness may further be conceptualised as an internal monitor; that is, monitoring consciousness (m-consciousness). Block also suggested that an entity may be m-conscious of inner perceptions, internal scanning, and meta-cognitive thoughts resulting from entering a particular cognitive state.

A commonality exemplified by the preceding notions of consciousness is that "When people are conscious, they are always conscious of *something*. Consciousness always has an object" (Benjafield, 1992, p. 58).[1] For example, one may be p-conscious of phenomenal properties; a-conscious of information that may be invoked to control actions; s-conscious of one's self-concept; or m-conscious of, for example, internal scanning. Benjafield's contention is by no means novel. Indeed, over a century ago, Husserl (cited in Sartre, 1958) argued, "All consciousness ... is consciousness *of* something" (p. li). Similarly, Sartre asserted that consciousness always attends to a "transcendent object" and is thereby precluded from being phenomenologically contentless.

---

1   One notable exception is an unmediated form of mystical experience referred to as the pure consciousness event (PCE) (e.g., Almond, 1982; Bucknell, 1989a; Franklin, 1990; Kessler & Prigge, 1982; Matt, 1990; Perovich, 1990; Prigge & Kessler, 1990; Rothberg, 1990; Woodhouse, 1990). Forman (1990a) defined the PCE as "a wakeful though contentless (nonintentional) consciousness" (p. 8). A substantial body of evidence has been produced that supports the purported existence of the PCE. For example, Chapple (1990) reported that descriptions of *kaivalyam* in the Samkhya system and *samadhi* in the *Yoga Sutras* are suggestive of the "attainment of a purified consciousness that is beyond characterisation" (p. 70). Griffiths (1990) surveyed the Indian Buddhist tradition and found evidence for a condition referred to as the attainment of cessation (*nirodhasamapatti*), which is defined as "the non-occurrence of mind and mental concomitants" (p. 78). Bucknell (1989b) suggested that the "third non-material *jhana*" encountered in Buddhist meditation is analogous to the introvertive mystical experience "in which both the thought-stream and sensory input have ceased, leaving zero mental content" (p. 19). Forman (1990b) examined the mystical theology of the Christian mystic Meister Eckhart, concluding that Eckhart considered one's encounter with the Godhead to be "phenomenologically contentless".

Sartre referred to this type of consciousness as "positional self-consciousness", stating that:

> All that there is of *intention* in my actual consciousness is directed toward the outside, toward the table; all my judgments or practical activities, all my present inclinations transcend themselves; they aim at the table and are absorbed in it. Not all consciousness is knowledge (there are states of affective consciousness, for example), but all knowing consciousness can be knowledge only of its object. (p. 1ii)

A survey of the cognitive psychology literature further supports Benjafield's (1992) contention. In brief, some cognitive psychologists (e.g., Matlin, 1998; Nairne, 1997; Solso, 2001) tend to define consciousness as the awareness of internal and external events (i.e., mental phenomena and stimuli in the environment, respectively). In contrast, others (e.g., Westen, 1999, p. G-4) limit the definitional boundary of consciousness to "the subjective awareness of mental events". It is arguable that these assertions constitute the core of consciousness concepts in cognitive psychology today. Commenting on the definition of consciousness as being aware of something, Natsoulas (1978) wrote: "It is difficult to emphasise sufficiently the fundamental importance of consciousness in the present sense. It is arguably our most basic concept of consciousness, for it is implicated in all the other senses" (p. 910).

The salient point exemplified by the preceding descriptions of consciousness is the distinction between consciousness and the content of consciousness. For example, Block's (2002) phenomenal consciousness is not composed of experiential properties such as sensations and perceptions (contents of p-consciousness), but rather refers to one *being p-conscious* of experiential properties such as sensations and perceptions.

The Consciousness/Content Fallacy

As stated above, consciousness is often defined as awareness of internal and external events (e.g., Matlin, 1998; Nairne, 1997; Solso, 2001) or merely awareness of something (e.g., Natsoulas, 1978). In contrast, a so-called "state" of consciousness (SoC) tends to be defined as "[the set] of mental episodes of which one can readily become directly aware" (Natsoulas, p. 912). While definitions of consciousness typically distinguish consciousness from the content of consciousness, the preceding definition of SoCs represents a theoretical confusion of consciousness and its contents by explicitly stating that an SoC *is* the content (i.e., mental episodes) available to conscious awareness. That is, when the qualifier "state" is affixed to consciousness, "it" [consciousness] is held to be content. Consequently, the term *states* of consciousness rests on a confusion of consciousness and content whereby consciousness is erroneously categorised in terms of content rendered perceptible, presumably, by "itself". We refer to this as the consciousness/content fallacy.

Implicit in the consciousness/content fallacy is the erroneous notion that during an SoC consciousness may observe "its" own qualities. For example, a privileged observer would be conscious only of the fact that he or she was experiencing a particular SoC (i.e., that consciousness exemplified state-like properties), if consciousness could observe its own properties. However, one cannot directly experience the conscious awareness process, CA_1, which functions to render an object perceptible, because this would require the postulation of a second conscious awareness process, CA_2, necessary to render CA_1 a perceptible object, thereby committing one to a vicious regress.

Furthermore, others (e.g., Feinberg, 2001; Kant, 1781/1933; Vasu, 1979) have argued that consciousness cannot directly experience "itself" as a perceptible object, for then it would cease to be the subject.[2]

---

2 For our purposes, consciousness is not considered a subject in the literal sense of a thing that attends to objects, but rather a process of subjectivity that renders objects perceptible.

Wilber (1993) stated that the circumstance is analogous to a sword that cannot cut itself, an eye that cannot see itself, a tongue that cannot taste itself, or a finger that cannot touch its own tip. This argument has been reiterated in Baladeva's commentary to the *Vedanta-sutras of Badarayana*, in which he wrote, "If the Self could perceive His own properties, He could also perceive Himself; which is absurd, since one and the same thing cannot be both the agent and the object of an action" (Vasu, p. 331). Similarly, in the *Brihadaranyaka-Upanishad* it is stated that, "You cannot see the seer of sight, you cannot hear the hearer of sound, you cannot think the thinker of the thought, you cannot know the knower of the known" (Swami & Yeats, 1970, p. 138). As Kant argued:

> I cannot know as an object that which I must presuppose in order to know any object, and that the determining self (the thought) is distinguished from the self that is to be determined (the thinking subject) in the same way that knowledge is distinguished from its object. (p. 365)

A variant of the consciousness/content fallacy may be found in Pekala's (1991) statement that, "By consciousness I mean one's awareness of one's subjective experience, including both the processes of being aware and the various contents of the awareness" (p. 1). That is, Pekala is contending that consciousness is *both* "one's awareness of one's subjective experience" *and* "the various contents of the awareness" (p. 1). Consequently, rather than committing the consciousness/content fallacy via a movement from a definition of consciousness to a definition of SoCs, Pekala has implicitly conflated consciousness and content within the context of a single definition.

From Shamanic States of Consciousness to Shamanic Patterns of Phenomenal Properties

A survey of the literature suggests that the key definitional elements of shamanic states of consciousness (SSCs) pertain to the objects or content of consciousness, rather than alterations in consciousness. For example, Peters and Price-Williams (1980) attempted to delineate trans-cultural factors indicative of shamanic ecstasy by examining the ethnographic literature pertaining to 42 different cultures. They concluded that so-called shamanic ecstasy is a specific kind of ASC involving "mastery" or control with respect to both the entrance and duration of the ASC, "post trance memory", and the ability to communicate with spectators during the ASC.

In challenging Silverman's (1967) contention that shamanism is a form of schizophrenia, Noll (1983, p. 443) utilised a "state-specific approach to the phenomenology" of SSCs and various schizophrenic states in order to demonstrate that they are qualitatively incompatible. A variety of important distinctions were identified. First, the shaman enters and leaves SSCs by his or her own volition, whereas the schizophrenic is the "helpless victim of his" (Noll, p. 450). Second, the shaman has the ability to discriminate between ordinary waking consciousness and non-ordinary states of consciousness such as SSCs, while schizophrenics often tend to lack this discriminative faculty. Third, the content of the schizophrenic's inner experiences tends to be "overtly negative" (e.g., delusions of persecution), whereas this affliction is generally absent in shamanism (Noll, p. 451). The shaman's reported perceptions are predominantly visual (e.g., "predatory creatures", "spirit helpers"), while those of the schizophrenic tend to be auditory (e.g., voices perceived to be external to the percipient). Finally, Noll stated that schizophrenia "is characterised by a flattening, blunting, or a contextually inappropriate expression of affect" (p. 454). In contrast, the shaman enters ecstatic states that result in an intensification of "contextually appropriate expressions of affect for public display" (p. 454).

Additionally, Noll (1983) attempted to distinguish between shamanic visionary states and those deriving from other traditions (e.g., Tantric yoga, ritual magic, alchemy, witchcraft). Noll acknowledged that controlled visionary states function as an integral component of various Eastern (e.g., Tantric yoga) and Western (e.g., ritual magic) traditions. SSCs may be conceptualised as visionary states characterised by vivid and spontaneous mental imagery to which the aspirant confers "absolute ontological validity" (Noll, p. 445). The aspirant adopts the role of participant-observer, exercising volitional control over the phenomenological effects associated with SSCs (Peters & Price-Williams, 1980). The shaman's penchant for active engagement distinguishes him or her from experts associated with other traditions that tend to passively attend to their visionary content. According to Noll, another crucial distinction concerns the "intrapersonal" and "interpersonal" aims associated with the shaman's entry into an SSC—expressly, the obtaining of knowledge on behalf of the community, the desire to heal one's self or others, and divination practices.

Peters (1989) asserted that SSCs may be likened to an imaginal or directed-daydreaming state that is tantamount to the "lucid" or "waking dream". Peters further contended that SSCs are not necessarily indicative of psychopathology nor do they involve a dissociative amnesia. Moreover, the aspirant can, to a large degree, apply volitional control over the imaginal content and duration of SSCs: "Significant for the psychological perspective is that both shamanistic embodiment and magical flight involve controlled visualisations, are lucid and [are] non-amnesic" (Peters, p. 120). Peters also asserted that SSCs are indicative of a transpersonal experience (i.e., transcendence of the spatial and temporal boundaries associated with the individual's self-identity).

Arguably the most sophisticated phenomenological research undertaken to date in the area of shamanism has been by Walsh (1990a, 1993a, 1993b, 1995), who engaged in the multidimensional mapping of shamanic journeying experiences and reported (1) an increase in concentration; (2) "fluid" (moves freely between selected visual images) rather than fixed or "one-pointed" (e.g., the Buddhist *jhanas*) concentration; (3) volitional control over entry and exit and partial control over one's phenomenology; (4) high levels of arousal and thus a decrease in calmness; (5) positive or negative affect that may be contingent upon the visual mental imagery encountered; (6) a self-sense experienced as a "soul" distinct from the physical body; (7) visual imagery that is highly organised, often multi-sensory (e.g., visual, auditory, somatic), and compatible with a shamanic cosmology; and (8) a reduced awareness of the environment. (This last characteristic, however, is considered to be minimal, as the shaman still possesses the ability to communicate with spectators.)

The salient point is that the key definitional elements of SSCs do not pertain to consciousness but rather to the objects of consciousness; that is, content of which a privileged observer may be consciously aware (e.g., visual mental imagery, body image, volitional control, affect). Consequently, if one uses "SSCs" as a subsidiary part of the notion of consciousness as being conscious of *something* (e.g., an internal or external event), then one has committed the consciousness/content fallacy on the ground that consciousness is implicitly held to be both: (1) the *process* that allows a privileged observer to be consciously aware of content, that is, constituents of a privileged observer's momentary experience (i.e., definitions of consciousness); and (2) the *content* itself (i.e., definitions of SSCs). That is, when the qualifier "shamanic states" is affixed to consciousness, "it" [consciousness] is held to be an object. Thus, the term "shamanic states of consciousness" confuses consciousness and its content (or objects) by erroneously conceptualising consciousness as an object rendered perceptible, presumably, by "itself". The erroneous implication is that consciousness can become an object for "itself". However, as previously stated, consciousness cannot directly experience itself as a perceptible object, for then it would cease to be the subject (e.g., Kant, 1781/1933; Vasu, 1979). As Schopenhauer explained:

> That the subject should become object for itself is the most monstrous contradiction ever thought of: for subject and object can only be thought one in relation to the other. This relation is their only mark, and when it is taken away the concept of subject and object is empty: if the subject is to become the object, it presup-

poses as object another subject — where is this to come from? (cited in Feinberg, 2001, p. 140)

If "shamanic states of consciousness" is not being used as a subsidiary part of the aforementioned notion of consciousness, then the definition of consciousness that has been used to extrapolate a definition for shamanic states of consciousness needs to be explicitly stated.

To reiterate: we have argued that, if the term "shamanic states of consciousness" is applied as an extension of the conscious awareness component of consciousness, then this results in a theoretical confusion of consciousness and its content; that is, consciousness is mistaken for the content of consciousness. Consequently, we argue that what has typically been referred to as a "shamanic 'state' of consciousness" is not a state of consciousness at all, but rather a specific pattern of phenomenal properties (e.g., visual mental imagery, body image, time sense, emotional feelings).

It is arguable, however, that phenomenal properties do not encapsulate the variety of perceptual, cognitive, and affective phenomena that may be objectified by consciousness. For example, as previously discussed, Block (2002) formulated the notion of access-consciousness whereby an entity is held to be conscious of non-phenomenal mental objects, for instance, information primed for the rational control of one's actions (Silby, 1998). Similarly, O'Brien and Opie (1997) suggested that "phenomenal experience" does not refer to objects associated with self-consciousness and access-consciousness (e.g., self-concept and information that may be invoked to control actions, respectively), but rather the "'what is it like?' of experience" (p. 269). For the purposes of this chapter, however, we will adopt Reber and Reber's (2001, p. 532) definition of a phenomenal field as "absolutely anything that is in the total momentary experiencing of a person, including the experience of the self," and apply it to "phenomenal properties". As a result, we will define "phenomenal properties" as the qualities of "absolutely anything that is in the total momentary experiencing of a person, including the experience of the self" (Reber &

Reber, p. 532). It is arguable that, if one defines "phenomenal proper-ties" in this way, then a "shamanic pattern of phenomenal properties" encapsulates what has been referred to by Block (1995) and others (e.g., Lormand, 1996) as phenomenal and non-phenomenal objects of con-scious awareness and, consequently, the content of which a privileged observer may be aware during an SSC.[3] One may then recommend that the term "shamanic states of consciousness" be supplanted by "sha-manic patterns of phenomenal properties." It would seem that, by reconceptualising the notion of an SSC in this manner, the theoretical confusion between consciousness and content is negated.

Implications

The consciousness/content fallacy has numerous theoretical implica-tions for "states of consciousness" research in general and shamanic studies in particular. Theories of SSCs, for example, would be enhanced by supplanting the term "shamanic states of consciousness" with "shamanic patterns of phenomenal properties." Theories contain-ing the consciousness/content fallacy would need to be revised to avoid fallacious contentions such as that consciousness is simulta-neously: (1) the "cognisor" of shifts in, for instance, "subjective experi-ence"; and (2) the shifts in "subjective experience" themselves. If a particular SSC theory did not incorporate the term "shamanic states of consciousness" as a subsidiary of the concept of consciousness as con-scious awareness of something, then this would need to be explicitly stated. Fundamentally, SSC theories would need to be reformulated so that the phenomenon being explained is alterations in phenomenal properties rather than alterations in consciousness.

In addition, the consciousness/content fallacy has implications for quantitative and qualitative research. A researcher who is cognisant of

3 It is not uncommon for scholars to use the term "phenomenal" or "phenomenological" to denote objects that, for example, Block (1995) would categorise as non-phenomenal. Similarly, Pekala's (1991) usage of the term "phenomenological experience" includes phenomena that Block would consider associated with self-consciousness (e.g., one's self as an object of consciousness).

this fallacy and wishes to develop a survey instrument to quantita-
tively measure, for example, shamanic experiences, would construct
items pertaining to alterations in phenomenal properties rather than
states of consciousness.[4] For instance, items such as "I experienced an
extremely unusual state of consciousness" would be omitted in favour
of items addressing a range of phenomenal properties (e.g., "My subjective time sense seemed to slow down"; "My visual imagery became
extremely vivid"; "I felt great joy"). Similarly, consider a research situation in which, for example, an existential-phenomenological study of
shamanic journeying experiences is conducted using semi-structured
interviews for the purpose of obtaining non-numerical data that may
be organised into comprehensive constituent themes. A researcher
who is mindful of the consciousness/content fallacy would not pose
open-ended questions about "shamanic states of consciousness" or
"alterations in consciousness". Instead, open-ended questions pertaining to phenomenal properties would be asked. For example, "Can you
please tell me about the visual mental images that you encountered
during your last journeying experience?"

Tart (1969) has posited three stages of induction that could be
applied to patterns of phenomenal properties rather than to altered
states of consciousness. First the current pattern of phenomenal properties is destabilised (as when one ingests a mind-altering substance or
when one's dream begins to become lucid). Second, there is a transition

4   Krippner and Meacham (1968) have suggested that "it may make more sense to
     speak of the 'objects' of consciousness than to speak of the 'states' of consciousness"
     (p. 150). It is noteworthy, however, that this recommendation was not arrived at via
     recognition of the consciousness/content fallacy, but rather the methodological
     difficulties associated with "searching" for a particular state — or altered state — of
     consciousness. For example, Krippner and Meacham assert that:

       The concept of "altered states of consciousness" would be valid if each
       state brought about similar subjective reports and similar
       neurophysiological reactions on the part of most individuals. With the
       exception of sleep and dream states, and with the possible exception of
       the "alpha state," these subjective and objective similarities have not
       been consistently noted (pp. 149–150).

to a new pattern (as when one observes perceptual changes after drinking ayahuasca). Third, the new pattern becomes stabilised (as when one is confident enough in a lucid dream to move it in a certain direction). Patterns of phenomenal properties can become destabilised by drumming, dancing, sleep deprivation, or any number of other conditions. The transition to another pattern is dependent on such variables as the dosage level of the drug that has been ingested, the participant's beliefs and personal myths, and the environmental setting. Finally, the stabilisation of the new pattern can lead to serenity, bliss, resolution of a problem, or in the case of shamans to victory over malicious entities, retrieval of a lost soul, or obtaining information needed for healing a community member.

Walsh's (2007) dimensions for mapping "states of consciousness" could just as easily be dimensions for mapping "patterns of phenomenal properties". They include degree of control, awareness of the environment, ability to communicate, level of concentration, degree of arousal, level of calmness, type of emotion, sense of identity, nature of inner experiences, and perceived separation from the physical body. These dimensions could lead to a map of one's pattern of phenomenal properties, a map that might have short-term or long-term stability. It could be applied to first-hand reports of shamanic journeying, to shamanic incorporation, or to any other shift in the shaman's pattern of phenomenal properties.

Conclusion

In this chapter, we have argued that the "states of consciousness" conceptual framework contributes to the mystification of shamanism, because it rests on a mistake, which we labelled the consciousness/content fallacy. Consequently, scholars of so-called "shamanic states of consciousness" have typically confused consciousness with phenomenological content. In contrast, our "patterns of phenomenal properties" conceptual framework reduces this mystification by avoiding the consciousness/content fallacy and allowing researchers of shamanic states to investigate the phenomenon that they are, in fact, purporting to investigate.

Chapter Four

Two Cross-Cultural Models for Studying Shamanic Healing Systems

For many centuries, Western investigators had little respect or regard for shamanic healing systems. However, in the 1980s such prominent psychotherapists as Jeanne Achterberg (1985), E. Fuller Torrey (1986), and Jerome D. Frank (Frank & Frank, 1991) found that many indigenous healing systems were extremely comprehensive, containing elements that could be instructive for Western psychotherapists and other mental health practitioners. In cross-cultural investigations, a "culture" is regarded as a particular group's shared way of life as manifested by language, customs, and material goods. Cross-cultural psychologists suggest that psychological generalisations cannot be made on the basis of research conducted in only one sociocultural context, but rather must be demonstrated through research that compares several cultural practices. Such practices as healing, teaching, crafts, food preparation, and dream interpretation have been described by native shamans from all the inhabited continents, many of them at conferences that focused on cross-cultural healing practices or on environmental activism. This chapter will focus on shamanic healing, a practice employed by most members of Winkelman's "shaman complex": shamans, shaman-healers, and healers.

Some shamanic practices were of value; it has been estimated that some 60 percent of the medicinal plants used by Rappahannock shamans were of demonstrable medical utility (Stein, 1942). The pharmacopoeia of the European invaders was less efficient, averaging 40 percent at the most (Krippner & Welch, 1992, p. 177). But many other interventions worked quite well because of the placebo effect; relaxation, ritual, and imagery have all been shown to have positive effects upon the immune system. Early humans who did not respond to placebos often died prematurely, and their genes dropped out of the gene pool. Dennett (2006) observed that the ailments that early humans took to shamans for treatment could have been precisely those hospitable to placebo-effect treatment. By the same token, shamans who could not shamanize — who, for example, were unable to engage in dissociation and imagination — could not be expected to serve their community well. Hence, trance phenomena, communication with the "spirits", and story-telling became adaptive traits; again, those who lacked these propensities retired at an early age, were exiled, or even were executed.

As previously noted, psychological generalisations cannot be made on the basis of research conducted in one cultural context, but rather must be demonstrated through cross-cultural research. This position is especially pertinent when applied to what Westerners would call "psychotherapeutic interventions"; thus a particular approach might be successful in one society but inappropriate in another. On the other hand, a comparison of interventions from non-Western cultural settings may yield information that can enhance Western practices.

The Siegler-Osmond Model

Siegler and Osmond (1974), in their book *Models of Madness, Models of Medicine,* proposed a 12-facet model for the purpose of comparing mental disorders, their etiology, and their treatment. In the social and behavioural sciences, the term "model" is used as an explicit or implicit structure that describes and/or explains a set of organised human behaviours and attitudes. By using this model, Krippner (1995a) attempted to improve understanding of the healing systems it represents. Models have been used to describe family interactions, personality dynamics, group conflict, and other phenomena.

Krippner modified the Siegler-Osmond model slightly, making it more amenable to cross-cultural comparisons of physical as well as mental disorders. The facets of this model are:

- Diagnosis
- Etiology
- Client's behaviour
- Treatment procedures
- Prognosis
- Personnel and institutional function
- Client's rights
- Client's duties
- Families' rights
- Families' duties
- Society's rights and duties
- Goals

The National Institutes of Health Model

In 1995, the Office of Alternative Medicine (OAM) of the United States National Institutes of Health convened a conference on research methodology. The purpose of this conference was to evaluate research needs in the field of complementary and alternative medicine (CAM). Several working groups were created to produce consensus statements on, and to identify factors critical to, a thorough and unbiased description of CAM systems, one that would be applicable to both quantitative and qualitative research in the United States and also in cross-cultural investigations on a variety of crucial topics. The panel on definition and description accepted a dual charge: To establish a definition of the field of CAM systems, for purposes of identification and research, and to identify factors critical to a thorough and unbiased

definition of CAM systems, one that would be applicable to both qualitative and quantitative research, both in the United States and in
cross-cultural investigations. The panel defined CAM in the following
way:

> Complementary and Alternative medicine (CAM) is a broad
> domain of healing resources that encompasses all health sys-
> tems, modalities, and practices and their accompanying theo-
> ries and beliefs, other than those intrinsic to the politically
> dominant health system of a particular society or culture in a
> given historical period. CAM includes all such practices and
> ideas self-defined by their users as preventing or treating ill-
> ness or promoting health and well being. Boundaries within
> CAM and between the CAM domain and the domain of the
> dominant system are not always sharp or fixed. (O'Conner et
> al., 1997)

The second charge of the panel was to establish a list of parameters
for obtaining thorough descriptions of CAM systems. The list con-
sisted of 13 categories first conceptualised by Hufford (1995). A 14th
category was omitted in this analysis, because it applied primarily to
researchers rather than practitioners.

1. Lexicon: What are the specialised terms in the system?
2. Taxonomy: What classes of health and sickness does the sys-
    tem recognise and address?
3. Epistemology: How was the body of knowledge derived?
4. Theories: What are the key mechanisms understood to be?
5. Goals for Interventions: What are the primary goals of the
    system?
6. Outcome Measures: What constitutes a successful
    intervention?
7. Social Organisation: Who uses and who practices the system?
8. Specific Activities: What do the practitioners do? What do
    they use?

9.   Responsibilities: What are the responsibilities of the practitio-
       ners, patients, families, and community members?

10.   Scope: How extensive are the system's applications?

11.   Analysis of Benefits and Barriers: What are the risks and costs
       of the system?

12.   Views of Suffering and Death: How does the system view suf-
       fering and death?

13.   Comparison and Interaction with Dominant System: What
       does this system provide that the dominant system does not?
       How does this system interact with the dominant system?

Research Question

Krippner (e.g., 1995a) asked if native healing traditions could be compared to each other, identifying both similarities and differences. In
carrying out this task, he followed a suggestion given by the World
Health Organisation's 1977 resolution to encourage the study and utilisation of traditional systems of medicine. This was followed by the
1980 revision in the American Medical Association's code of ethics,
permitting physicians to consult with, take referrals from, and make
referrals to health care practitioners who lacked orthodox medical
training. That same year, an editorial in *Lancet*, one of the world's most
influential medical journals, stated that "even where modern medical
care is available the people may still prefer to consult their traditional
practitioners for certain troubles. This decision may be quite reasonable, because systems of traditional medicine have a holistic approach
to illness, in which the patient is seen in relation to the environment,
ecological and social" (Traditional Medical Practitioners, pp. 963-964).

Research Methodology

Krippner decided to use both the Siegler-Osmond and the NIH models
of healing systems, as each seemed to be comprehensive. He also
decided to use the former model to describe Western allopathic medicine in order to compare it with a designated traditional healing

model, that of the Pima Indians of the American southwest. He has utilised this model to describe Candomblé, an African-Brazilian folk healing system (1998/1999), and another folk healing system still utilised
in rural and small town areas of Calabria, a province in southern Italy
(Krippner, Budden, Bova, & Galante, 2010). The model was also
applied to *curanderismo*, Mexican-American folk healing, and traditional Chinese medicine (Krippner, 1995a). The NIH model, in contrast, was used to describe Filipino Christian Espiritistas. Krippner
was assisted in this task by Scott Taubold, a clinician who had conducted extensive field work in the Philippines (Krippner & Taubold,
2005; Taubold, 2003). He has also used the NIH model to describe traditional Islamic healing in Morocco (Krippner, 2005) and the Andean
Kallawaya healing system (Krippner, 2002a). Krippner made first-
hand observations of each of the healing systems he selected for this
study.

Results

The results of this investigation are presented here in the following
manner. First, the Siegler-Osmond model will be applied to Pima shamanism, followed by an application of the same model to Western
allopathic biomedicine. Finally, the NIH model will be applied to the
Filipino Espiritista system, which has a shamanic base—even though
that orientation has been diluted by Christian influence over the years.
Nonetheless, one of shamanism's remarkable characteristics is its ability to retain its core while assimilating aspects of other systems, a strategy often deemed necessary for its survival. The term "client" will be
used to describe the former system when it is applied to shamanism,
but "patient" will be used when applied to biomedicine. For the latter
system the term "client" will be used.

Pima Indian Shamanism

Pima Indian shamanism is often said to be as subtle and sophisticated
as Western systems of medicine and psychotherapy (Krippner, 1995a,

p. 23). The principles of Pima shamanism have been recorded in some detail as a result of a study in which an anthropologist collaborated with a Pima shaman, a Pima translator, and a Pima linguist. This procedure made native people co-investigators of the study rather than passive subjects of the investigation. Some anthropological studies have been flawed because tribal respondents have lied to or played tricks on the investigators, or simply told them what they wanted to hear. Apparently, these anthropologists did not give credit to the intelligence of their respondents or to the possibility they would deliberately provide incorrect information.

The Pima (who refer to themselves as the *Akimel O'odham*) are a group of American Indians living in an area consisting of what is now Arizona and Sonora, Mexico. They are often called the "River People" because of their propensity to live in villages along a river. Before the European invasion they had built canals; afterwards, they had little contact with the Europeans, which allowed them to maintain much of their cultural identity, including their healing system. Following a series of droughts and disasters, the Pima revitalised their farming economy after the Second World War and constructed a water delivery system across their reservation. This diversion of water has had negative as well as positive results, and the Pimas' health problems include a high rate of Type 2 diabetes, perhaps the highest in the world (Waldman, 1999). Nonetheless, their traditional healing system has survived and has been able to incorporate salient aspects of allopathic biomedicine.

1. Among the Pima, *diagnosis* is as important as treatment; both are carried out by the shaman. A client's body is seen as the stratified repository of a lifetime's acquisition of strengths and weaknesses. It is the task of the shaman to make an accurate diagnosis, and then turn the client over to other practitioners for specialised treatment. In making the diagnosis, shamans believe that they are assisted by benevolent spirits. Typically, these are the same spirits who originally recruited and trained the shaman.

2. *Etiology* depends on the type of sickness that is being treated. One type of sickness is not treated because the body's self-healing capacities will deal with it. These sicknesses include constipation, indigestion, and minor insect bites. Another type of sickness is not treated because no change is possible, for example, mental retardation and infant body deformities. There are two major types of treatable sicknesses. One is "wandering sickness", caused by impurities that "wander" through the body. The other is "staying sickness", which "stays" in the body because it is triggered by spiritual factors. Causes include improper behaviour toward sacred materials, such as buzzard feathers, roadrunner birds, and jimson weed. When the Europeans arrived, it was noted that they did not fall ill when they violated sacred materials. The Pima Indians assumed that these items were not sacred to the Europeans; hence they could not be punished for treating them with disrespect. Treatment for "wandering sickness" is not carried out by the shaman but by other practitioners. In general, shamans are in charge of healing rituals for "staying sickness".

3. The *client's behaviour* provides important clues for diagnosis and treatment. "Wandering sickness" involves such symptoms as fever, hives, piles, or sores. "Staying sickness" can be identified by compulsive behaviour, erratic actions, lethargy, or self-destructive activity. The former sicknesses can be communicable, but not the latter. When the Pima found out about "germs", they simple assigned them to the category of the impure agents that caused "wandering sickness".

4. *Treatment procedures* for "wandering sickness" usually involve herbal teas, mixtures, and poultices. Once the Europeans arrived, their medicines were added to the treatments for "wandering sickness". The treatment for "staying sickness" involves chanting, singing, praying, blowing the harmful agents away from the body, sucking the harmful agents from the client's body, eating the sacred object whose violation caused the sickness, or placing the client on a sand painting. Sand painting is often recommended for "wind sickness", while a community feast is often recommended for "deer sickness" or "rabbit sick-

ness". Shamans usually will treat "staying sickness" using such implements as crystals, tobacco smoke, or eagle feathers to connect the shaman's "heart" power with the client's self-healing capacities. Such other implements as rattles appeal to benevolent spirits, requesting that they bless the herbal remedies that are used to follow-up the healing rituals for "staying sickness".

5. *Prognosis*, or anticipated outcome, is positive if the treatment is appropriate, immediate, and powerful. If not, death or suicide may result, or the sickness may continue. Suicide can result from "wind sickness", while fatal heart attacks may result from "horned toad sickness". "Deer sickness" and "dog sickness" are dangerous, often fatal, conditions.

6. The *personnel* involved in healing can range from the allopathic physician or nurse to the Pima shaman or herbalist. The *institutional function*, whether it be in a structure or natural setting, is to provide a conducive healing environment.

7 and 8. In the Pima system, *clients* have a *right* to treatment, as well as the *duty* to cooperate with the practitioner. They also have the *duty* to refrain from further violation of the sacred objects that could bring about a return of the "staying sickness". Each person has internal "strengths" that are located in specific parts of the body. In "staying sickness", the "strength" of each sacred object that has been violated interfaces with the client's internal "strengths" or self-healing capacities. Such treatments as sucking out the impurities or massaging the body can enlist these "strengths" for self-healing.

9 and 10. The client's *family* has the *right* to obtain treatment for its indisposed family members. Parents have the *duty* to avoid violating the dignity of sacred objects, as this might result in their own sickness as well as endanger the health of their children. Parental misdemeanours are seen as a frequent cause of infant birth defects.

11. Pima *society* has both the *right* and the *duty* to have healing practitioners available for its members. *Society* also has the *duty* to obey tradi-

tional spiritual laws so that its people will not be at risk for plagues and epidemics.

12. The *goal* of the healing model is to uphold the custom or "way" of the Pima tradition. This "way" was given to them by the Great Spirit at the time of creation. The Pima tradition attempts to be of assistance in the life of individuals to keep the tribal unit "proper". This propriety results in a balanced life of health and happiness.

The Allopathic Biomedical Model

The allopathic biomedical model stands in stark contrast to the Pima healing model. *Diagnosis* is almost always made by the physician and follows logical procedures that are carried out with or without input from the patient. It rarely involves input from the family and almost never requests advice from the community. *Etiology* is considered to be natural rather than "supernatural" or "magical".

The *patient's behaviour* is connected to the diagnosis through symptoms, the patient's reported experiences, and signs resulting from examining the patient's body. The *treatment* of symptoms and signs sometimes proceeds with a known etiology, especially in emergencies. For example, a physician may prescribe medication to lower a patient's fever before identifying the cause of the fever, especially if the fever is unduly high.

Medical or surgical treatment is specific for each disease, but when a diagnosis is unclear, treatment may proceed by trial and error. Treatment is oriented toward specific objectives and is adjusted to the response of the patient.

Prognosis (the physician's perspective on the course of the patient's disease) is based on diagnosis. The physician considers such matters as chances of recovery, probable period needed for recovery, and chances of a relapse. The physician offers hope but cannot promise a cure. Death is seen as the failure of the diagnostic and treatment aspects of the system, or simply as the inevitable result of aging or of a serious sickness that is not responsive to the best available treatment. Suicide typically is the outcome of a serious psychiatric disturbance.

The *function of the institution*, whether it is the physician's office, a clinic, or a hospital, is to provide care for patients. *Personnel* in the allopathic biomedical system include physicians (who treat patients), nurses (who care for patients), and various rehabilitationists (who teach patients how to regain lost or damaged bodily functions).

The allopathic model holds that it is the *priority of patients* to assume the role of patient, which includes obeying the physician, nurse, and/or rehabilitationist. In this "sick role", the patient can receive care and is not expected to assume his or her ordinary responsibilities. It is the *priority of the patient's family* to seek and receive help and sympathy, and to receive information about the patient's condition and progress. The family is expected to cooperate with medical personnel who are carrying out the treatment. Society has the priority to be protected from sick people who put themselves and others at risk. It has the role of providing medical care in one form or another to those who need it. In the allopathic model "priority" is a more appropriate term than "rights" and "duties".

The *goal* of this model is to treat patients and attempt to restore them to ordinary functioning or at least to prevent the condition from getting worse. A secondary goal is the accumulation of medical knowledge so that more diseases can be cured and so that treatment can be increasingly effective.

Filipino Christian Spiritism

Christian Spiritism in the Philippines is a term that refers to a cluster of religious and philosophical orientations, all of them representing a syncretism of Roman Catholicism and the writings of the French pedagogue Allan Kardec.

1.Lexicon. What are the specialised terms in the system?

The "Union of *Espiritistas* of the Philippines" is an organisation founded for the purpose of training men and women with alleged mediumistic propensities to become practitioners known as *Espiritistas*. However, not all of the practicing *Espiritistas* are members of the Union, nor have all mediums been trained by Union members. The Union was incorporated in 1909 and almost immediately initiated mediumship training (Taubold, 2003).

The term *espiritista* is of Spanish origin, referring to persons allegedly infused by the Holy Spirit, having the ability to "channel" so-called "spiritual energy" for alleviating problematic physical or mental conditions of their clients or *pasyente*. Various *espiritistas* claim to be able to perform various interventions, including "magnetic healing" and "psychic surgery". In addition to their contact with the Holy Spirit, *espiritistas* believe that they have special relationships with a "spirit world" filled with discarnate entities who work through them to produce effects on the "physical plane".

"Magnetic healing" is the method by which an *espiritista* purportedly manipulates "subtle" electromagnetic forces for the purposes of alleviating a client's condition. The "laying-on of hands" is one way in which magnetic healing is practiced.

"Psychic surgery" is the method by which an *espiritista* allegedly enters a client's body with his or her bare hands, supposedly extracting tumours and other pathological growths or obstructions. There are some accounts of psychic surgery dating back to pre-Colonial days, but it is said to have emerged spontaneously among *espiritistas* in about 1948. The term "psychic surgery" was coined by the U.S. author Harold Sherman in his 1967 book, *Wonder Healers of the Philippines*.

"Witchcraft", or *gayuma,* and "sorcery", or *panggagaway,* are practiced by witches (*aswang*) and sorcerers (*mangkukulam*). Although sometimes used for benevolent purposes, these practices are typically described by local villagers as the use of personal power, malevolent spirits, and/or demons to inflict psychological or physical harm to others. One of the most commonly described practices is *barang*, the transmission of rocks, glass, insects, and other foreign objects into the body of the intended victim. So-called psychic surgery attempts to extract these objects; it has been speculated that this practice was influenced by Filipinos' exposure to Western surgical methods during World War II.

2. Taxonomy. What classes of health and sickness does the system recognise and address?

Someone is determined to be in good health (*kalusugan*) when actively engaged in a process of spiritual development (*banal*). *Kalusugan* is conceptualised not only as being free from negative physical symptoms but as manifesting spiritual growth and balance of one's "vital energy" (*bisa*).

On the other hand, sickness or *sakit* results from *gayuma*, from *panggagaway*, or from *sala*, living a sinful lifestyle, i.e., harbouring thoughts or carrying out activities that separate the individual from God. *Sakit* can also be directly inflicted by malevolent spirits (*enkantos*).

Natural ailments (*likas*) can be diagnosed by Western medicine, but an ailment is considered unnatural (*di-kilala*) when it cannot be diagnosed by a Western-trained physician. In such instances, *gayuma*, *panggagaway*, or *sala* are suspected.

3. Epistemology. Is there a canonical body of knowledge? How was this body of knowledge derived?

The canonical body of knowledge embraced by the Union can be found in the treatise, *A Short Spiritist Doctrine*, by Juan Alvear (1998), who founded the Union in the first decade of the 20th century. It is based on the longer treatises of Allan Kardec, who is referred to as the author of "true spiritism" (p. 68). *Espiritistas* are described as allowing the Holy Spirit to make itself known so that the spiritual progress of humankind can be furthered. Kardec, not a medium himself, based his writings on answers derived from over 1,000 mediums who were asked questions pertaining to the nature of the universe.

Filipinos had a spiritual tradition long before the arrival of the Spanish, beginning with shamanic practices. Most of these folk traditions blended easily with Roman Catholic doctrine; those that did not were discarded or continued discreetly. Even after Western biomedicine became the accepted treatment modality, folk beliefs in witchcraft, sorcery, and mediumship remained. The biblical description of "speaking in tongues" was interpreted as mediumship, and other biblical passages were seen as descriptions of spirit communication both in dreams and in wakefulness, e.g., "automatic writing" or use of the Ouija Board.

In 1955, a group of *espiritistas*, influenced by Western psychical research books and articles, broke away from the Union, incorporating themselves as the Christian Spiritists of the Philippines. Another group, the Philippine Healers' Circle, Inc., was organised in 1981 and accepts associate members from overseas. Smaller groups have been influenced by Eastern religions and other non-Christian paradigms, breaking away from the Union as well.

4. Theories. What are the key mechanisms understood to be?

The *espiritistas* believe that there are two human systems, physical and spiritual; the Holy Spirit, in the form of "magnetic energy", is held to be the mechanism of action for each system. Mediumship is a "gift" from the Holy Spirit; the medium learns how to "direct" the Holy Spirit's magnetic energy for both magnetic healing and psychic surgery.

Everyone has some mediumistic talent, but the skill must be developed. Conceptualising oneself as an instrument of the Holy Spirit's healing power removes the limitations of dualistic thought, the belief that physical and spiritual systems are separate entities.

This belief system reflects the philosophy of Allan Kardec (1971), who described a semi-material body, the *perispirit*, composed of "magnetic fluid" that serves as an intermediary between one's physical and spiritual systems. The *perispirit* is composed of a magnetic fluid; hence, magnetic healing is an especially effective intervention.

5. Goals for Interventions. What are the primary goals of the system?

The goals of Christian Spiritism are to successfully treat physical, psychological, and spiritual ailments, including those brought about by human agency, i.e., witchcraft and sorcery, and to promote wellness and peace of mind. Additional goals are to encourage belief in God among clients along with their spiritual growth.

6. Outcome Measures. What constitutes a successful intervention?

Interventions are considered successful if the magnetic energy in the client's body is more equitably balanced and/or if diseased tissue or foreign matter in the body is dissolved or removed. Successful interventions result in a remission of symptoms, removal of a hex or a curse, enhanced peace of mind, restoration of balance and harmony, induction or restoration of faith, and/or the revitalisation of the client's energy.

Word-of-mouth or personal testimonials are the basic evaluation modes within this healing system. Outside testing has produced various results, from in-depth case studies to allegations of trickery to conflicting information regarding blood and tissue samples taken from clients during or after psychic surgery (see Martin, 1999).

The successes of the Philippine faith healers and psychic surgeons are attributed to the glory of God and the healing capacities of the Holy Spirit, not to individual practitioners. Failures are attributed to "God's will", to "fate", or to the failure of the client to adhere to the follow-up directions required to maintain the benefits of the interventions.

7. Social Organisation. Who uses and who practices the system?

The Philippine province of Pangasinan in Northern Luzon is the heartland of Christian Spiritism, the place where the practice of psychic surgery is most prevalent. However, there are several practitioners in Manila and other locations. *Espiritistas* have travelled abroad, but it is often claimed that their abilities are weakened by the problems of adjusting to a new location, and by the legal hurdles they face if they conduct an intervention in which they attempt to open the body in some manner. Healing chapels are common in the Philippines, some of which are located near or adjacent to the practitioners' homes.

The *espiritistas* are easily available to local Filipinos, as well as to tourists once they arrive in the Philippines. Referral is basically handled by word-of-mouth among Filipinos, and by travel agencies for tourists. These "tours" have diminished in number since a network of graft was uncovered, one that involved fraudulent practitioners and the taxi drivers who took tourists to see them.

Practitioners have different specialties; not all of them employ psychic surgery. Some of them use "magnetic healing", while others specialise in "spiritual injections", "distance healing", or "materialisations". Some healers devote a great deal of time to providing "blessings" for coloured water that clients take home with them for internal or external use. Practitioners are compensated through "donations", the specific amount of which is often agreed upon in advance. Sometimes there are referrals to other healers, or even to allopathic biomedical physicians.

8. Specific Activities. What do the practitioners do? What do they use?

These practitioners perform "magnetic healing" through the laying-on of hands, and some of them engage in spirit-directed "psychic surgeries", generally while experiencing altered patterns of phenomenal properties. They believe that the Holy Spirit works through them to diagnose and treat illness, even when they are using sleight-of-hand to obtain a positive outcome. *Espiritistas* may also perform "distant healing", "distant surgery", "spiritual injections", "cupping and sucking", expelling "evil spirits" from the client's body and/or "energy field", and other techniques.

The paraphernalia most often seen in the office of a Christian *espiritista* include candles, banners, religious icons, and oils that purportedly have been blessed in a local Roman Catholic church or by a powerful *espiritista* healer. Clients often will bring their own oil and water to the practitioner's office to obtain a blessing. Those practitioners who engage in "psychic surgery" have a cot or table available, as well as sheets, cotton balls, towels, and, often, medical supplies.

Sometimes, herbal preparations are recommended, dietary advice is given, and admonitions to live a Christian life are included as part of the treatment.

9. Responsibilities. What are the responsibilities of the practitioners, patients, families, and community members?

The responsibilities of the *espiritista* practitioners are to worship God, continue their personal spiritual development, and serve others. Because their goal as healers is to assist the client, sleight-of-hand often is regarded as a legitimate therapeutic technique. In other words, these practitioners often model themselves after the ubiquitous "trickster" seen in shamanic healing traditions worldwide (Hansen, 2001). Practitioners do not have the responsibility to tell clients that sleight-of-hand may be used, as this would negate the placebo effect that a dramatic intervention usually evokes.

The clients' responsibilities are to follow the suggestions of the practitioner, whose work is assumed to be directed by the Holy Spirit. They may be passive during the treatment session, but their post-treatment assignments are often extensive. They may be told to drink holy water and apply sacred oil daily, to chew up the paper on which the practitioner originally wrote their "prescriptions", and to repent of their sins. If lifestyle changes are not forthcoming, the sickness may return in one form or another.

The responsibilities of family members include praying for the relative who has been treated by an *espiritista*. Family members may be asked to help pay for the treatment, buy supplies, provide transportation for the client, and maintain family ties with the ailing relative.

10. Scope. How extensive are the system's applications?

The applications of this healing system are varied and specialised. Fairly unique elements of this system include mediumship, "psychic surgery", "distant healing", "distant surgery" (which purportedly involves cutting through the skin), "spiritual injections", and the expulsion of "evil spirits".

Practitioners rarely specialise in particular ailments or problems; instead, they specialise in their own particular mode of healing. For example, some "psychic surgeons" appear to go "deeper" into their clients' bodies, while others focus on tumours and cysts that are close to the body's surface. *Espiritistas* claim that they can treat virtually any condition, and work with any gender, age group, or nationality.

11. Analysis of Benefits and Barriers. What are the risks and costs of the system?

Proponents of allopathic biomedicine typically claim that there are considerable risks involved when clients choose this type of treatment, refusing standard medical practices. By neglecting orthodox medical procedures, clients are taking great risks and are losing valuable time (Nolen, 1974). The *espiritistas'* emphasis on spiritual shortcomings as a causal factor in sickness may increase a client's sense of guilt, and the resulting emotional turmoil may undermine his or her self-repair mechanisms. Further, the trip to the Philippines is costly, forcing clients to use money that could better be spent on effective medical care.

Advocates of the *espiritistas* note that, once clients reach the Philippines, the cost is minimal. Most of the *espiritistas* ask only for "free will" donations, which typically amount to a few pesos for local clients. These advocates claim that the practitioners' purported emphasis on sin and guilt is inaccurate, and that a large number of overseas clients have already been treated by allopathic physicians, seeing the ministrations of the *espiritistas* as their last resort.

12. *Views of Suffering and Death. How does the system view suffering and death?*

Christian Spiritism takes a conservative Christian position on suffering; that is, God allows it so that lessons of compassion and humility can be learned. Unlike most Christians, however, they believe in reincarnation; death is simply a transition, one stage in a person's continual spiritual growth.

Mediumship, to the *espiritistas*, provides evidence for the existence of a "spiritual realm" in which spirits can interact as well as communicate with selected individuals on the Earthly plane.

13. *Comparison and Interaction with Dominant System. What does this system provide that the dominant system does not provide? How does this system interact with the dominant system?*

Christian *espiritistas* provide services that the dominant biomedical system does not address. These include offering "spiritual healing" instead of symptom reduction, counteracting "witchcraft" (which is seen as superstitious nonsense by biomedical physicians), and furnishing low-cost treatment instead of the costly medicines and drugs prescribed by physicians. This healing system includes a strong spiritual component to treatment that is lacking in allopathic medicine, which does not recognise any aspect of treatment that cannot be explained from a biomedical perspective.

There is little interaction between *espiritistas* and allopathic practitioners, and minimal interaction between *espiritistas* and members of the middle and upper economic classes. However, there are notable exceptions to both generalisations. Some of the best known *espiritistas* have referred clients to medical practitioners.

On the other hand, *espiritistas* often find themselves in conflict with members of the Philippine Medical Association, especially when they treat clients with serious illnesses. *Espiritistas* and their supporters counter with the claim that most of these clients had been seeing (and paying) physicians for long periods of time with no discernable results, or that they had been hospitalised for months, again without positive outcomes. Some attempts have been made to document these outcomes (e.g., McDowall, 1996).

For decades, the World Health Organisation (Mahler, 1977) has promoted communication between traditional folk healers and allopathic biomedicine, noting that more people in developing countries rely on the former for their health care than the latter.

Discussion

The Philippines, whose cultural roots reflect an indigenous shamanic tradition, is the only Asian country where the majority of the populace is at least nominally Christian. In addition, Filipinos have been influenced by U.S. culture, having been a territory of the United States following Spain's defeat during the Spanish-American War. The result of this unique blend of Asian, European, and North American influence has produced a great diversity in worldviews. Christian Spiritism claims to heal with the power the *espiritistas* obtain from the Holy Spirit. Their mediumistic practices date back to the shamanic legacy as well as the impact of the books by Allan Kardec (e.g., 1971), the French chronicler of spiritism and mediumship.

Hansen (2001) has pointed out that folk healers work on the "margins" of society in Westernised countries. The status of Christian *espiritistas* is definitely marginal, even though many of them have attained fame and status. Nevertheless, they have been persecuted by the Roman Catholic church, Evangelical Protestants, and allopathic physicians; they have also been reviled by Western journalists because of their utilisation of sleight-of-hand. They have been ignored by medical anthropologists, even though basic outcome research has yielded provocative results in other parts of the world (e.g., Greenfield, 1987). This state of affairs is typical of the "trickster" healer whose qualities include disruption, deception, and non-conformity to rules of conduct set up by the local establishment (Hansen, 2001, pp. 28–36).

Walsh (2007) has described how many indigenous healers use trickery not only to enhance their own reputation but also to elicit a client's self-healing capacities and put them to work. These capacities often depend upon faith, belief, catharsis, and other processes that a dramatic intervention can evoke, even if sleight-of-hand is involved (pp. 104–109). The percentage of "psychic surgeries" due to sleight-of-hand, as well as the number of successful interventions, due to either chicanery or some other type of intervention, is unknown. A few eyewitness accounts (e.g., Krippner, 1976) include suggested research strategies.

Conclusion

Frank and Frank (1991) contended that three main factors are present in an effective healing process: (1) the installation of hope through "naming" the problem and making the diagnosis in a context understandable by the client; (2) emotional arousal, dynamic healing techniques, and the creation of catharsis, hope, and confidence; and (3) a feeling of control and a sense of mastery gained by the client in regard to the presenting problem. Because most shamanic healing systems cover these three bases, they have survived the encroachment of Western medicine (Krippner, 2002b). Nevertheless, formal investigations of the practitioners, their worldviews, and their technologies seem necessary before globalisation, industrialisation, and political opportunism erode the unique aspects of these singular systems of healing. This chapter has helped to demystify shamanism by observing how its healing practices touch the bases of two models constructed to compare healing systems cross-culturally. Colonisation eliminated or compromised many of the shamanic healing systems, and its 21st century counterparts threaten to continue this destructive process.

Chapter Five

Applying a 10-Facet Model to North and South American Shamanic Dream Systems

In delineating his four basic "modes of consciousness", Winkelman (2010) listed dreaming along with sleep, wakefulness, and "integrative consciousness", the latter said to characterise intense shamanic activity (p. 22). Although Winkelman specifically described dreaming as occurring in "rapid eye movement" (REM) sleep, it is known that dreams can occur during just about any time of the night but are rare in the very deep stages of sleep (Domhoff, 2003, p. 15). Nonetheless, Kramer (2007) provided support for Winkelman's categories by concluding that "dreams can be as reliably measured as their sibling, the psychophysiology of sleep, and the two are equally stable" (p. 73). He and his colleagues also found an orderly development of dream content within a given REM period. It is this narrative that has provided grist for the mill of shamans, psychotherapists, and other practitioners who attribute meaning to dream reports.

A close examination of North and South American shamanic dream systems reveals a remarkable complexity and erudition that exceeded the simplistic systems brought to the Americas by European conquerors. European dreamers were urged to ignore their dreams, since the dreamer would not know which dreams were divinely inspired and which were "demonic" (Moss, 2005, p. 33; Savary, 1990, p. 6). Native

American shamans, on the other hand, had no such dilemma, as they had centuries of traditional dreamwork to fall back on in allowing them to determine the nature of a dream report. In most of these traditions, individuals and family members were encouraged to work with their own dreams. As Kilbourne (1990) observed when discussing indigenous dream systems, "Dreams raise precisely the same questions concerning their truth and falsehood as do the data from sense perceptions" (p. 200). There are still a few commentators who insist that dream content is completely random and without meaning. This position was demolished by Krippner and Combs (2007) who drew upon anthropological, psychological, and neuroscientific data to demonstrate not only that dreams are patterned but that they demonstrate continuity with the dreamer's waking behaviour and attitudes. To tell a shaman that dreams lack meaning would elicit laughter at best and derision at worst.

In Shakespeare's *Romeo and Juliet*, dreams are poetically dismissed as "the children of an idle brain, begot of nothing but vain fantasy". Although this statement serves a dramatic purpose in the Elizabethan tragedy, it portrays a point of view that is not consistent with 21st century dream science. Indeed, Hobson (2002) has described the scientific study of dreaming as "a true renaissance, a genuine revolution ... [that] can be seen as a crucial part of a larger project, one that will shake the foundations of philosophy, psychology, and psychiatry" (pp. 160–161). This visionary declaration is one that can motivate both scientists and practitioners, laboratory and field researchers, writers driven by theory and those bound by data. The only folks left behind are those who, in the face of evidence from multiple disciplines, still cling to the notion that dream reports "signify nothing".

A Contemporary Model for Comparing Dream Systems

These considerations motivated Stanley Krippner and April Thompson (1996) to compare shamanic dream systems with those popular with Western psychotherapists, using a model proposed by Montague

Ullman and Nan Zimmerman (1979). The original focus of Ullman and Zimmerman's model was to compare three Western dream interpretation systems, those of Sigmund Freud, Carl Jung, and Montague Ullman. Krippner (1994) added two facets to the model and revised several others to provide a better basis for cross-cultural comparison. As a result, there is now a 10-facet model that permits a comparison of shamanic and Western dreamworking practices. The term *system* will be used in this discussion to describe a body of dreamworking practices prior to being cast into a *model*. The latter term is descriptive, often using terminology and concepts that may or may not fully represent a system. Hence, a system, according to this definition, is more organic, complex, and complete than the ensuing model later used to describe it. Further, a *theory* is explanatory and yields itself to confirmation or refutation. There may be theoretical elements in a system or in a model. When "spirits" are asked for specific assistance, the implicit theory holds that spirits exist and that they are capable of providing assistance to those in need. The former part of this theory may not be tested directly, but the latter part yields itself to empirical investigation. A collection of theories is often referred to as a *paradigm* or "super-theory". Each of these terms, if properly used and applied, can be helpful in demystifying shamanism.

Comparison of Freud's, Jung's, and Ullman's Dream Systems Using the Revised 10-Facet Ullman-Zimmerman Model

1. What is the function of dreaming?

Freud: To discharge repressed instinctual responses.
Jung: To disclose unacknowledged aspects of the self.
Ullman: To serve as an adaptive form of consciousness during sleep.

2. What motivates people to recall their dreams?

Freud: People often try not to recall dreams because they contain repressed material, but in psychoanalysis the dream is the "royal road to the unconscious" and helps people to understand their personal psychodynamics, e.g., the role of wish fulfilment in dreams.

Jung: By recalling dreams, people can work toward individuation, e.g., by understanding how, in dreams, they compensate for the undeveloped parts of their psyche.

Ullman: Through dream recall, dreamers can become aware of their waking life predicament and their feelings about it.

3. What is the source of dreams?

Freud: Dreams come from the unconscious, which contains repressed desires.

Jung: Dreams come from the unconscious, which contains the undeveloped aspects of the psyche.

Ullman: Dreams come from the unconscious, which consists of material that dreamers ignore or repress.

4. How do dreams convey their meanings?

Freud: Imagery is the language of the unconscious and of dreams.

Jung: Imagery is the language of the unconscious and of dreams.

Ullman: Imagery is a vehicle for expressing dream content and feeling as visual metaphors.

5. Are the meanings of dreams universal?

Freud: Sexual symbols occur, in various forms, in all cultures.

Jung: Archetypal symbols are universal; personal symbols are not.

Ullman: There are no universal symbols; dream imagery is rooted in one's daily experience and in one's culture.

6. What is the role of one's current life situation in dreams?

Freud: Day residue elicits memories of an earlier conflict.

Jung: Day residue reveals undeveloped parts of the psyche.

Ullman: Day residue opens up and often resolves issues not attended to while awake.

7. What approaches are used to work with dreams?

Freud: Free association is used in working with dreams.

Jung: Direct association and amplification are used in working with dreams.

Ullman: Dreamworking assesses metaphors through exploration of the associative context.

8. What is the role of the dreamworker?

Freud: Psychoanalysts tell dreamers their dreams' meanings.

Jung: Psychotherapists function as guides, as dreamers explore their dreams.

Ullman: Psychotherapists and other dreamworkers serve as guides, but the dreamer is the final arbiter of the dream's meaning.

9. What role does dreaming play in the dreamer's culture?

Freud: Dreams reflect a culture's repressed material, including social taboos.

Jung: Dreams reflect a culture's mythic archetypes including "shadow" aspects of the culture.

Ullman: Dreams are socially grounded in the culture and reflect unsolved social issues.

10. How are anomalous and visionary dreams viewed?

Freud: Anomalous dreams are subject to the same psychodynamics as other dreams.

Jung: Anomalous dreams reflect archetypal material and synchronicities.

Ullman: Anomalous dreams are valuable resources, e.g., in understanding emotional interactions.

Bourguignon (1979) has identified two basic strategies employed in cross-cultural work: (1) archival research (investigating material in such archives as libraries and journal collections), and (2) field studies (going into field settings to observe and interact with people from the culture being studied). Both archival and field studies can compare diverse societies in order to test hypotheses about human behaviour, activities, and attitudes. Cross-cultural psychology has been defined by Triandis (1980) as the systematic study of behaviour and experience as they occur in different cultures, are influenced by culture, or lead to changes in existing cultures (p. 1).

In addition to experimental and quasi-experimental techniques, cross-cultural psychology has utilised ethnographic and systematic observational field studies, survey and archival methods, and "whole culture" approaches. However, Ward (1989) warned against a "sole reliance on the medical oriented psychopathology model", as it may be "unduly restrictive and fails to capture the dynamic character" of many unique cultural processes (p. 127). Further, in discussing such phenomena as alleged spirit possession, Lee (1989) cautioned that "our present methods of cross-cultural observation cannot determine the actual state of the possessed or entranced person. Observation of such behaviors [sic] is not the same as personally experiencing them," (p. 251) and much the same could be said about dreaming. In other words, cross-cultural research often employs implicit assumptions that distort the lived experience of the people being studied. The correction of this bias is the goal of cultural psychology and its research methods (Shweder & Bourne, 1986).

When the Ullman-Zimmerman model is utilised in archival or field research with indigenous groups, it is important to differentiate function and motive. The function of the dream might be conceptualised as adaptive (e.g., to assist the myelinisation of nerve cells, to develop the eyes' binocularity) or informational (e.g., to assist in problem-solving, to download emotional residues, to bring new information to the dreamer). The case for emotional regulation as a key function of dreaming has been made by Nielsen and Lara-Carrasco (2007), who cite nightmares as an instance of the temporary or chronic failure of this function (p. 274). At least five different interpretations of the functional significance of dreams and other human activities have been described (Moffit, Kramer, & Hoffman, 1993), ranging from "high survival value" to "needed to build another characteristic which eventually will have high survival value" to "does not have survival value" (pp. 1–3). Often there will be more than one function and more than one motive. In addition, there might be a natural function of dreaming (e.g., consolidation of what was learned during the day) and an overlaid function (e.g., the use of lucid dreams to assist in physical and emotional healing). Degarrod (2004) has described how dreams assist shamanic practitioners in both diagnosis and treatment, noting that both are identified in dreams. He then provided a stirring account of the Sharanahua Indians of Peru, whose shamans enter into the dream world of their clients in order to heal them (p. 93).

On the other hand, the motive to recall one's dreams might be to find game during the hunt, to make contact with deceased relatives, or to receive direction about one's vocation. *Function* refers to the operation of the total human organism within a given historical and geograph-ical context, while *motive* refers to more specific personal and commu-nity goals. D'Andrade (1990) has used the term *motivation* to provide the link between a culture and the ensuing actions of its members (pp. 117–118). The motivation to recall and work with dreams would be an example of D'Andrade's analysis.

It is also necessary to differentiate *source* from function. The source of dreams is their origin, as well as the mechanism and agency of this source. Aristotle differentiated between efficient causes and final causes; in contemporary science, a similar distinction is made between mechanisms and functions. Psychoanalysts typically describe the source of dreams as the unconscious, while neuroscientists find the source in the brain's neural mechanisms; the two perspectives are not always interchangeable. In much the same way, the Western concept of the unconscious has no exact counterpart in the worldview of indig-enous people. However, the Western notion of the unconscious may be comparable in some ways to such shamanic concepts as "the spirit realm", "the other world", or "the unknown".

For Western dreamworkers, the dream's "language"" refers to its apparent use of symbols and metaphors to carry meaning (e.g., Hill-man, 1990). Shamans employ similar concepts; for example, the appearance of various animals and birds in dreams often has specific meanings. In considering the association between the dream and a dreamer's life situation, indigenous people often dream about community activities, e.g., hunting, harvesting, fighting, worshiping, as well as individual concerns. Therefore, "dream language" need not be symbolic or metaphorical to convey meaning.

Nowak and Dentan (1983) have described the difficulty of finding transcultural terms to use in the absence of accepted operational definitions. As a result, we used the least pejorative terms we could find — "dreamworker" and "dreamworking" — to encompass both Western and indigenous practices. A variety of dreamworking approaches are carried out by shamans and other spiritual practitioners, the family, or the community as a whole. The dreamworkers in native cultures might be shamans, medicine people, or similar practitioners, and their approaches to working with dreams include both individual and group processes (O'Neil, 1976).

As mentioned earlier, Krippner added two facets to Ullman and Zimmerman's model, namely, the role that dreaming plays in the culture and the role of anomalous and visionary dreams. Dreamworking plays a more important role in most indigenous societies than it does in Western culture, as do anomalous and visionary dreams. For example, the direct effect of dreams and dreaming on waking life is a theme that runs through several indigenous dream models. Western psychodynamic dream models, on the other hand, focus on the ways that waking life affects dreaming. Among indigenous groups, the effects of dreams on waking life can be observed in their cultural myths, their social rituals, and their enactment of dream scenarios; in each instance, dreams can channel the dreamer's social behaviour and community identity in ways harmonious to both the individual and the group.

An anomalous phenomenon is something regarded by a social group (such as Western behavioural scientists) as something rare and/or puzzling (Cardeña, Lynn, & Krippner, 2000). A vision may occur in daytime or night-time and is generally regarded as a message from deities, deceased relatives, or other incorporeal agencies. From their perspective, shamans and other indigenous practitioners do not consider any type of dream anomalous, because these dreams are easily encompassed in the culture's worldview. Perhaps "unusual" or "extraordinary" would be a more accurate description of these dreams. "Rare" is not accurate, because many shamans consider so-called precognitive and telepathic dreams to be fairly common. On the other hand, *visionary* is a term that identifies specific types of dreams in many indigenous traditions, several of which regard them differently from other dreams.

The overlap among several aspects of the 10-facet model is unavoidable. This is bound to occur when a unitary system with a homogeneous cultural base is segmented for the purposes of study. Furthermore, this model was originally used to compare Western dream systems; thus it does not do full justice to either the Western or indigenous systems that were compared and contrasted.

Research Question

Krippner and Thompson (1996) asked if the Ullman-Zimmerman model would be a useful cross-cultural tool for studying Native American dreamworking systems, and—if so—how they would resemble and how they would differ from each other. The investigation was delimited to Native American tribal groups in today's Canada and the United States. However, native societies in Mexico, Central America, South America, and the Caribbean are equally worthy of study.

For example, the Xavante Indians of the Mato Grosso plateau of central Brazil live in a mosaic of ecosystems, sharing the land with jaguars, pumas, anteaters, termites, parrots, and a variety of other wildlife. The dream world is an essential element of Xavante life, because dreams allow them to maintain contact with their ancestors. When Xavante elders dream about the "immortals", they share the dream with the entire village, which begins preparing a re-enactment of the dream, with the elders playing the roles of the ancestors. These dream ceremonies help to align the present with the past, providing cultural continuity. On other occasions, tribal members will sing and dance each other's dreams, thus developing a sense of trust among tribal members (Graham, 1995).

The Guarani Indians in the southeast part of Brazil also have a venerable dream tradition. The tribal legends hold that in primordial times native people divided themselves into three groups, the People of the Sun, the People of the Moon, and the People of Dreams. The Xavante and the Guarani are members of this latter group; some Guarani communities hold Dream Circles, or morning dream-sharing sessions. Often, a dream is shared that begins to give direction to the daily life of the village, and it is not necessarily the dream of a *pajé* or shaman. Indeed, a child can have a dream that indicates a new direction for a community (Jecupé, 1998).

The cultural roots of dreaming have been discussed by Ullman (1960), who observed how myths serve to make experience intelligible, and that the unsolved problems of individuals in that culture are worked through within the particular mythic framework. Myths often come to life in a dream as sources of support or as sources of anxiety, depending on the underlying nature of the immediate conflict (p. 184). In the case of the Northern Iroquois, for example, it is interesting to observe that several centuries before Freud these societies understood the "secret wishes of the soul" (Wallace, 1958). As an observant Jesuit priest wrote after a visit to the Hurons, these people believe that:

> Our souls have other desires which are, as it were, inborn and concealed…. They believe that our soul makes these natural desires known by means of dreams, which are its language. Accordingly, when these desires are accomplished, it is satisfied; but, on the contrary, if it be not granted what it desires, it becomes angry, and not only does not give its body the good and happiness that it wished to procure for it, but often it also revolts against the body, causing various diseases, and even death. (Moss, 1992, p. 32)

The importance of dreams and visions for Native Americans was first noted by Ruth Benedict (1923), who identified their use as the most basic expression of their spirituality. Irwin (1990) confirmed Benedict's thesis in his work with Native American dreams and visions. D'Andrade (1961/1990) stressed the importance of learning about indigenous peoples' dreams if their cultures were to be adequately fathomed — finding, for example, that societies using dreams to seek and control supernatural powers were more likely to live by hunting, gathering, and fishing than by agriculture and animal husbandry. Although denigrated by European colonists, Native American dream systems have gradually won the interest and respect of social sciences as well as significant numbers of the general population. Indeed, some "pop psychologists" have appropriated Native American spiritual practices, including dreamwork, and passed them off as authentic, often charging considerable amounts of money in the process (Krippner & Welch, 1992; Shaw, 1995). Bruchac (1993) has observed that, even when financial gain does not seem to be a motive, "sometimes enthusiasm has far outstripped the knowledge and ability of the non-Native people who involve themselves in and even lead these ceremonies" (p. 20). As a result, this investigation is both timely and consequential.

Research Methodology

The archival method was used in an attempt to answer the research question. Archival data collections have been used for both hypothesis testing (e.g., Zusne, 1989) and exploratory research (e.g., Zung, 1985), as they provide the investigator with an unobtrusive means to reduce a researcher's bias. Archival data are usually convenient to collect and to work with, and are often the only source of information on a topic. There are also limitations to the archival method — for example, the data collected may themselves be biased or incomplete.

A number of other cross-cultural studies have utilised the archival method in studying what we have referred to as patterns of phenomenal properties. Bourguignon and Evascu (1977), in an archival study, reported that almost all of the traditional societies they investigated displayed naturally occurring "trance" behaviour traditionally linked to visions or spirit intrusion.

Krippner and Thompson (1996) read several accounts of the ways in which dreams were used by dozens of Native American societies, finding 16 that provided enough data for analysis: the Alaskan Eskimo, Blackfoot, Crow, Dakota Sioux, Hopi, Klamath, Kwakiutl, Mandan, Maricopa, Menominee, Mojave, Navajo, Northern Iroquois, Ojibwa, Yuma, and Zuni. These 16 societies were selected because they are (or were) located in various parts of what is today Canada and the United States, and because there was enough archival material on their dreamworking systems to make meaningful comparisons. Although they found references to dreams in archival accounts of several other Native American tribes, the accounts were too sparse to create a model that would represent the use of dreams by those peoples.

For the purposes of this exploratory study, Krippner and Thompson defined dreams as narrative reports of imagery, thoughts, and/or feelings occurring during sleep. This definition excluded apparitions, reveries, daytime visions, and other forms of waking imagery, even though many of the same dreamworking approaches would be used by tribal members to understand these experiences. They shared Tedlock's (1991) differentiation between dreams and dream reports in that "dreams are private mental experiences which have never been recorded during their occurrence, while dream reports are public social performances which are accessible to researchers" (p. 161). Tedlock has reminded researchers that "dream narratives are not dreams, and neither narrating nor enacting dreams can ever recover dream experiences" (p. 163).

Krippner and Thompson delimited their data sources to anthropological accounts of native practices, admitting that Western social scientists often make errors in describing complex activities of the people they are studying. They would have preferred to have based their analysis on accounts by native people, but too few of these were readily available. The limitations of this study were the reductive and

ethnocentric posture taken towards indigenous dreamworking practices. The term *dreamworking* was originally coined in an attempt to
mitigate not only the customary Western devaluation of dreams but to
encompass practices by people other than psychoanalysts and psychotherapists. Even so, it does not fully describe the lived experience of the
groups whose records were studied. Perhaps such a term as *dream living* would be more appropriate, because not only were dreams told
and discussed, they often became part of the daily life of the dreamers
and their community.

When investigating 16 societies that emphasised the use of dreams,
Krippner and Thompson relied on a variety of sources, most of them
written by anthropologists and ethnologists (e.g., Eggan, 1966;
Hallowell, 1966; Irwin, 1994; Sandner, 1979; Spier, 1970; Spindler &
Spindler, 1971; Tedlock, 1987, 1992). Many of these sources (e.g., Lincoln, 1935) were not original accounts but drew upon other sources
(e.g., Forde, 1931). Some of them did both; Moss (2005), for example,
combined archival material with his own personal contacts, producing
a highly readable account of Iroquois dreamwork, especially the ways
in which it is used to acquire *orenda*, or power, a hallmark of shamans
as well as their tribal peers (p. 9).

Few sections in these reports were written by Native Americans
themselves. As a result, some accounts were presented from Freudian
(e.g., Devereux, 1951) or Jungian (e.g., Bruce, 1975) perspectives. In
addition, these sources use a variety of terms to denote what speakers
of English call "spirits" and "deities". Krippner and Thompson
regarded those terms as useful social constructs, but bracketed their
own opinions as to their veridicality. They also avoided the word
supernatural. Although the term appears in the anthropological literature, Native Americans did not make as rigid a division between spiritual and earthly domains as have the Westerners who studied them.

Several of these societies no longer work intensively with dreams
due to European-American influence, but Krippner and Thompson
presented each system in the "anthropological present." Many of these

groups place daytime "visions" and other unusual waking experiences in the same category as dreams; however, Krippner and Thompson emphasised night-time dreams in describing these systems. They took an extremely modest stance in presenting their results because of the many limitations inherent in the research data.

Results

The specific systems that Krippner and Thompson investigated have been published elsewhere (Krippner & Thompson, 1996), but here is a synthesis of their findings.

Synthesis of 16 Native American Dream Systems Using the Revised 10-Facet Ullman-Zimmerman Model

1. What is the function of dreaming?

Dreams are sources of power (e.g., healing, hunting, war), cultural knowledge (e.g., myths, rituals, songs, omens), and/or personal information (e.g., occupations, social roles, future events, guardian spirits).

2. What motivates people to recall their dreams?

Remembering dreams provides the dreamer with power and information that are not otherwise available.

3. What is the source of dreams?

The spirit world is the source of dreams; it can be accessed by "soul travel" or by "spirit visitations". Thus dreams are "real" in that they portray actual events that occur in their own "reality". In some cases, they are more "real" than everyday life.

4. How do dreams convey their meanings?

Dream power and information are conveyed by stories and images that reflect events in the past, present, future, and/or the spirit world. The roles of these four settings vary from tribe to tribe.

5. Are dream meanings universal?

Some dreams have the same meaning for every member of the group, while other dreams convey personal meaning; in either case, the same story or image may have several potential meanings depending on the context. In some tribes, the importance of individual dream meanings was emphasised, while in others it was not.

6. What is the role of one's life situation in dreams?

Dreams may serve a problem-solving function, reflecting the dreamer's past, present, or future. Dreams also may affect dreamers' waking life situations; for example, the dreamer may be directed to carry out injunctions or scenarios presented in a dream or, conversely, to avoid a situation depicted in a dream.

7. What approaches are used to work with dreams?

Dreams can be induced among individuals or groups through such procedures as ritual, fasting, sleep deprivation, or shamanic suggestion and/or instruction. Dreamwork can consist of acting out, sharing, exchanging, and/or selling the dream. In most tribes, dreams are so clear that dreamers can understand them; in other instances, tribal experts are consulted, usually the shaman or tribal elders, although these experts are present in each society. Unwelcome dreams are prevented in some tribes by placing "dreamcatchers" near one's bed.

8. What is the role of the dreamworker?

Shamans, parents, elders, and/or dream societies, as well as dreamers themselves, can work with dreams. The social role of dreamworkers is highly respected, but the individuals or groups who work with dreams vary widely.

9. What role does dreaming play in the dreamer's culture?

Dreaming plays a valuable role, providing beneficial information and power to community members as well as to shamans and other practitioners who use dreams in their vocation. Dreams are a frequent topic of discussion among members of the community in most tribes, but in some there is reluctance to discuss dreams openly.

10. How are anomalous and visionary dreams viewed?

Dreams can reflect distant, future, or former life events. Visionary dreams, which contain power or information that is valuable for the entire community, can be differentiated from ordinary dreams that are relevant only to the individual. The specific type and use of these dreams vary from tribe to tribe.

An Example of the Model: The Mapuche Dream System

Following Krippner's serendipitous contact with a Mapuche shaman during a trip to Chile in 1993, he was able to locate a doctoral dissertation by Degarrod (1989), "Dream Interpretation among the Mapuche Indians of Chile". The author of this study collected 380 dreams and their interpretations over a period of 17 months in the field. As an example of how the Ullman-Zimmerman model can be used cross-culturally, Krippner applied it to Degarrod's data (Krippner, 1995b).

Degarrod identified four levels of analysis in the dream: (1) the *intratextual* level that focuses on specific dream imagery; (2) the *contextual* level that deals with the social and personal life of the dreamer, as well as the dreamer's reactions to his or her dreams; (3) the *intertextual* level that relates a particular dream to other dream texts of the same individual or those of others; (4) the *retrospective* level where the dreamer examines the events following the dream for the purpose of understanding its meaning. Within this framework, Krippner applied his modification of the Ullman-Zimmerman model and its 10 questions:

1. What is the function of dreaming?

A dream (*peuma*) provides the Mapuche with information about present or future actions of others on the dreamer, guides decision-making and provides a rationale for one's actions, and/or serves as a channel of communication between the dreamer and other people, and between the dreamer and the spirit world. Hence, dreams can be divided into present-oriented and future-oriented dreams.

2. What motivates people to recall their dreams?

Dreams are extremely important to the Mapuche. They can validate knowledge and the assumption of traditional roles and careers. For ordinary dreamers, prestige is obtained if the meaning of a dream is presented in a way that seems effortless. Dreams can be used to diagnose illness, especially alleged "sexual possession" by a spurned or jealous lover. Dreams are often sought by the Mapuche, especially in times of stress. Especially valuable are the dreams of shamans (*machi*, who traditionally are women), diviners (*pelon*), chiefs (*lonco*), ritual leaders (*niempin*), and the "official" tribal dreamers (*peumafe*). These dreams often express the traditional codes of Mapuche society, as dictated by the spirits (the "supernaturals"). In addition, the diviners would often locate lost objects in dreams by sleeping with an object that once was in physical contact with what had been lost.

3. What is the source of dreams?

Among the Mapuche, dreaming is an activity of the soul (the *poulli*) that leaves the body at night, wandering about encountering other souls. The soul's night-time experiences are recalled at dawn when it reunites with the body. In the case of ordinary individuals, the soul wanders without volition and is a mere receiver of its experiences. Through dreams, the soul encounters benign spirits who may give good advice, or malicious spirits who may do it harm. Through these encounters, the dreamer learns about the present or the future, and —

upon recalling and interpreting the dreams—takes the appropriate action.

4. How do dreams convey their meanings?

Dreams can convey their meanings either literally or symbolically. A dead relative coming to take the dreamer on a journey can symbolise death. Sometimes the decision is made by default; dreams narrated to public audiences are accompanied by literal interpretations, while those narrated in the privacy of the home often undergo symbolic interpretation.

5. Are the meanings of dreams universal?

The Mapuche are very flexible in their interpretation process. They examine dreams in relationship to the circumstances of the people around them. The intervention of others in the interpretation process permits the dream's meaning to be modified and manipulated. The contextual waking reality is taken into account during interpretation. Mapuche dream interpretation is an open system; dreamers can modify and manoeuvre the meanings of the dreams according to their specific social context.

6. What is the role of one's current life situation in dreams?

Dreams guide Mapuche actions and decisions, because dreaming, imagining, and thinking are on the same continuum. In imagining and thinking, the soul also leaves the body but with volition, embarking on a much shorter journey. (Death is the longest journey of them all; night terrors and visions are visits to the dreamer by spirits.) Waking reality is balanced with dreaming reality during the interpretation process.

7. What techniques are used to work with dreams?

Dream interpretation among the Mapuche uses several perspectives. Through various modes of interpretation dreamers can relate to different levels of time, to different aspects of their culture, to other members of their tribe as well as to outsiders, and to the world of the spirits.

a. For example, through intratextual analysis, the dreamer connects his or her dream imagery with common cultural and personal symbols. Contextual analysis integrates the dream with the dreamer's social and individual life situation. Intertextual analysis integrates the dream with the dreamer's previous dreams and sometimes with the dreams of other family members. Retrospective analysis permits the full meaning of dreams to be found and new symbols to be created. Any of these types of analysis may permit conversions from a metaphoric reversal to a literal system of analysis.

b. Dreams considered to be negative (*wesa peuma*) are shared as soon as possible; the interpretation is usually communal, within the family. This allows dreamers to intervene in each other's problems and may facilitate healing. The interpretation of positive (*kume peuma*) dreams is more likely to be a private matter. The classifications are made on the basis of prophecies in the dream. If the dream is ambiguous, the dreamer may wait for future events to assist in the interpretation.

c. There are informal gatherings at which these dream reports are narrated as part of four different types of oratory: ritualised speech, improvised emotionally-toned songs, accounts of heroic deeds, and narratives of folk tales.

8. What is the role of the dreamworker?

Most Mapuche dream interpretation is conducted within the family each morning and before important events. Difficult and troublesome dreams are taken to the shaman or some other knowledgeable interpreter. All families and individuals participating in the process bring to it their own idiosyncrasies and beliefs. A Mapuche shaman can determine the direction of the individual's dreams, bringing volition to the process in order to visit the spirit realm and communicate with his or her spirit advisors. Shamans sometimes use mind-altering substances to heal through dreams, to obtain specific information about the future, or to contact the spirits. Contextual analysis can determine who has the prerequisite characteristics for becoming a shaman and legitimise shamanic initiation through dreams. However, in Mapuche society, everyone is considered to be a potentially important dreamer.

9. What role does dreaming play in the dreamer's culture?

Dreams are fully intertwined with all aspects of Mapuche culture. Dream interpretation is not an isolated event; it is integrated into all aspects of the dreamer's life through multilevel analysis. Through intertextual and contextual analysis, the dreamer establishes communication with other people. This sharing and interpretation of dreams affects different types of communication between the narrators and the participants of the event. The dreamer's social position and the nature of the dream influence the rendition of the dream report, where the dream report is discussed, and the type of interpretation used. Dreams also are used to validate various aspects of the culture such as myths, songs, and social rankings.

10. How are anomalous and visionary dreams viewed?

Through the dream experience itself and various means of analysis, the Mapuche can link and integrate different people and time periods. Retrospective analysis, by providing information about the future, links the dreamer's present activity to future events. Intertextual analysis links past dreams to those of the present. Because of these intertemporal links, the interpretation system helps to shape and influence the Mapuche views of the past, the present, and the future. It is customary for dreams about the "supernaturals" to be interpreted literally. It is typical for positive dream reports to be communicated only after their prophecy has been fulfilled. This retrospective analysis permits the verification of premonitions received in dreams and thereby perpetuates the use of dreams as forecasting devices. It also establishes the dreamer as a competent channel of communication with the spirit world.

As an example of Mapuche dreamwork, Degarrod (1989) cited a puzzling dream that was reported during her fieldwork by "Julio":

> They dressed me with white clothing like a Catholic priest. The
> clothing fit me very nicely. It wasn't loose like priests usually
> wear, but a little tighter. It felt very good on my body as if it
> belonged to me. (p. 94)

Julio was confused, because to dream of clothes is a negative sign, but
white is positive. However, he felt good in the dream and enjoyed its
imagery, so he decided to postpone labelling the dream. Two weeks
later, a ceremony was held among people from two Mapuche reservations. The Roman Catholic Church, which was organising the event,
planned to have both chiefs and priests lead the ceremony. To Julio's
delight, he was one of the individuals chosen to lead prayers. He felt
proud because of his position in the ritual, being surrounded by important people. Retrospective analysis had enabled him to interpret the
dream. It had indicated that he would act like someone of importance
in front of the community. In addition, he had found a new symbol;
henceforth, for him to dream of white clothing would be a positive
sign.

The Mapuche often change their dream reports over time, following
the contributions of family and community members. This practice is
reminiscent of research studies that investigated the connection
between dream content and the dreamer's personality. In a study that
compared dream content analysis data with personality test scores for
a sample of university students in Canada, no significant relationships
were found. However, when the students filled out questionnaires that
asked them about dream content, significant relationships were found
in such areas as extraversion, agreeableness, conscientiousness, and
openness. The authors of this study concluded that "one's personality
may tell us little about what a person actually dreams, but it can tell us
a great deal about what a person thinks she/he dreams" (Bernstein,
Belicki, & Gonzalez, 1995, p. 139). These research results and the
Mapuche proclivity to relate dreams in ways that reinforce their status
correspond with postmodern distinctions between "fixed texts" and
"fluid texts", the latter term being more descriptive of dream reports.

It is apparent that the Mapuche dream legacy is a complete model of dreaming and dreamworking, even when described in Western terms. However, unlike Westerners, the Mapuche integrate their dreams into every major facet of their waking life (Faron, 1968). For these people and their shamans, there is no rigid division between dream life and waking life. The same can be said for many Native American dream systems, especially those practiced before the arrival of the Europeans (Krippner & Thompson, 1996). Among most North and South American Indian tribes, the shaman was the focal dreamworker, but it was acknowledged that "everyone who dreams has a bit of shaman" within them (Kracke, 1987, p. 65).

This presentation of the Mapuche dream model is in keeping with Tedlock's (1991) well-grounded perception that social scientists can learn more from native people's dreams by "studying dream theories and interpretation systems as complex psychodynamic communicative events" than by making typological or statistical comparisons between so-called Western and non-Western dreams (p. 174). If contemporary dreamworkers are motivated to learn from native people, the Mapuche culture is still accessible, and the cooperation that Degarrod attained in her dissertation research serves as testimony to what can be ascertained by contemporary scholars. Or could it be that prejudice against the indigenous people of the Americas propels the general public, the popular media, and perhaps the academic community itself toward the "mysterious East"? If so, the field of dream studies in general and Western dreamworkers in particular will lose a splendid opportunity to explore the deeper dimensions of the human psyche from a unique perspective.

Discussion

For many of the North and South American tribes surveyed by Krippner, dreams do not typically require systematic interpretation; their message is direct and undisguised. For those dreams that require some type of interpretation, the variety of approaches in these models represents the plurality and polymorphic nature of Native American traditions in general (Irwin, 1994, p. 21). Some tribal dreamworking approaches resemble those used by Western dreamworkers, e.g., psychodrama, dream sharing, role-playing. Among the Northern Iroquois, dreams often reveal desires that one cannot comprehend during wakefulness, and the dreamer was often permitted to act out directly or symbolically these "secret wishes" in private or in a community setting (something quite alien to Freudian psychoanalysts, whose model also postulated dreams saturated with desire). Those native dream systems that posited universal symbols are reminiscent of the Jungian notion of archetypes. For the Jungians as well as for such societies as the Hopi, Kwakiutl, Mojave, and Navajo, individual permutations of the symbol are recognised and taken into account during dreamworking.

There are instances of Native American dreamers taking extreme measures to change the outcome of a dream by "play acting" the event. A Mohawk warrior who dreamed he was taken captive and tortured by fire insisted that his peers restrain him and burn him with red hot metal (Moss, 1992, p. 32). During the Ononharoia, a sacred midwinter ceremony still held on some Iroquois reservations, tribal members engage in dream-guessing contests that often turn into dream giveaways. Treasured possessions, husbands, and wives have been known to be given away during Ononharoia, which translates as "Upturning of Minds".

Admittedly, this approach to Native American dreaming is what anthropologists call "etic", imposing a Western model on accounts written by Western anthropologists, rather than the "emic" approach in which accounts are given by tribal peoples themselves. In studies of this sort, there is an "equivalence problem" regarding the construction of meaning units that might not be comparable in different cultural settings (Shweder & Bourne, 1986). It would be a valuable exercise for indigenous dreamworkers to construct their own models of dreaming, imposing them on writings by Freud, Jung, Ullman, and others. In addition, we support Tedlock's (1991) suggestion that researchers interact within natural communication contexts of dream sharing. In such contexts, the introduction of the researchers' own dreams would be quite natural, even expected, and might reveal unconscious reactions to the peoples they are attempting to study (p. 161). This "participant-observation" method would abandon the viewing of native people's dreams as what postmodernists refer to as the "other" in favour of an interaction in which both the researcher and the research participant comment on each other's dream reports.

If there was any facet of Native American dreaming that was not adequately represented in the Ullman-Zimmerman model, it was the way that many tribal societies categorise dreams. Several systems distinguish between ordinary dreams and visionary dreams, such as the Northern Iroquois, Mandan, and Menominee. Some groups treat nightmares differently from dreams in general (e.g., Zuni), and some categorise dreams on the basis of their purported origin (e.g., Yuma). Some classify them in terms of various types and degrees of power and knowledge represented (among the Mojave, there are "omen" dreams and "power" dreams). The Ojibwa have at least a dozen categories of dreams, such as bad, beautiful, impure, ominous, painful, and visionary. In addition, we suspect that shamans and other dreamworkers have often had lucid dreams, but it is doubtful that anthropologists knew how to ask the questions that would have indicated their frequency and their use.

Lincoln (1935) distinguished between "culturally patterned" and "individually patterned" dreams; in the former instance, the dream content is largely determined by the demands of the culture. As examples of "culturally patterned" dreams, Lincoln cited Crow vision dreams and Yuma mythic dreams. On the other hand, Sandner (1979) found Navajo dreams to be largely individual, with "no culturally prescribed requirements for dreaming" (p. 263). Even so, Navajos shared a common symbology when dreams were interpreted (Morgan, 1932). Dreams, of course, are only one aspect of a culture's "indigenous psychology" (Kim & Berry, 1993), but they may provide a key to other facets.

This examination of Native American dream societies illustrates the value of studying dream systems from other cultures, especially those that take dreams seriously (Eggan, 1949, 1952; Kracke, 1991). It demonstrates the plasticity of dreams, and how dreamers tend to report dreams that conform to cultural expectations. The 16 systems Krippner and Thompson described provide evidence of the limitations imposed by cultural frameworks in which the individual dream operates, thus either suppressing or enhancing the idiosyncratic elements that dreamers bring to their dream experience. As a result, Ullman (1960) noted that the prevailing myths in the dreams of non-Westerners are "readily detectable to an outside observer".

Although scepticism and divergent thinking are not unknown in native societies, the power of traditional myths is accepted by most of the dreamers in these cultures. Myths may come to life in the dream "as sources of support or as sources of anxiety, depending on the underlying nature of the immediate conflict" (Ullman, 1960, p.184). Krippner and Thompson's 16 North American systems, as well as the South American Mapuche system, demonstrate a variety of ways in which this support or anxiety is handled by community dreamworkers.

There is an urgent need for more information in these areas, and cross-cultural psychology can play an important role in this quest. Are there universal human processes that are mediated by cultural settings? Or are human processes heavily dependent on time and place? These questions are the focus of much cross-cultural research; dreaming is a universal human process and our investigation demonstrates some of the variations in its canalisation. However, native cultures are changing in the wake of acculturation; those still retaining their traditional ways of living and dreamworking present critically important research opportunities.

Irwin (1994) discussed Native American dream traditions in the context of the late 20th century intellectual changes in the sciences and the

humanities from a "causally conditioned and mechanistic world order
... toward a more holistic, indeterminate, interactive ... patterned
world of interpersonal events" (p. 22). It is likely that such postmodern
perspectives will make unique contributions to the understanding of
non-Western dream models. Helpful research methods would include
cultural psychology (the study of how cultural traditions and social
practices regulate, disclose, modify, and infuse human behaviour and
experience) and hermeneutics (the analysis of texts on the basis of their
particular historical epochs and contextual situations). For cultural
psychologists, cross-cultural psychology "is not heretical enough",
because it depends on methods that may do an injustice to the many
alternative expressions of the human condition, assuming an "intrinsic
psychic unity" and "central processing mechanism" that may not exist
(Shweder & Bourne, 1986, pp. 12–13). Hermeneutical analysis claims to
add to a cross-cultural anthropologist's understanding of other cultures by its insistence that all social science theories must be interpretive. Hermeneutics holds that an understanding of those human
actions and cultural products objectified in ordinary language cannot
be exhausted by means of social theories (Ulin, 1984, p. xv).

As mentioned earlier, for postmodernists, dreams can be conceptualised as cultural texts. To be appreciated, the content of these texts
needs to enter an ongoing discourse. Like other cultural products, they
can be best understood within the historical and geographical conditions of which they are a part, and may be most meaningful within
their own context. We suspect that an understanding of remote societies can be best attained through context-dependent interpretations,
because the search for abstract universal laws of social development
has not provided satisfactory outcomes (Shweder, 1990).

Spindler and Spindler (1971) contended that the Menominee
employed a language that was subtle, complex, and radically different
from any Western language in its organisation of action and object,
time and occurrence. This language permeated Menominee dreams,
providing these people with "a social map within which all persons

could be placed [and] a philosophy of education, rules for teachers, a theory of man [and woman] in nature, a set of values to live and die by" (p. 14). Hence, an intensive study of the complex Menominee myths and rituals on their own terms might be of greater value than a comparison with other worldviews.

Conclusion

In conclusion, each of the dream systems investigated placed a value on dreams; some can rightfully be termed "dream cultures". The Navajos and the Mojave had especially well-developed dreaming systems. Dreaming life was considered to be more "real" and/or more important than waking life among the Northern Iroquois and the Yuma. Most Western dream models, by contrast, see dreaming as a biologically-driven altered state of consciousness which, nonetheless, may produce useful information in the hands of a skilled interpreter. Although Western psychodynamic models allow consideration of a dream report's potential value, these models stand in opposition to the general cultural stance that this is "nothing but a dream". Westerners, in general, are acculturated to ignore their dreams and rarely consider integrating their dreaming and waking experiences, a process considered routine in Native American dream systems (Laughlin, McManus, & d'Aquili, 1990, p. 155).

In most shamanic dream systems there is no distinct separation between the dreamed world and the lived world. The dream often represents the dreamer's merging with the "unknown" visionary realm, which can enlighten and empower the dreamer. In contrast, Western models of dreaming sharply demarcate dreaming from waking consciousness; the former is seen, at best, as an imaginative cognitive process and, at worst, as the elimination of "waste products" of information processing or as "chance" combinations of randomly evoked imagery.

This chapter has demystified shamanism by underscoring the complexity and the sophistication of indigenous descriptions of dreaming and the way that shamans and other dreamworkers put dream reports to practical use. But traditional people need to enter the discourse on the nature of dreaming by telling their own stories, writing their own histories, and describing their own dream models. Our comparison of shamanic dream systems does not do them full justice.

In addition, Valsiner (1995) speculated as to the role played by research participants and informants in the construction of psychological and anthropological knowledge, and cites a number of possible confounding variables, such as lack of information, desire to please, and need to impress. If the postmodern paradigm achieves salience in the social sciences, dream traditions and other aspects of Native American wisdom may come to be even more instructive than they have been in the past.

The study of indigenous North and South American dream systems using the 10-facet model was an attempt to implement Tedlock's (1991) suggestion to discard the practice of making statistical comparisons between "Western" and "non-Western" dreams in favour of "studying dream theories and interpretation systems" (p. 174). Tedlock also advised that these dream systems be studied "in their full social context" (p. 174); hence, this investigation provides less of a finale than a beginning.

Chapter Six

The Construction of an Ontology and Epistemology of Shamanic Journeying Imagery

An integral feature of shamanism is the utilisation of "… techniques for inducing, maintaining, and interpreting the experience of enhanced visual mental imagery" (Noll, 1985, p. 45). Indeed, Peters (1989) stated that, "The shaman is a visualiser …" (p. 130), who relies on this modality to access transpersonal realms. In support of this contention, Houran, Lange, and Crist-Houran (1997) analysed 30 phenomenological reports concerning shamanic journeying, derived from Harner (1980), and found that 93.3% emphasised visual phenomena. Shamanic visualisations (i.e., journeying imagery) typically reflect one's cultural cosmology (Krippner, 1990b; Walsh, 1995, 2007), which tends to be a multi-layered universe consisting of an upper world, middle world (the terrestrial world or Earth), and lower world (Ellwood, 1987).[1] Sometimes there are several upper worlds or lower

---

1   Shamanic journeying imagery is not restricted to any particular sensory modality; that is, journeying imagery may be visual, auditory, gustatory, olfactory, tactile or multi-modal (Walsh, 1995). However, for the purpose of the present chapter, shamanic journeying images will be delimited to their visual modality because these are arguably the most abundant (Houran, Lange & Crist-Houran, 1997; Noll, 1983).

worlds, and the inhabitants of these realms are not consistent across cultures.

In recent years, shamanic practices have generated increasing interest as a complementary therapeutic strategy in the conventional medical and psychological arenas (Bittman et al., 2001; DuBois, 2009, pp. 264–290). Consequently, it may prove prudent to investigate further the nature of shamanic patterns of phenomenal properties (e.g., journeying imagery). At the same time, to our knowledge, a lacuna exists in the literature with regard to a systematic analysis of the philosophical problems hampering the development of an ontology and epistemology of shamanic journeying imagery. This is crucially important at a time when neo-shamanism has made purported "shamanic journeying" available to neophytes. Traditional shamans may or may not report imagery similar to that reported by well-meaning but poorly-seasoned neo-shamanic practitioners.

Ontology may be defined as "the matter of what there is in the world" (Chalmers, 1996, p. 41); it is concerned with "an overall conception of how things are" (Heil, 1998, p. 6). The term "ontological foundations" refers to the fundamental nature or essence of a particular variable, X (e.g., a shamanic journey image). For example, an ontologist might be concerned with whether the kind of "thing" that a shamanic journeying image is referentially linked to is imaginal (e.g., derived from material stored in one's long-term memory system) or transpersonal (i.e., independent of the percipient's mind-body complex) (Walsh, 1990a).

In contrast, epistemology may be defined as the study of the "origins, nature, methods and limits of human knowledge" (Reber & Reber, 2001, p. 246). With regard to shamanic patterns of phenomenal properties, one might, for example, investigate the epistemic process that results in a percipient becoming aware of a shamanic journeying image. While epistemological debates in the philosophy of religion have tended to focus on mystical experience (e.g., Evans, 1989; Forman, 1996; Gill, 1984; Katz, 1978, 1983; Stoeber, 1991), one might contend that the epistemological problems discussed are also applicable to shamanic patterns of phenomenal properties. For example, there is no reason in principle why the epistemological issue of whether mystical experience is "shaped" conceptually and linguistically by one's cultural milieu is not applicable to shamanic patterns of phenomenal properties. Indeed, a recent series of papers (e.g., Rock & Baynes, 2005, 2007) investigated the extent to which shamanic journeying imagery on the part of volunteer participants was "shaped" by contextual influences (e.g., the shaman's cultural cosmology or autobiographical memories).[2]

The purpose of this chapter is to demonstrate how various philosophical problems impede the formulation of an ontology and epistemology of shamanic journeying imagery. We will proceed by demonstrating that the problem of induction constitutes an inherent limitation associated with recent experimental studies investigating the origin of such imagery. Subsequently, we develop and critique a deductive argument concerning the ontology of shamanic journeying imagery. Wittgenstein's (1958) "private language" argument and the fallacy of reification are also considered in the context of such imagery.

Previous Experimental Research Concerning the Origins of Shamanic Journeying Imagery

Attempts to elucidate the kinds of "thing/s" that the term "shamanic journeying image" is referentially linked to may prompt addressing two intimately related questions: (1) What is the fundamental nature of shamanic journeying images? (2) How might one "find" the origin of a shamanic journeying image? The first question is ontological; that is, it is concerned with the nature and essence of the shamanic journeying image. In contrast, the second is an epistemological and methodologi-

---

2   One might argue that philosophical problems, by definition, resist empirical testing. It is noteworthy, however, that motivation and learning were once conceptualised as philosophical problems and, thus, held to be incongruent with the methodology of science (Eacker, 1972).

cal question; it relates to how one might acquire certain knowledge. It is arguable that 1 and 2 are inextricably bound at a fundamental level —that is to say, answering 2 presumably provides one with the methodology necessary to address 1.

Rock and Baynes (2005, 2007) addressed 2 by developing a non-hypnotic version of Watkins's (1971) "Affect Bridge" (a hypnotic technique used to "uncover" the origin of an emotion) for the purpose of investigating the origins of shamanic journeying imagery. The Modified Affect Bridge was developed as one potential *partial* solution to 2; it was not designed to facilitate unrestricted access to one's unconscious material, but rather to facilitate ordinary remembering among ordinary participants in a non-clinical context. The Modified Affect Bridge was first applied in an experimental context by Rock, Casey, and Baynes (2006) and, subsequently, by Rock (2006).

Rock, Casey, and Baynes (2006) reported that ostensibly shamanic journey images encountered by naïve participants journeying to the "lower world" with the aid of monotonous drumming at 8 beats per second for 15 minutes were just as likely to be derived from autobiographical memories as spontaneous visual mental images reported by naïve participants assigned to the control condition of sitting quietly with eyes open for 15 minutes. This finding suggests that the epistemological process that results in one being consciously aware of an ostensibly shamanic journeying image involves memory recall and superimposition "within" one's phenomenal space. Consequently, the journeying images may be tentatively assigned an imaginal ontological status. Subsequently, Rock (2006) randomly allocated 6 participants to counterbalanced factorial combinations of a within-group factor (technique: monotonous drumming, Ganzfeld-type sensory deprivation, relaxation, sitting quietly with eyes open) and a between-group factor (instruction: no instructions, or journeying to the "lower world" instructions with and without religious components). It was concluded that visual mental images encountered while journeying to the "lower world" were derived primarily from autobiographical memories. Interestingly, other visual mental images were tentatively labelled as symbolic, transpersonal, and indeterminate. Again, we need to emphasise that the results from this study were not derived from shamanic practitioners, and must be delimited to naïve participants.

The results of Rock, Casey, and Baynes (2006) and Rock (2006) facilitated the development of a tentative four-fold *ostensibly shamanic journeying imagery origin* typology consisting of autobiographical, symbolic, transpersonal, and indeterminate sources. An ostensibly shamanic journeying image may be categorised as "autobiographical" if it appears to be the derivative of an autobiographical memory — that is, a "memory for events that have occurred in one's life" (Reber & Reber, 2001, p. 423). The "symbolic" characterisation of an ostensibly shamanic journeying image is invoked if the image seems to perform a symbolic function without appearing to mentally represent a previous sensory experience. An ostensibly shamanic journeying image may be conceptualised as "transpersonal" if the image appears to be linked to some "thing" that exists independently of the participant's mind-body complex. Finally, an "indeterminate" status is conferred upon an ostensibly shamanic journeying image when the participant is unable to isolate its origin (Rock & Baynes, 2007).

Given that the Modified Affect Bridge was formulated as a potential *partial* solution to 2, and has yielded four imagery-origin categories, thereby addressing 1, it might be asked, "How might one resolve the ontological foundations of shamanic journeying imagery?" In this context, it may be efficacious to consider Mercante's (2010) suggestion that a persuasive argument for considering imagery associated with the ayahuasca experience an "involuntary and spontaneous process is that voluntary events rely on memory" (pp. 6–7). Extrapolating from Farthing's (1992) discussion of mental imagery to the Portuguese term *miração*, Mercante (2010) wrote:

> If the arrival and dissipation of *mirações* were subject to the command of the individual, it would follow that no "alien" ele-

ments (outside a person's familiar universe) would be present.... The idea is that one can only voluntarily manipulate
images that are impressed upon the memory through sensa-
tion. Not that a person cannot assemble new patterns from
recorded sensory data, but he or she cannot manufacture fundamental data beyond the pale of experience. The revelatory
qualities of the miração would be lost or at least considered illu-
sory if the experience of it were limited to the cache of existing
memory. (pp. 6–7)

One may apply Mercante's (2010) argument to shamanic journeying
imagery and contend that, if shamanic journeying images are immune
to voluntarily manipulation, then these images are not constructed
from material derived from a percipient's long-term memory system.
Ethnographic data, however, suggest that shamans tend to cultivate a
mastery over journeying images (e.g., Noll, 1985), thus indicating —
provided one accepts Mercante's preceding argument — that shamanic
journeying imagery is the result of an epistemological process involving memory recall and superimposition "within" a percipient's
phenomenal space.

Furthermore, it is arguable that, even if the "outward" appearance
of a shamanic journeying image, X, is derived from material stored in a
percipient's long-term memory system, this does not necessarily preclude the ontological foundations of X from being transpersonal. For
example, if a shaman or experimental participant encounters a "predatory creature" during a journey to the "lower world" — and the "outward appearance" of this predatory creature is the derivative of an
autobiographical memory — it remains possible that the "predatory
creature" is the manifestation or "persona" of an external "entity", or
even a combination of a memory and an "entity". Strassman (2001),
for instance, has suggested that "entities" encountered during
dimethyltryptamine-induced patterns of phenomenal properties tend
to manifest in forms recognisable to the percipient (e.g., "elves",

"aliens", "angels", "deceased relatives"), and yet may reside in parallel universes or dark matter realms.

Problems of Induction and Deduction

Let us assume, for the sake of argument, that there are six necessary conditions for a visual mental image to qualify as a shamanic journeying image and that the conjunction of N_1–N_6 constitutes a sufficient condition. Let us further assume that N_6 states that the ontological foundations of a visual mental image, X, must be Y. An ontologist might be interested with whether the kind of "thing" (i.e., denoted by Y) that a shamanic journeying image is referentially linked to is imaginal or transpersonal (Walsh, 1990a, 2007).

Future research might formulate an *a posteriori* derived definition for Y by comparing Xs that satisfy N_1–N_5 (group 1) with Xs that satisfy four or fewer of the aforementioned necessary conditions (group 2). Specifically, one may investigate whether group 1 is associated with different categories of Ys compared to group 2. Given that group 2 does not satisfy N_1–N_5 (N_6 notwithstanding), the ostensible shamanic journeying image status of this group is falsified. In contrast, the constituents of group 1 have not been falsified because they do satisfy N_1–N_5. If it is observed that all of the constituents of group 1 are derived from, for example, a transpersonal source, then one might tentatively infer that Y is a transpersonal source and, thus, N_6 would state that the ontological foundations of a visual mental image, X, must be transpersonal. However, if, for instance, some constituents of group 1 appear to be derived from a transpersonal source, while other constituents of group 1 do not, then it may be that the transpersonal constituents of group 1 are shamanic journeying images and, thus, Y is a transpersonal source, whereas the non-transpersonal constituents of group 1 are merely visual mental images. That is, if N_6, in fact, states that the ontological foundations of a visual mental image, X, must be transpersonal, then the transpersonal constituents of group 1 satisfy N_1–N_6, which is a sufficient condition for qualifying as a shamanic journeying image. In contrast, the ostensible shamanic status of the non-transpersonal constituents of group 1 would be falsified on the ground that these constituents fail to satisfy N_6. It is, of course, logically possible that Y, in fact, denotes a non-transpersonal source and, thus, the non-transpersonal constituents of group 1 satisfy N_1–N_6, while the transpersonal constituents of group 1 would be falsified.

However, if one were able "definitively" to demonstrate that shamanic journeying images X_1, X_2, X_3 ... X_{10} were all derived from, for example, transpersonal sources, then to presuppose that X_{11} is also derived from a transpersonal source is to commit the fallacy of induction; that is, moving from particular instances to general principles. For example, Rosenberg (2000) suggests that the observation "that the sun has risen many days in the past is good grounds to believe it will do so tomorrow, but does not make it logically certain that it will" (p. 177). Consequently, induction is inherently limited. Additionally, if the ontological foundations were different for X_1, X_2, X_3 ... X_{10} (e.g., autobiographical for X_1 and X_2, symbolic for X_{10}, indeterminate for X_7 and X_8), then one might contend that such variability hampers N_6's usefulness as a necessary condition.

Similarly, deductive models (i.e., moving from general principles to particular instances) are inherently limited. For example, one may formulate a logically valid argument concerning the identity of Y, but there is no guarantee that such an argument is logically sound. Consider the following deductive argument:

1.   All shamanic journeying images are derived from transpersonal sources;

2. X is a shamanic journeying image;

3.   Therefore, X is derived from a transpersonal source.

It may be observed that, while the preceding argument's conclusion follows logically from its premises, it may of course be that *not* all shamanic journeying images are derived from transpersonal sources.

The aforementioned problems associated with attempts to formulate an ontology and epistemology of shamanic journeying imagery using inductive or deductive reasoning are further complicated by Wittgenstein's (1958) private language argument and the fallacy of reification.

The Private Language Argument

In a private language, it is held that terms "refer to what can only be known to the person speaking; to his immediate private sensations. So another person cannot understand the language" (Wittgenstein, 1958, pp. 88–89). The notion of a private language is underpinned by an argument for solipsism: "I can only believe that someone else is in pain, but I know if I am" (Wittgenstein, 1958, p. 102). A privileged observer (i.e., first-person) may, for example, establish a link between the term "pain" and the phenomenal properties of pain. However, it is possible that the privileged observer's private definition may be erroneously applied in subsequent instances due to false memory impressions concerning the phenomenal properties of pain (Malcolm, 1981). Consequently, Wittgenstein (1958) asserted that one should "always get rid of the idea of a private object in this way: assume that it constantly changes, but that you do not notice the change because your memory constantly deceives you" (p. 207).

To summarise, Wittgenstein's (1958) private language argument undermines the following: First, the ability of a non-privileged observer to correctly apprehend the meanings of terms applied to phenomenal properties by a privileged observer; and second, the reliability of a privileged observer's application of terms to the phenomenal properties known by his or her conscious awareness.

The epistemological presuppositions associated with shamanic journeying imagery are two-fold and inextricably related at a fundamental level: (1) a privileged observer can, via introspection, know a shamanic journeying image; and (2) a privileged observer may communicate the introspected shamanic journeying image to a non-privileged observer.

Clearly, in order to categorise an image as shamanic one must first learn the meaning of the term "shamanic". A non-privileged observer might endeavour to learn the meaning of "objecs" commensurate with a shamanic journeying image, X, by attempting to correctly apprehend the meanings of linguistic terms applied by a privileged observer to the set of constituents associated with X, xyz. However, while a non-privileged observer may be informed that X exhibits a certain set of constituents, xyz, Wittgenstein's (1958) private language argument undermines a non-privileged observer's ability to correctly apprehend the meanings of linguistic terms applied to xyz by a privileged observer. Consequently, while it is possible that a non-privileged observer may subsequently engage in the privileged observation of xyz, and thus X, it is impossible to verify that such a mental event has occurred. This epistemological problem is compounded by the suggestion that a privileged observer's false memory impressions concerning xyz, and thus X, may result in the unreliable application of linguistic terms to xyz, and thus X, in future instances (Wittgenstein, 1958).

This raises a further epistemological problem. Tart (1975) has emphasised the state-specificity of knowledge, while Fischer (1980) asserted that one may experience difficulty recalling events that occur "in another state of arousal" (p. 306). Consequently, the probability of a privileged observer unreliably recalling a phenomenal property associated with what Tart (1975) has referred to as a particular "state" of consciousness, SoC_1, due to a false memory impression, may exponentially increase when functioning in an SoC other than SoC_1 (e.g., $SoC_{2...n}$). Consequently, this may compromise a privileged observer's ability to assess retrospectively an image as shamanic while functioning in ordinary waking consciousness.

The Fallacy of Reification

Reichenbach (1951) employed the axiom *substantialisation of abstracta* to denote the fallacy of reification, whereby an abstract noun (e.g., consciousness) is confused with a thing-like entity. Similarly, Whitehead

(1946) referred to reification as the *fallacy of misplaced concreteness*, which he defined as "… the accidental error of mistaking the abstract for the concrete" (p. 66).

An awareness of the fallacy associated with reifying consciousness may be observed in James's (1890) contention that "consciousness does not exist", which Chalmers (1996) suggested is interpretable as an attempt to argue that consciousness does not exemplify the property of "thing-ness". Indeed, Klein (1984) stated that James (1890) avoided committing the fallacy of reification by asserting that consciousness is a "function" or "process" of knowing, rather than a thing-like entity.

One might argue, with some justification, that experimental studies of shamanic journeying imagery that use, for example, Pekala's (1991) retrospective phenomenological assessment instrument, the *Phenomenology of Consciousness Inventory* (a 53-item questionnaire that purports to quantify the structures of consciousness), commit an ontological mistake by concretising mental phenomena (e.g., visual mental imagery), thereby conflating mentalism with materialism. Pekala (1991) has committed the fallacy of reification (Eacker, 1972) or misplaced concreteness (Whitehead, 1946) by attempting to "quantify consciousness", and thus contravenes James's (1890) contention that consciousness is not a thing-like entity, but rather a "function" or "process" of knowing (Klein, 1984). Indeed, Pekala (1991) has routinely engaged in the kind of fallacious reasoning whereby an abstract noun (e.g., "state absorption", "rationality", "positive affect") is reified and ascribed a numerical value. The problem of reification would appear difficult to circumvent, however, given that, at present, mental phenomena cannot be investigated by means of mainstream scientific methods — and thus measured — until they are reified by the assignment of operational definitions commensurate with the ontological status of thing-like entities.

While Wittgenstein's (1958) private language argument and the fallacy of reification problematise the findings of shamanic research, it does not necessarily follow that these findings are rendered spurious.

Indeed, a more measured approach might be to develop an appreciation of these issues and merely interpret one's results with a suitable
level of caution. In the next chapter, we present a methodology that
arguably constitutes a preliminary step towards the formulation of an
ontology and epistemology of shamanic journeying imagery.

Conclusion

In this chapter, we distinguished between the linguistic term "shamanic journeying imagery" and the "entity" or "entities" signified by
the term. We made a preliminary step towards demystifying shamanic
journeying imagery by clarifying the ontological and epistemological
issues associated with elucidating the nature of the aforementioned
"entity"/"entities". In addition, we demonstrated how inductive and
deductive reasoning, the private language argument, and reification
perpetuate the mystification of shamanic journeying imagery. However, the study reported in this chapter was conducted with volun-
teers, not with shamans. One would expect considerable differences if
this type of study were to be repeated with shamanic participants, or
even with neo-shamans. Depth of experience would need to be measured; the element of risk would need to be considered in the case of
encountered malicious entities; and the purpose of the journey would
need to be identified. It is likely that many potential shamanic participants would refuse to engage with a researcher in this project unless it
would serve some clearly stated and mutually agreed upon need.
Finally, the neat categories that we have identified in this chapter
might break down when shamans are studied; shamanism tends to
combine groupings and blur boundaries that investigators previously
took pride in constructing.

Chapter Seven

Necessary Conditions For Shamanic Journeying Imagery

Despite renewed interest in shamanism and shamanic journeying imagery (Walsh, 1989b) these phenomena are neither well-defined nor sufficiently understood. It is, of course, a common-sense point that a shamanic journeying image is one that occurs in the context of a shamanic journeying experience. Clearly, this statement is true by definition, or tautology, and is, thus, redundant. What is needed is a formal statement of the criteria for the necessary conditions for shamanic journeying imagery. Our proposed criteria are derived from a review of generally accepted examples of shamanic journeying found in the anthropological and psychological literature. That is to say, the criteria will be validated by showing that they are features of imagery that are considered by scholars (and by shamans themselves) to be shamanic. Furthermore, it will become evident that our criteria are indicative of an experientially consistent journeying experience with regard to:

(1)   the way the images are integrated to form a "geography" or "landscape",

(2)   shamanic cosmology,

(3)   the purpose of the journey, and

(4)   the function of the journeying image.

The purpose of this chapter is to propose criteria for the necessary conditions for shamanic journeying imagery. Before proceeding, however, a qualifying statement is required. Shamanic journeying imagery is not restricted to any particular sensory modality — that is, journeying imagery may be visual, auditory, gustatory, olfactory, tactile, or multi-modal (Walsh, 1995). However, for the purpose of this chapter, shamanic journeying images will be delimited to the visual modality because these are arguably the most abundant (Houran, Lange, & Crist-Houran, 1997; Noll, 1983).

We will propose that four necessary conditions exist for a visual mental image to be deemed a shamanic journeying image:

N_1:   The visual mental image, X, must be integrated with other visual mental images;

N_2:   The "outward appearance" of X must be consistent with a shamanic cosmology;

N_3: X must be consistent with the purpose of the shamanic journey; and

N_4:   The function of X must be consistent with X.

N_1–N_3 were formulated *a posteriori*, while N_4 was constructed *a priori*. An example of an ostensible — yet ultimately non-shamanic — journeying image might be an X that satisfies, for instance, N_1 (i.e., the visual mental image, X, must be integrated with other visual mental images), but fails to satisfy one or more of the remaining necessary conditions.

N_1: X must be integrated with other visual mental images

We are using the term "integrated" to emphasise that during shamanic journeying experiences various visual mental images combine to form cohesive "geographies" or "landscapes", wherein events unfold in a sequential manner. Consequently, during journeying the shaman does not, for example, aim to cultivate — and subsequently focus on — a single visual mental image while attempting to eliminate all other thought-forms. By way of illustration, one may consider the following narrative provided by a Magyar shaman detailing a journey to the "lower world" or "underworld":

> The shaman travels to a high mountain pass, and from there descends into the "underworld." Many of the geographical names used are both real and symbolic. For example, just beyond Dhorpatan is a large stone with a natural groove around its middle. The stone is called "The Tying Place of the Death Sacrifice," and as such is a symbolic road marker for the road of death. The groove is attributed to the wear of the ropes of animals which have been tied there for the "Casting-Away-the-Soul Sacrifice." Further on, at the mountain pass, is a dividing of watersheds. The water which runs toward the village is known as "The Waters of Remembrance," and the water flowing the other way as "The Waters of Forgetfulness." In retrieving the soul, it is said that if the shaman can overtake it while it is still within the Waters of Remembrance, its capture and subsequent reinstallation is comparatively easy. If, on the other hand, the soul has reached the Waters of Forgetfulness, it will forget its home and family and wander into the underworld. (Waters; cited in Desjarlais, 1989, p. 291)

It is noteworthy that, in the preceding example, visual mental images such as a "large stone", "mountain pass", "watershed", and a "village" are integrated to form the "geography" of the Magyar shaman's "underworld". Consequently, these visual mental images satisfy N_1. An example of a visual mental image that does not satisfy N_1 is any image that is not a constituent of a coherent "geography" or "landscape". For instance, if an individual reported a single visual mental image (e.g., a "large stone") manifesting in a vacuum, then this would be inconsistent with N_1.

N_2: The outward appearance of X must be consistent with a shamanic cosmology

By "outward appearance" we are referring to the form or "garb" of X. For example, Strassman (2001) has speculated that "entities" encountered during dimethyltryptamine (DMT, i.e., a hallucinogenic drug) "trips" may manifest in forms (e.g., "elves", "aliens") recognisable to the percipient. Thus, to invoke Kant's (1781/1933) noumenal/phenomenal distinction, one may distinguish between the "entity" as a thing-in-itself (i.e., the noumenon) and the "entity" as perceived by the percipient (i.e., the phenomenon, "outward" appearance, form, "garb").

It is important to emphasise that the proposed criteria for this necessary condition consist of a specific shamanic cosmology rather than shamanic cosmologies in general, because the latter implies an arguably erroneous universality. During a shamanic journeying experience, the aspirant purportedly "travels" to "realms" or "worlds" located within the shaman's cosmos (Walsh, 1995). While each shamanic culture has developed its own cosmology, Ellwood (1987) suggested that a typical shamanic cosmology tends to consist of a three-tiered universe of varying ontological status. In addition, Harner (1980) considered it instructive to divide the shaman's universe into bipolar opposites: ordinary and non-ordinary reality. During shamanic journeying experiences, the shaman purportedly accesses what is technically referred to as the "lower world" and the "upper world" (non-ordinary realities) (Door, 1989; Walsh, 1990b, 1994). In ordinary waking consciousness (ordinary reality), the shaman experiences what is known as the "middle world", which is simply one's everyday existence on Earth (Harner, 1987).

Eliade (1989) stated that all three "worlds" are interconnected by a "central axis" (e.g., a "pillar", "tree", "mountain"). Moreover, the "upper" and "lower worlds" are believed to be multi-layered in many shamanic cultures (Walsh, 1990b). For example, Peters (1990) stated that, according to Tamang cosmology, the universe is held to exhibit a configuration of nine "lower worlds" and nine "upper worlds". Furthermore, six planets are understood to surround the terrestrial world in various directions. Rather than the "central axis" assuming the form of a "world pillar", "cosmic mountain", or "world tree" (Eliade, 1989), the Tamang shaman utilises a "rainbow rope" that emanates from the top of the cranium (Peters, 1990).

The three "worlds" of shamanic cosmology are referred to quite frequently, as they were some of the first elements observed by outside reporters, elements that they could comprehend and describe. As a result, many scholars (e.g., Eliade, 1989; Kalweit, 1988; Walsh, 1989b) emphasise the similar elements of shamanic cosmologies, overlooking their differences. Kalweit (1988) stated that the "upper world" is a realm that generally is associated with experiences of light and celestial beings. Walsh (1989b, p. 27) asserted, "The upperworld is a place where teachers and guides may be found" and is "perhaps populated with strange animals, plants, and people". Additionally, Shirokogoroff (1935; cited in Kalweit, 1988, p. 70) wrote that, in the cosmology of the Tungus, the "upper world" is where the "stars, the sun, the moon, and a few spirits and souls" reside.

The shaman's "lower world" is commonly referred to as the "underworld" (Eliade, 1989) and its geography is frequently characterised as a burial ground (Eliade, 1989, p. 509). Indeed, the cosmology of Tamang shamanism makes reference to "a black castle of death in the middle of a cemetery" (Peters, 1990, p. 78), whilst amongst the shamans of North Asia the geography of the "underworld" contains graves decorated with inverted objects (Eliade, 1989). However, there are exceptions to these generalisations; hence, each cosmology deserves individual attention.

Symbolic death and rebirth is a prevalent theme in the shaman's "lower world" (Dobkin de Rios & Winkelman, 1989; Peters, 1989; Winkelman, 1986). Amongst the shamans of western South Australia, the neophyte is inserted into a water hole, swallowed by a mythical snake, and subsequently ejected in the form of a newborn child (Drury,

1987). Similarly, in Labrador Eskimo shamanism, Tongarsoak the Great Spirit purportedly manifests in the guise of an enormous white bear and consumes the candidate (Eliade, 1989). As Campbell (1993) explained, "This popular motif gives emphasis to the lesson that the passage of the threshold is a form of self-annihilation" (p. 91).

Whilst descending to the "lower world", the neophyte routinely encounters "obstacles" such as rivers, bridges, and mountains (Desjarlais, 1989). Eliade (1989) held that aquatic symbolism often fulfils the negative performative function of an "obstacle". Eliade (1989, p. 312) contended that the "infernal river" is a classic motif of the "descent to the underworld", which is "present in nearly all the variants". Indeed the "Waters of Death" are held to be a prevalent theme amongst, for example, Asiatic, Oceanic, and palaeo-oriental mythologies (Eliade 1959, p. 135). For example, the Altaic shaman's descent to the "lower world" is characterised by seven "subterranean regions", referred to as *pudak* (i.e., "obstacles"), of which the fifth and the seventh *pudak* incorporate aquatic symbolism (i.e., waves and rivers, respectively) (Eliade, 1989). This is consistent with Walsh's (1990a, p. 147) assertion that the "lower world" is "often a place of tests and challenges".

Walsh (1993b, p. 750) stated that "the experiential content of the shamanic journey is ... consistent with the shaman's learned cosmology". Thus, a shamanic journeying image is, at least in part, a visual mental image consistent with the shaman's cosmological framework. An example of shamanic journeying imagery would be the Mazatec shaman María Sabina's journeying imagery (Wasson, Cowan, Cowan, & Rhodes, 1974). When treating a young man, she once asked some basic questions (e.g., "What happened to your foot?" p. 31) and then provided diagnostic answers (e.g., "It isn't a sickness ... it is a blow of fortune that hit him" p. 33). And, as the psychotropic mushrooms both the shaman and her client had ingested began to take effect, she launched into her healing journey. For example, "Oh Jesus, clock woman am I, eagle woman am I" (pp. 64–65). "I am going to thunder, I am going to sound. Even below the water, even the sea" (p. 83); "woman lord of the holy clown am I, the mushroom says" (p. 91); "lawyer woman, affairs, Mexican flag" (p. 103); "woman of the whirlpool, in the lake am I" (p. 107); "woman of the star of the Southern Cross am I ... woman of the shooting stars am I, lawyer woman am I, woman of affairs am I, I am going to the sky. Yes, Jesus Christ says, there my paper book is, there my Book is, my clean Book, my good Book" (p. 109); and, "There is where my prayers are, and where my little nuns are, and I go to the sky" (p. 111).

At the end of the session, María Sabina asked the young man "Has your body become lighter now?" (p. 201), and he answered in the affirmative. However, the healing was not complete, and she concluded that her client "probably needed many more" mushrooms (p. 203). Back from "the sky", María concluded the session by saying, "We are left only perplexed" (p. 205). These excerpts qualify as shamanic journeying images because they were a series of images that occurred during a shamanic ceremony, and they seemed to reflect shamanic cosmology – in this case, the traditional Mazatec shamanic "lower world" of the whirlpool, sea, and lake, as well as the "upper world" of the eagle, shooting stars, and the sky. In contrast, the overlay of Roman Catholic symbolism (Jesus Christ, nuns, and the Book), Mexican folklore (clock woman, holy clown), and politics (lawyer woman, Mexican flag) do not satisfy N_2 and, thus, do not qualify as shamanic journeying images, even though they might have played a role in connecting the young man with familiar icons.

N_3: X must be consistent with the purpose of the shamanic journey

Walsh (1995, p. 37) suggested that the mental images encountered during shamanic journeying are consistent with "the purpose of the specific session". For example, a Siberian shaman, Semyon Semyonov, described the following sequence:

> My ancestors made me into a shaman. They set me up like a
> wooden pole and shot arrows at me until I became uncon-
> scious. They cut the flesh off me. They separated my bones and
> counted them. My flesh they ate raw. When they counted my
> bones, they found that there was one too many. Had there not
> been enough bones I could not have become a shaman.
> (Ksenofontov, cited in Kalweit, 1988, p. 106)

It is arguable that the purpose of Semyon Semyonov's journeying session is what Eliade (1989, p. 59) has referred to as "ritual death and resurrection". Consequently, the entire series of images (e.g., ancestors
cutting and eating the shaman's flesh) may be regarded as consistent
with the task at hand, thus satisfying N_3. In contrast, if the purpose of a
shamanic journeying session was "ritual death and resurrection"
(Eliade 1989, p. 59) and the imagery sequence was inconsistent with
this purpose (e.g., the shaman traversed a "jungle"), then the imagery
would fail to satisfy N_3. Additionally, a close reading of this account is
inconclusive regarding intention; Semyonov may himself have
intended to become a shaman but, on the other hand, the ancestors'
intention to generate a shamanic initiation appears to have been
stronger.

N_4: The function of X must be consistent with X

We are using the term "function" to denote the action or activities
expected of X according to a particular shamanic cosmology. It is arguable that Xs perform either literal or symbolic functions. If some X performs a literal function, then X functions "in exact accordance with or
limited to the primary or explicit meaning of a word" (*Collins Concise
Dictionary*, 1999, p. 854). Consider a Siberian shaman's description of
the features of a journey to the "lower world":

> His soul is taken to the shaman ancestor, and there they show
> him a kettle full of boiling tar. There are people in it. There are
> some who are known to the shaman. A single rope is fastened
> across the kettle and they order him to walk over it. If he suc-

ceeds, he will live long. If he falls into the kettle, he might still become a Kam (shaman), but usually they do not survive. (Dioszegi, cited in Kalweit, 1988, p. 231)

The function of the "shaman ancestor" image is to impose tests that the neophyte must pass. This function is consistent with the explicit meaning of the term "shaman ancestor". That is to say, one literal function of a shaman ancestor is to provide shamanic training. Consequently, the "shaman ancestor" image satisfies N_4. If, for example, the "shaman ancestor" exhibited the behaviour of a court jester (e.g., juggling red balls for the purpose of entertaining spectators), then this would be inconsistent with the literal function of a shaman ancestor and, thus, N_4.

In contrast, if some X performs a symbolic function, then the function of X is to "represent or stand for something else, usually by convention or association" (*Collins Concise Dictionary*, 1999, p. 1507). One may consider the "rope across the kettle of tar" image from the previous example. This image may be conceptualised as a symbol of hell (Kalweit, 1988), thus satisfying N_4. In contrast, if the shaman, for instance, drank from the "kettle of tar" and claimed that his/her thirst had been quenched, then this would be inconsistent with the symbolic function of this image and, thus, constitute a violation of N_4.

Scoring With Regards to Shamanic Journeying Image Status

The formulation of N_1–N_4 constitutes a set of criteria that allows one to investigate whether a visual mental image is not a shamanic journeying imagery. If the visual mental image fails to satisfy any of the necessary conditions, then it is falsified and regarded as a non-shamanic image. However, even if all the proposed necessary conditions are satisfied, it does not necessarily follow that the visual mental image is a shamanic journeying image, because the conjunction of N_1–N_4 may not constitute a sufficient condition (i.e., there may exist necessary conditions that we have overlooked). One might invoke a dichotomous "yes/no" scoring format with regards to each necessary condition and code "yes" as 1 and "no" as zero. The image would be scored out of 4 (i.e., four viable necessary conditions). Thus, any score less than 4 would result in the falsification of a visual mental image's purported shamanic status. Consider a Tamang shaman's description of his initiatory calling:

> I took my father's [also a shaman] magical dagger and went to where the three rivers cross [a cemetery].... In the cemetery, I saw many evil spirits, some with long crooked fangs, others with no heads and with eyes in the middle of their chests, still others carrying decayed corpses. They attacked me and, before I knew it, they were all over me devouring my body. I was scared to death and, in a last hope, cried for the gods to save me, pleading that I was only a young boy. I drew out my father's magical dagger to defend myself, but it fell to the ground and struck a rock. This created a spark of light and everything changed. Suddenly it was daytime and the demons were gone. I was alive! (Peters, 1982, p. 23)

One may proceed to assess, for example, the "evil spirit" images as follows. The "evil spirits" satisfy N_1 on the ground that they are integrated with other visual mental images (e.g., a "cemetery", "decaying corpses", a "magical dagger", and a "rock"). "The "outward appearance" of the visual mental image (e.g., "evil spirits" with "crooked fangs") is consistent with Tamang shamanic cosmology (i.e., the shaman often encounters predatory creatures), thereby satisfying N_2. The "evil spirits" satisfy N_3 on the ground that they appear consistent with the purpose of the journey, which is arguably shamanic death/rebirth. It is noteworthy that the shaman stated that the "evil spirits" "attacked me ... I was scared to death ..." (Peters, 1982, p. 23). This mental imagery sequence is consistent with the contention that "predatory creatures" such as "evil spirits" perform the symbolic function of representing the shaman's fear (Kalweit, 1988), thus satisfying N_4. Given that the "evil spirits" satisfy N_1–N_4, a score of 4 is awarded and the purported shamanic journeying status of the visual mental image is not falsified. It may also be observed that, when N_1–N_4 are satisfied, the journeying imagery experience is arguably more coherent and, thus, more likely to be productive and meaningful for the shaman and his/her community. That is to say, if one or more of the necessary conditions are not satisfied, then the experiential consistency of the journey is compromised. For example, if the purpose of a journeying session is ascension to the "upper world" to communicate with one's power animal, then being attacked by "evil spirits" in the "lower world" is inconsistent with this purpose and, thus, a contravention of N_3. Consequently, it might be argued that, given the purpose of the session, being attacked by "evil spirits" detracts from the experiential consistency of the journey.

Shamanic societies rarely differentiated between waking journeys and night-time dreams, so these criteria could be used to evaluate any of a shaman's reported imagery. These criteria could also be applied to waking visions, meditation imagery, or the colourful panoramas emerging from ayahuasca sessions. But shamanic imagery does not allow itself to be easily categorised and pigeonholed; these criteria need to be used provisionally, or they will truncate the richness and complexity of the shamanic imagination.

Conclusion

In this chapter, we argued that shamanic patterns of phenomenal properties, and therefore journeying images, are neither well-defined nor sufficiently understood. We attempted to reduce the mystification surrounding journeying images by formulating a series of necessary conditions for a visual mental image to qualify as a journeying image. These necessary conditions allowed us to extrapolate a scoring system that permits empirical testing, via falsification, of a visual mental image's ostensible shamanic status. Essentially, the aforementioned necessary conditions provide future researchers seeking to examine shamanic journeying imagery with the conceptual tools needed to identify the phenomena that they are intending to investigate. Needless to say, a thorough knowledge of a particular shaman's cosmology, and that of his or her culture, is a requisite for accurate identification. Finally, the identification arrived at needs to be modest and subject to revision, should new information become available.

Chapter Eight

The Issue of Realism and Shamanic Journeying Imagery

As metaphysicians, shamans are typically realists (Walsh, 1990b) in the sense that the content of journeying imagery is conceptualised as real, objective, and independent of the percipient's *mind-body state(s)*, which Combs and Krippner (2003) have defined as "the entire set of mental and physiological aspects of a person's moment-to-moment experience" (p. 50). Indeed, Peters and Price-Williams (1980, p. 405) asserted, "Whereas Western psychiatry explains the visions as symbolic of internal processes, the shaman sees them as objective events". Furthermore, in a survey of the ethnographic literature, Noll (1985) stated that during a North American Indian vision quest, "a vision was taken to be a real perception: an encounter with an order of reality independent of the perceiver" (p. 446). Similarly, Harner (1987) suggested that the shaman's cosmos is not a mental projection, but rather exists independently of the perceiver's mind. Such a possibility is often perceived as a threat to the Western worldview.

Noel (1997) has maintained that many contemporary publications about shamanism represent Western fantasies that romanticise the topic, often ignoring shamanic journeys to the "lower world", encounters with dangerous entities, and other experiences too bizarre and diverse for simplistic generalisations. This issue is especially critical now that "neo-shamans" claim to be journeying, taking the realist position, since they may be ill-prepared to face an encounter with the malevolent forces and hazards that traditional shamans have learned how to combat.

Tart (1987) contended that it is "humanly important" to "test the essential claims of religion" by investigating "the reality (or lack of it) of ostensibly independently existing 'non-physical' worlds (NPWs)" (p. 145). However, Tart's call has largely gone unanswered. Indeed, while numerous scholars (e.g., Achterberg, 1987; Harner, 1987; Noll, 1985) concur that shamans tend to be realists, previous research has neglected to critically examine the ontology of shamans' claims for veridicality, for example, the upper world and lower world are independently existing NPWs. It would, of course, be advantageous to investigate the ontology (i.e., nature or essence) of shamanic NPWs using *a priori* or *a posteriori* methods, rather than merely to assume that the shaman's perceptions are veridical. Similarly, it would be disadvantageous to uncritically accept Western psychiatry's previously stated anti-realist position that shamanic NPWs are projections of the percipient's mental set at best and hallucinations at worst.

In Chapter 6 we explicated the inherent limitations associated with using empiricism to investigate the ontology of shamanic journeying imagery. Consequently, the aim of this chapter is to adopt a rationalist approach and, thus, analyse the logical coherence of a realist interpretation of shamanic NPWs (i.e., the referents of shamanic journeying images). By *logical coherence* we mean simply a logical agreement among parts of an argument. For example, does A follow from B? We will proceed by determining which variant of realism is most consistent with the shaman's purported views regarding the ontological status of the aforementioned NPWs. Subsequently, we consider shamanic journeying imagery in the context of the key definitional elements of the term "mental image". Finally, we formulate three premises concerning shamanic journeying imagery and NPWs with the aim of assessing the logical coherence of the shaman's realist ontology.

Shamanism Situated Within a Realist Framework

Lauden (1996) suggested that the term "realism" has many variants. "Scientific realism", for example, may be conceptualised as a strong form of realism that denotes the proposition that "entities, states and processes described by correct theories really do exist" (Hacking, 1983, p. 21). A weaker version promoted by Popper and his advocates is "conjectural realism", which refers to the claim that, while "the aim of science is to discover the truth about what really exists and theories are to be appraised for the extent to which they fulfil that aim", it should be acknowledged that knowledge is fallible as demonstrated by falsified theories supplanted by improved theories that view the universe rather differently (Chalmers, 1999, p. 240). In contrast, "structural realists", in brief, espouse the view that the degree to which a theory is held to approximate the structure of physical reality is contingent on its predictive success. For instance, the predictive success of quantum-mechanical theories intimates that the structure of the physical universe may approximate something quantum-mechanical (Worrall, 1996).

As previously stated, numerous scholars (e.g., Harner, 1987; Noll, 1985; Peters & Price-Williams, 1980; Walsh, 1990a, 1990b, 2007) have suggested that the shaman's ontological perspective is consistent with realism. More specifically, it is often argued that shamans conceptualise the content of journeying imagery as real, objective, and independent of the percipient's mind-body state(s) (Walsh, 1989a). Indeed, while it seems reasonable to accept that shamans are realists, it is perhaps prudent to explore with which variant of realism the shaman's perspective is most aligned. Blackburn (1996) suggested that the varieties of "realism" may be grouped into five claims:

> A realist about a subject-matter S may hold (i) that the kinds of thing described by S exist; (ii) that their existence is independent of us, or not an artefact of our minds, or our language or conceptual scheme; (iii) that the statements we make in S are not reducible to other kinds of statement, revealing them to be

about some different subject-matter; (iv) that the statements we make in S have truth-conditions, being straightforward descriptions of aspects of the world and made true or false by facts in the world; (v) that we are able to attain truths about S, and that it is appropriate fully to believe things we claim in S. (p. 320)

Blackburn uses the word "we" to refer to a community of scholars, but a case could be made for its applicability to a community of shamans as well.

Claim (i) holds that S is referentially linked to some "thing" that is. In contrast, claim (ii) is opposed to epistemological constructivism, which states that metaphysical entities (e.g., *En-sof*, *sunyata*, *Brahman*) are partially constructed or "shaped" by a percipient's religio-cultural-linguistic beliefs and values (incomplete constructivism, e.g., Hick, 1989, 1993; Katz, 1978), or are one hundred percent reducible to the percipient's religio-cultural-linguistic beliefs and values ("hard" constructivism, e.g., Gimello, 1978, 1983). We suggest that the assertion that shamans are realists seems consistent with claims (i) and (ii) on the ground that, as previously stated, scholars (e.g., Harner, 1987; Noll, 1983, 1985, 1987; Walsh, 1990b) often refer to the position that shamanic NPWs are real, objective, and independent of the perceiver (i.e., ii), and it is rather obvious that (i) is a necessary condition for (ii). That is, the kind of "thing(s)" described by the term "shamanic NPWs" cannot be, for example, independent of the perceiver (i.e., ii) if the thing(s) denoted by the term "shamanic NPWs" do not exist (i.e., i). Consequently, we will take the statement "shamans are realists" to mean that shamans subscribe to (i) and (ii) with regard to the kind of thing(s) to which shamanic cosmological terms (e.g., upper world, lower world, anthropomorphic spirit helper) are referentially linked.

Now that we have clarified the realist claims to which shamans purportedly subscribe, we are in a position to start our assessment of the logical coherence of a realist interpretation of shamanic NPWs. However, given that shamanic NPWs are experienced as shamanic journeying images, which are held to be mental images (e.g., Noll, 1985), it may be advantageous first to elucidate the key definitional elements of the term "mental image".

What Are Mental Images?

The ontological status of mental images continues to perplex philosophers of mind and cognitive psychologists (Heil, 1998). Indeed, numerous scholars (e.g., Haberlandt, 1994; Medin, Ross, & Markman 2001; Reed, 1992; Robinson-Riegler & Robinson-Riegler, 2004) purport to discuss the concept of mental imagery, while neglecting to formulate a definition of the term. Nevertheless, a survey of the literature suggests the delineation of a number of key definitional elements. First, mental imagery may be conceptualised as a mental representation (e.g., Solso, 2001). Second, mental imagery constitutes stimuli that do not originate from the percipient's sensory apparatus. As a result, the visual system is not involved in the production of the mental image (Best, 1995), and the mental representation pertains to a "nonpresent object or event" (Solso, 2001, p. 292), as opposed to being referentially linked to an object or event in the external world. For this reason, mental imagery is sometimes referred to as a quasi-sensory or quasi-perceptual experience (Richardson, 1969). Furthermore, Sternberg (2003, p. 215) suggested that "mental imagery may represent things that have never been observed by your senses at any time".... Consequently, for the purpose of this chapter, mental imagery will be defined as "the mental representation of things (e.g., objects, events, settings) that are not currently being sensed by the sense organs" (Behrmann, Kosslyn, & Jeannerod, 1996, cited in Sternberg, 2003, p. 215).

As stated in the previous chapter, shamanic journeying imagery is held to be consistent with the shaman's cosmology (Krippner, 1990a; Walsh, 1995), which typically consists of a multi-layered universe often exemplified by what is technically referred to as the lower world (often called the underworld), upper world (typically the sky), and middle world (the terrestrial world or Earth), although variations of this schema exist. Indeed, it would be an oversimplification to assume that all shamanic traditions equate the lower world with the Land of the Dead, because others equate the upper word with the abode of the deceased. For example, Lepp (2004, pp. 218, 217) stated that Mongolian shamans "travel to the Lower World to talk with the dead" (p. 218), but Na-hki and Moso shamans (in the Tibet area) believed that souls "rise to heaven".

The various worlds are considered to be connected by a pole that may manifest as, for example, a world tree, cosmic mountain, or world pillar (Eliade, 1989). Walsh (1989b, p. 27) asserted that the upper world tends to be associated with spirit guides and teachers and may be populated with strange animals, plants, and people, as well as celestial beings (Kalweit, 1988).

In contrast, as noted in chapter 7, the geography of the lower world is frequently conceptualised as funerary (e.g., Magyar, Tamang, and North Asian shamans routinely report graveyards or cremation grounds: Desjarlais, 1989; Eliade, 1989; Peters, 1990). Furthermore, shamans often experience symbolic death and rebirth at the hands of symbolic predatory creatures while travelling through the lower world (Dobkin de Rios & Winkelman, 1989; Peters, 1989; Winkelman, 1986). For example, in the Siberian shamanic experience the shaman-ancestors or other mythical beings may reduce the neophyte to "the state of a skeleton" (Eliade, 1989, p. 63). Similarly, in the South Australian Aboriginal and the Labrador Eskimo shamanic traditions, a mythical snake or other creature may swallow the aspirant (Drury, 1987; Eliade, 1989). Indeed, Walsh (1990a,) suggested that the lower world is "often a place of tests and challenges" (p. 14), one that is further populated by various *obstacles* that may be encountered by the shaman (Desjarlais, 1989; Harner, 1980; Kalweit, 1988; Peters, 1989, 1990).

On the Logical Coherence of a Realist Interpretation of Shamanic NPWs

As previously stated, many scholars (e.g., Noll, 1985; Walsh, 1990b) have suggested that shamans are realists in the sense that they conceptualise shamanic NPWs as real, objective, and independent of the perceiver. Furthermore, as previously discussed, it is routinely asserted that shamanic NPWs are experienced as shamanic journeying images, which are held to be mental images (e.g., Noll, 1985). We have suggested that mental images may be defined as mental representations of non-present events or objects (e.g., an *earlier* sensory experience). If shamanic journeying images are mental images — as opposed to retinal images — and one accepts that what is typically referred to as a "state of consciousness" may be defined as a "[set] of mental episodes" (Natsoulas, 1978, p. 912), a "stream of mental episodes" (Pressman, 1992, p. 12), or "a pattern of mental functioning" (Tart, 1969, p. 1), then it would seem to follow that a particular property (e.g., a mental image) is instantiated in a particular "object" (i.e., consciousness). Expressed another way, "mental episodes" (e.g., mental images) are attributes that organise a "compound" (i.e., consciousness). Consequently, mental images do not exist independently of consciousness, which is inconsistent with a realist interpretation of shamanic journeying imagery. Nevertheless, a realist might contend that properties may exist independently of their instantiation in objects. For example, a realist might argue that the colour red exists independently of the red ball that exemplifies it. Furthermore, it might be asserted that the property red can be exemplified multiple times; that is, it can be simultaneously instantiated in other entities (e.g., a red shoe, a red car) (Loux, 1998).[1] However, an anti-realist might rebut that, while the property of redness is not an epiphenomenon of the object that instantiates it, mental images are indeed an epiphenomenon of consciousness. A realist might reply that a retinal image cannot exist independently of one's

---

1   Thus, the ontological status of shamanic journeying images is further complicated by the problem of universals and particulars.

perceptual apparatus and yet is referentially linked to an object in the external world.

However, we argue that a realist position might be defensible if one distinguishes between: (1) shamanic journeying images, and (2) the entities or constituents of NPWs, to which shamanic journeying images are referentially linked, or which they mentally represent. While shamanic journeying *images* are clearly not independent of the percipient's mind-body state(s), it is arguable — the realist maintains — that shamanic *NPWs* are not an artefact of one's mind-body state(s) and, thus, exist independently of all sentient beings (Harner, 1987; Noll, 1983, 1985, 1987; Walsh, 1990b). Yet if shamanic journeying images are mental images — and, thus, *not* linked to concurrent sensory impressions — then what shamanic journeying images *are* referentially linked to (e.g., a *temporally prior* sensory impression, idea, dream, and so on) are *not* independent of a percipient's mind-body state(s) because they are stored in — and subsequently retrieved from — a percipient's working memory or long-term memory (depending on the temporal interval between the *initial* sensory impression, idea, dream, etc., and its subsequent retrieval). In other words, consensual reality is accessed in a particular mind-body state with particular rules of interaction with that reality and the laws regarding what passes as evidence. The shamans' NPWs are accessed in their own particular mind-body state with different rules and laws. The two worlds do not exist on a continuum but represent different realities.

In order for shamanic NPWs to be amenable to a realist interpretation, aspects of it must exist as either (1) sensory impressions, or (2) non-sensory impressions of exosomatic (i.e., independent of a person's mind-body state(s); H. Irwin, 1985) entities linked to concurrent shamanic journeying images. However, if shamanic journeying images are linked to concurrent *sensory* impressions, then this would violate definitions of the term "mental image" (e.g., a mental representation of a non-present event or object), and shamanic journeying images would be held to constitute retinal images (Rey, 1981). Clearly, shamanic journeying images do not involve "the (approximate) point-by-point picture of an object cast on the retina when light is refracted by the eye's optical system" (Reber & Reber, 2001, p. 341). Consequently, it seems rather obvious that shamanic journeying images are not retinal images.

In contrast, shamanic journeying images may be linked to non-sensory impressions accessed from a source independent of the percipient's mind-body state(s) (i.e., an exosomatic entity). If one invokes Kant's (1781/1933) noumenal/phenomenal distinction, then it is plausible that these impressions, for example, are phenomenal, while shamanic deities as things-in-themselves are noumenal, the latter being consistent with a realist position.

Thus, based on the preceding analysis, one may formulate at least three premises concerning the ontology of shamanic journeying imagery:

1. *Shamanic journeying images and their referents (i.e., NPWs) are reducible to the percipient's mind-body state(s).*

Premise (1) clearly holds that the referents of shamanic journeying images are not independent of the percipient's mind-body state(s). This is consistent with Gimello's (1978, 1983) "hard" or complete constructivism, which asserts that, for example, a mystical experience is one hundred percent reducible to the percipient's mind-body state(s). Thus, one tacit assumption underpinning "hard" constructivism is that there are no independently existing or exosomatic shamanic entities or NPWs, only artefacts of the percipient's mind-body state(s). Consequently, (1) is incompatible with realist claim (ii).

2. *Shamanic journeying images are referentially linked to exosomatic entities whose "outward" appearances are reducible to the percipient's mind-body state(s).*

By "outward appearance" we are referring to the form or "garb" of exosomatic entities. For example, Strassman (2001) has speculated that ostensibly exosomatic entities encountered during dimethyltryptamine- induced experiences may manifest in forms or "garb" (e.g., "elves", "aliens") recognisable to the percipient. Thus, once again invoking Kant's (1781/1933) noumenal/phenomenal distinction, one may distinguish between the entity as a thing-in-itself (i.e., the noumenon) and the entity as perceived by the percipient (e.g., the phenomenon, outward appearance, form, "garb").

Premise (2) is consistent with realist claim (ii) and also commensurate with Katz's (1978) incomplete constructivism and Hick's (1989) religious pluralism, whereby it is held that, while a metaphysical entity exists independently of a percipient, the outward appearance, or "garb", of that entity will be "refracted" through the percipient's religio-cultural-linguistic "lens" (i.e., a conceptual framework consisting of beliefs, values related to the percipient's mythology and cosmology). However, (2) is incompatible with Gimello's (1978, 1983) "hard" constructivism, which states that there are no independently existing or exosomatic metaphysical entities. One might tentatively argue that the constituents of the outward appearance are drawn from material stored in the percipient's memory system. Furthermore, the material selected is perhaps partially contingent on demand characteristics (e.g., embedded cues) derived from the environment, and the percipient's mind-body state (e.g., personality traits, cognitive schemata, religious belief systems, bodily sensations).

Thus, it is logically possible that the journeying image satisfies the criteria for a mental image (i.e., mental representation, non-sensory) given that: (a) the journeying image is a mental representation in the sense that it is a "refraction" of the exosomatic entity through the percipient's perceptual lens, and this "refraction" would, clearly, take place in the percipient's phenomenal space by virtue of the fact that the "refraction" constitutes a cognitive activity (a mental "action" associated with knowing); and (b) the journeying image is referentially linked to a non-present "object" or "event"; that is, non-present in the sense that the "object" or "event" is non-material. Furthermore, exosomatic entities may be considered non-present in the sense that they may be located in *other* space-time continua or in a space-time location inconsistent with the percipient yet *within the same* continuum as the percipient (e.g., my lost tennis ball is non-present to me by virtue of its being lost, yet it does not necessarily reside in another space-time continuum). Usually, the shaman embarks on solo journeys, but there are reports of encounters, deliberate or by chance, with other shamans who have accessed the same NPW (e.g., Kalweit, 1988).

3. Shamanic journeying images are referentially linked to exosomatic entities whose outward appearances are not reducible to the percipient's mind-body state(s).

In premise (3), journeying images continue to satisfy the mental representation and non-sensory criterion points of a mental image satisfied by (2). Furthermore, the contention that the entities are exosomatic is consistent with realist claim (ii). In contrast, to (1) and (2), however, the epistemological process that results in a percipient experiencing a shamanic journeying image does not involve superimposition within the percipient's phenomenal space and is, thus, incompatible with both incomplete (e.g., Hick, 1989; Katz, 1978) and "hard" (e.g., Gimello, 1978, 1983) constructivism. Thus, one of the tacit assumptions underpinning (3) is that the "outward" appearance of an exosomatic entity is intrinsic to that exosomatic entity; that is, the "outward" appearance is not an artefact of the percipient's mind-body state(s). Rock and Baynes (2005), however, have argued that the epistemological structure of shamanic experiences is not "pure" but rather mediated by a variety of cognitive processes. For example, during journeying the shaman typically exhibits the ability to communicate with spectators (Peters & Price-Williams, 1980) using grammatical rules governed by syntactical structures, which suggests that his or her linguistic system remains functional. Similarly, the shaman's ability to recollect the phenomenological content of, for instance, soul-flight implies that his or her memory systems remain operational during these experiences (Peters & Price-Williams, 1980). Given the level and complexity of

cognitive functioning during shamanic experiences it seems reasonable to suggest that, in contrast to (3), the "outward" appearance of
exosomatic entities is, in various epistemological ways, "shaped" by
the percipient's cognitive processes, which is consistent with (2).

To summarise: we have formulated three premises concerning the
ontology of shamanic journeying imagery and NPWs. Premise (1) was
that shamanic journeying images and their referents are reducible to
the percipient's mind-body state(s), which is inconsistent with realism
claim (ii). In contrast, we demonstrated that both (2) and (3) reveal that
shamanic journeying images may constitute mental images – in the
sense that journeying images can be shown to satisfy the mental representation and non-sensory criterion points – yet this does not necessarily preclude shamanic NPWs from existing independently of the
percipient's mind-body state(s). Consequently, it is not logically incoherent for scholars to claim that: (a) shamanic journeying images are
mental images; and (b) shamanic NPWs are not an artefact of the shaman's mind-body state(s). In other words, a realist interpretation of
shamanic NPWs is not necessarily logically incoherent even if shamanic journeying images are mental images. It will be observed that
premise (1) consists of less metaphysical baggage – on the ground that
it does not include exosomatic entities in its ontology – than (2) or (3)
and is, thus, more parsimonious. It is noteworthy, however, that the
violation of Occam's razor is not a sufficient condition for disproving
(2) and (3).

Conclusion

In this chapter, we have considered shamans' claims of veridicality
regarding the ontological status of "spirit worlds", which we referred
to as "non-physical worlds" (NPWs). Numerous scholars have con-
tributed to the mystification of these claims by merely concurring that
shamans tend to be realists, while neglecting to analyse the ontology of
shamanic NPWs. Our analysis reduces this mystification by invoking

three ontological premises that, ultimately, allow us to demonstrate that a realist interpretation of shamanic NPWs is not necessarily logically incoherent even if shamanic journeying images are mental images.

Chapter Nine

Methods for Studying Shamanic Reports of Psychic Phenomena

Over the millennia, shamans have reported experiences that parapsychologists would consider possible psychic or "psi" phenomena—reported interactions between organisms and their environment (including other organisms) in which information and influence have taken place that cannot be explained through conventional science's understanding of sensory-motor channels. In other words, these reports appear to challenge the constraints of time, space, and energy. Any attempt to demystify shamanism needs to consider these reports and the best means of evaluating them (Van de Castle, 1977, p. 274).

Key Issues and Question

Ever since shamans have reflected on their experiences, they have described reveries that appeared to transmit thoughts of another person, dreams in which the shamans seemed to become aware of faraway events, rituals in which future happenings supposedly were predicted, and mental procedures that were said to produce direct effects on distant physical objects or living organisms (Rogo, 1987). Are these occurrences instances of what parapsychologists now refer to as *telepathy, clairvoyance, precognition,* and *psychokinesis*? Or are there less contentious explanations of these phenomena? Do these experiences represent human potential or human illusion? (Krippner & Friedman, 2010).

When shamans attempt to locate lost objects, they may be utilising clairvoyance. When they seek to communicate with someone who is not nearby, they could be manifesting telepathy. When they try to divine the future, they might be displaying precognition. When they attempt to heal someone at a distance, they could be practicing psycho-kinesis. Purported psi phenomena are the most dramatic of the special abilities that provide shamans with their authority, prestige, and stat-ure. Can these alleged capacities be demonstrated under conditions that would rule out such conventional explanations as logical infer-ence, perceptual cues, subliminal perception, deception, and coinci-dence? This is the challenge faced by parapsychology when it turns its attention to shamanism.

From a philosophical standpoint, presumptive psychic (or psi) phe-nomena in shamanic practices differ from "supernatural" or "miracu-lous" phenomena. These terms describe phenomena that, if they exist, stand apart from nature and may even suspend or contradict natural laws and principles. Parapsychologists assume that the phenomena they investigate are lawful and natural and — at some point — will "fit" into the scientific body of knowledge, either with or without a revision of the current scientific worldview. Furthermore, parapsychologists discriminate between unverified psychic experiences and verified psy-chic events. Critics of the field insist that there are no psychic events, only psychic experiences that can be explained from the standpoint of conventional psychological mechanisms such as coincidences, optical illusions, misattribution of ordinary events, misperceptions, faulty memory, or downright fraud.

Research Finding

Weiant, however, in a paper delivered at an American Anthropologi-cal Association convention in 1960, reviewed some ethnographic accounts of possible parapsychological phenomena, remarking:

I feel very strongly that every anthropologist, whether believer or unbeliever, should acquaint himself with the techniques of parapsychological research and make use of these, as well as any other means at his disposal, to establish what is real and what is illusion in the so-called paranormal. If it should turn out that the believers are right, there will certainly be exciting implications for parapsychology. (as cited in Van de Castle, 1977, p. 668)

The literature in scientific parapsychology presents a variety of research directions, ranging from second-hand reports, to informal observations, to controlled observations, to controlled experiments, and to phenomenological accounts. Most of the reports in these categories would describe psychic experiences, but controlled observations and controlled experiments may themselves yield psychic events. In giving examples (and evaluations) of each category, we do not pretend to provide a comprehensive review. However, we have cited representative studies, mainly from the anthropological literature, that illustrate the problems and the prospects inherent in this field of study.

Interviews and Second-hand Reports

When Halifax (1979) interviewed the Mazatec shaman María Sabina in 1977, Doña María's precognitive experiences were among the topics they discussed. Doña María remarked, "And you see our past and our future which are there together as a single thing already achieved, already happened. So I saw the entire life of my son Aurelio and his death and the face and the name of the man that was to kill him and the dagger with which he was going to kill him because everything had already been accomplished" (pp. 134–135). The loss of her young son was a tragedy from which Doña María never fully recovered, yet she used this grief to empathise with the misfortunes of her clients.

Carpenter and Krippner (1989) interviewed Rohanna Ler, an Indonesian shaman, who told them of her "call" to heal. According to her narrative, one of Ler's sons began to lose his sight and did not respond to conventional medical treatment; when the boy's eyes began to bleed, she was close to utter despair. Then she had a powerful dream in which an elderly man appeared and told Ler that it was her fate to become a healer. Her son was the first person she would heal, but if she turned down the call he would go blind and never recover his sight. The dream visitor gave Ler a stone; upon awakening she found a stone in her bed and placed it on her son's eyes, whereupon he recovered completely. Subsequent dream visitors purportedly gave Ler a ring that she used as a "power object" in her healing sessions.

Murphy (1964) wrote about a St. Lawrence Island Eskimo informant who recalled a shaman producing sounds as though spirits were walking underneath and around the floor of his house, until "the house seemed to shake and rattle as though it were made of tissue paper and everything seemed to be up in the air, flying about the room" (p. 60). Murphy's informant described another shaman who was noted for his "power animal", a fox that purportedly could be seen running around the rim of the drum while the shaman conducted a ceremony. Murphy (1964) attributed these feats to conjuring, claiming that "some shamans were more imaginative or better ventriloquists than others, while some were more dexterous at sleight of hand" (p. 60). Murphy gave no specific explanations of the alleged techniques of legerdemain that could have been involved in these deeds.

Critique

Interview material and second-hand reports can be valuable reflections on the life and beliefs of native people. However, interviewers need to be well-trained so that they do not give inadvertent cues signalling the interviewee what is "expected" or what the interviewer "wants to hear". Many anthropological reports that have been considered to be valid some time later have fallen into disrepute, as other investigators, conducting research in a more rigorous manner, have provided quite different descriptions and reports. On the other hand, an investigator who concludes that conjuring is at work needs to provide at least one plausible scenario for readers to consider. In fact, the Parapsychological Association has urged its members to consult with magicians when conducting research in which sleight-of-hand may surreptitiously have been utilised or, better yet, to add a magician to the investigative team.

Eyewitness Observations

A 1914 report by Father Trilles, a Roman Catholic missionary to the Middle East, concerned a practitioner who told the priest that he intended to make an out-of-body journey to a magician's palaver in a distant village. The missionary, who expressed his scepticism, asked the practitioner to tell a student, who lived along the way, that he should come to see him at once, as he needed a new supply of shotgun cartridges. "After gesticulation, words, chants, and having rubbed himself all over with a reddish liquid smelling like garlic, he fell into a lethargic sleep. His body was perfectly rigid." The priest passed the night in the shaman's hut to be sure that there was no subterfuge. Three days later, the missionary's student arrived with the requested shotgun cartridges (as cited in Van de Castle, 1974, pp. 276–277).

Erdoes (1972) related attending a shamanic ceremony in a converted railroad car with members of his family and about 40 local Sioux residents. Once the kerosene lamp had been extinguished and the drumming commenced, Erdoes claimed that tiny lights began to appear throughout the room. The shaman's rattles flew through the air, and Erdoes's electronic flash unit began flashing of its own accord (pp. 280-281).

Hallowell (1971), who worked with the Salteaux Indians in Manitoba, Canada, described a shamanic session held for a woman whose son had been missing for a week. Shortly after the ceremony began, the voice of a young man seemed to manifest through the shaman, explaining that he was in good health and giving the location where he was camping. Two days later, the son arrived home; he confirmed that during the night of the session he had been asleep at the very location indicated by the shaman (p. 68).

Boshier, an amateur South African anthropologist who refused to take medication for his epileptic seizures, found that these seizures attracted the attention of the local natives, who saw them as "signs" that he should become an apprentice for extensive training. Telling a parapsychological conference about his apprenticeship in 1973, Boshier (1974) reported that he had visited one shaman who ritually "threw" the divination bones and told him details about his past and future "that were absolutely correct". Boshier was recognised as a bona fide shaman by his compatriots, and his biography is replete with other remarkable observations as well as personal experiences (Watson, 1985).

Schwartz (2009), while visiting Virginia Beach, Virginia, observed the intertribal medicine man Rolling Thunder work with a boy whose wounded leg resisted healing.

> Suddenly, I notice that there is a white mist-like form taking shape around and in front of Rolling Thunder's body. Sometimes I can see it, sometimes not. But it becomes stronger, steadier, until it is continuously present. It is almost dark now, but the fire gives enough light to see. Then it takes form, slowly at first, but as if gathering energy into itself it takes form. I can clearly see the smoke-like form is a wolf. Rolling Thunder moves as rhythmically as a clock. Sweep. Sweep. Flick. Sweep. Sweep. Flick.
>
> After about 30 minutes the form begins to fade, first losing shape, then becoming increasingly insubstantial. Finally, it is nothing more than a chimera, there and not there. Then it is gone. Rolling Thunder straightens up, and stops. He makes a kind of gesture, and somehow we are released to come forward. The boy is very peaceful. His mother has come forward, and she leans over him, kissing his forehead. The wound is completely healed. It looks like your skin does when a scab falls off leaving smooth unlined pink skin, shiny in its newness. I am astonished. (p. 10)

Critique

These observations are provocative indeed, suggesting directions that future research could take. By themselves, they are barely evidential, because the reader does not know how to assess their veracity. An observer requires a background not only in conjuring but in critical analysis. Could the practitioner subtly be eliciting information from the observer that was later used in making a prediction or a statement about the observer's personal life? Nor does the reader know how many sessions observed by the writer produced material that was not accurate, how many dreams provided incorrect data, or how many clients of the shaman did not obtain useful details about their lives and problems. Hyman (1977) has demonstrated how a performer can give a "cold reading" by using vague statements and sensory cues to construct a seemingly accurate description of a client. In many cases, the "hits" so impress the client he or she forgets or ignores the "misses".

Schwartz's observation is extremely remarkable, especially since it was witnessed by a group of individuals. However, none of them recorded their observations after Rolling Thunder's work was done. Schwartz himself waited several decades before transcribing his notes, writing his report, and submitting it for publication.

Controlled Observations

Bogoras, an ethnologist, made one of the first attempts to obtain controlled data on the unusual abilities of shamans. Bogoras (1904–1909) had heard reports of "spirit voices" that whistled and spoke during Siberian Chuckchee ceremonies. Bogoras, who attributed these phenomena to ventriloquism, decided to record a session, obtaining permission to observe a shaman famous for his alleged ability to evoke "voices" from the spirits. Bogoras placed a recording funnel some distance from the shaman, who sat in a stationary position during the demonstration and conducted the ceremony in almost total darkness. Several supposed spirit voices were heard. Soon Bogoras realised that the voices came from various points in the tent, not only from the area where the shaman was sitting. This distance effect also was apparent to people who heard the recording of the session, and Bogoras admitted that there was a marked difference between the voice of the shaman himself, who seemed to be speaking away from the funnel, and the spirit voices that seemed to be talking directly into the funnel. However, Bogoras never admitted that anything he had witnessed could have been anomalous, i.e., inexplicable by mainstream scientific paradigms; in his final report, published by the Museum of National History, Bogoras concluded that everything he observed was due to trickery.

Laubscher (1938), a South African psychiatrist, attempted to test the claims of Solomon Baba, a Tembu diviner. Unseen by anyone, Laubscher buried a small purse wrapped in brown paper, covered it with a flat stone, and placed a gray stone on the brown one. He then drove to the home of Baba, who lived 60 miles away. Shortly after Laubscher's arrival, Baba began to dance. He then accurately described the purse, the wrapping paper, and the stones. On another occasion, Baba described the appearance of some missing cattle from a distant region, and even predicted the exact day of Laubscher's forthcoming trip to England, although the specified date was several months after the time for which the original passage had been booked.

When Boshier (1974) was working with a museum in Swaziland, he had an opportunity to test a local "witchdoctor" named Ndaleni in the company of another native practitioner and Boshier's friend, a "Miss Costello". The "target" item to be identified was the skin of a gemsbok, a South African antelope. Boshier recalled:

> Leaving her in my office with the other witchdoctor and Miss Costello, I went to a neighboring [sic] building and took out the skin of a gemsbok. This I hid beneath a canvas sail on the back of my Landrover. Then I called her outside and told her I had hidden something that she must find. With the aid of the other witchdoctor, she knelt down and began to sing softly. Then, in a trance state, she informed me that I had hidden something

across on the other side of that building over there. She told me that it had more than one color [sic], that it came from an animal, that it was raised up off the ground. Suddenly she got up, ran around the building, out into the front where the Landrover stood and knelt down beside it. Again she began singing softly, and within five minutes of this she tore off one of her necklaces, and holding it in front of her like a divining rod, she walked around the Landrover, climbed into the back and took out the skin (p. 27, paraphrased).

Critique

Boshier's study is impressive but flawed; because he knew the identity of the "target" item, he may have passed nonverbal cues to Ndaleni, who picked them up, consciously or unconsciously, as a stage magician will locate an object hidden in the audience by observing the gestures and eye movements of the crowd. As for Laubscher's work, another person should have interviewed Solomon Baba. Laubscher knew the identity of the hidden object, and the reader of his report has no guarantee that Solomon Baba did not elicit clues from Laubscher during interactions that might have occurred before, during, or after the trance dance. Bogoras's account is presumptive in concluding that ventriloquism was at work and in not providing an explanatory mechanism for the differences that he and others purportedly observed on the recording. Investigators who claim that fraud has occurred need to present a plausible scenario for their claim. They, too, should have a background in conjuring, if they are to write knowledgeably about trickery and deception. Chari (1960) has provided a guide to sleight-of-hand effects for which one must be on guard, basing his report on his investigations of fakirs in India, while Wiseman and Morris (1995) have compiled an excellent set of guidelines for testing psychic claimants, i.e., people who claim to have psychic abilities.

Experimental Studies

Rose (1956) conducted a series of telepathy and psychokinesis tests with Australian aborigines using specially designed cards and plastic dice, which were placed in a shaker and tossed on a table with the goal of having certain die faces appear uppermost. He obtained statistically significant results in several of his telepathy experiments; at above chance levels, participants were able to guess the design on which Rose's wife was focusing, out of their sight. Psychokinesis tests yielded chance results; Rose reported that the aborigines did not believe they could influence psychokinetic phenomena, since that was a prerogative of the tribe's "clever men" (i.e., shamans). Two of these "clever men" were given telepathy tests, but their scores were not statistically significant.

Giesler (1986) conducted several studies, each with a different group of Afro-Brazilian "shamanic cultists." In one study the participant was asked to describe the location where someone (an "out bounder") had been taken—a location that was determined after the shaman and the out bounder had parted company. In another task, a glass of water, a white candle, and a spirit statuette (taken from the Afro-Brazilian pantheon) were displayed, and the research participant was asked to guess the order in which the three objects appeared, an order that had been recorded on a hidden list. The results were suggestive but not conclusive.

In Garhwal, India, Saklani (1988) screened a number of shamans who claimed to incorporate various deities (e.g., "Muslim Pir", "Goddess Dhari"). One shaman, Yashoda Devi, was selected for parapsychological studies. Tests in which Devi attempted to match "token objects" with the name of their owner yielded non-significant results, as did an examination for psychokinetic effects on methanol. However, the height of plants from seeds was significantly greater in the group "treated" by being held by Devi while she chanted than in the control group, which had no contact with her. A significant effect in the absorption of saline solution "treated" by the same shaman was observed when compared to containers of control saline. The growth of seeds sown in the field and "treated" by flasks of water previously held by Devi was somewhat more rapid on certain days of the study than that of control seeds given ordinary water. Saklani did not make clear whether the person making the measurements was "blind" to the "treated" and control materials; even fair-minded experimenters can inadvertently "tilt" the results if they know which group represents the experimental condition and which is the control.

Critique

Giesler's and Saklani's work are among the few experimental parapsychological investigations that have been made of native practitioners who claim to have psychic abilities (i.e., psychic claimants). The results of these inquires are neither compelling nor conclusive, but there were a few provocative outcomes. In addition, their experimental designs, as well as their suggestions for improvements, might pave the way for future studies. Giesler (1984, p. 315), for example, has called for a "multi-method" approach that would (1) focus more attention on what he termed the "psi-relevant" contexts in native cultures; (2) combine ethnographic and experimental methodologies so that the strengths of one offset the weaknesses of the other; and (3) incorporate a "psi-in–process" method into the field research design so that the investigator can observe the effect, if and when it occurs. Giesler proposed that, with this approach, the researcher may study ostensible psi processes and their relationship with other variables in the contexts of shamanic rituals and practices such as divination, trance mediumship, and healing. This procedure would allow for control of the conditions of a psi task, and the results could be evaluated with a minimum of interference or disturbance of the psi-related activity.

Phenomenological Accounts

For the shaman, there are no rigid boundaries between "waking life" and "dream life"; both are regarded as "real", but full admission to the latter "reality" usually depends on training and discipline. Malidoma Patrice Somé (1994), an African Dagara shaman, remarked, "Nothing can be imagined that is not already there in the inner or outer worlds" (p. 233). Somé's autobiography is a phenomenological account of his preparation, initiation, and apprenticeship, often marked by presumptive psi phenomena. For example, Somé (1994), remembered that, at a crucial period in his initiation, he was told to enter a cave. He recalled:

> I went that way, jumping from rock to rock until I reached the entrance to the magical cave. The floor was sandy and dusty; I noticed with surprise that the walls were perfectly carved out of red granite. My fire went out. I closed my eyes in an effort to blot out images of what would happen if I had to back out. When I opened them again, I could see a light a little distance ahead of me. It grew bigger and bigger, and soon I realised that I had reached the other side of the mountain. Writing about what came next is an extremely difficult task. I saw a tree that distinguished itself from the others by its unusual size. Under the roots of the tree was a bluish-violet stone that glowed as I looked at it. It had a very bright center [sic] whose light increased and decreased, making the stone seem as if it were breathing. My hand had taken on a violet color [sic] as if the irradiation of the stone were infectious. The violet was so powerful that I could clearly see it shining through the back of the hand stuck on top of it. Soon I felt as if I were in the middle of a huge violet egg that had no shell. Inside this egg there was a whole world, and I was in it. In that moment of awareness, I had an epiphany that the light we encounter on the road to death is where we belong. I could remember the entire experience I had just lived through, but it bore the aftertaste of a fantastic dream. Actually, I felt more like myself than I had ever felt before. Suddenly, out of nowhere, I saw a girl and found myself asking her for directions. She said, pointing west, "You see those mountains over there? Go to the one in the middle, and cross to the other side of it. There is a cave there. That is your way home." I found the cave the girl had told me about and ran in. It became dark as soon as I reached its interior. I could see the stony ceil-

ing two or three feet above me. I had crossed back through the mountain almost instantaneously. Something bit me inside my hand. It was the blue stone, my only proof that what had happened had been real (p. 244, paraphrased).

Critique

Phenomenological accounts are not evidential because they lack the controls necessary to rule out prevarication, memory distortion, self-deception, and the like. However, there are very few accounts as graphic and as detailed as that offered by Somé. Obtaining a shaman's "inside" view of a psychic experience is a unique opportunity that should be encouraged by future investigators.

Implications

"Magic" is a term used to describe a body of applied technology used to influence domains a society believes are ordinarily incalculable, uncertain, or unaccountable (Malinowski, 1954, pp. 139–140; Reichbart, 1978). If "magic" represents "natural" principles that are lawful, it is amenable to scientific investigation by parapsychologists and other investigators utilising scientific methods and procedures (Winkelman, 1982). As the term is usually employed, human beings perform "magic", but so-called "supernatural" entities (e.g., spirits, deities) perform "miracles". "Magical" practices and phenomena would be amenable to scientific study because they follow natural laws, but "supernatural miracles" would not be amenable to science, except at a descriptive or phenomenological level. In our attempts to demystify shamanism, we have bracketed claims of "supernatural miracles", which might or might not exist despite our scepticism. If so, they fall into the domains of "faith" and "belief", rather than the domain of science.

Explanations for the Phenomena

In his anthropological survey of unusual experiences among tribal people, Jensen (1963) remarked, "There can be no doubt that man actually possesses such abilities" (p. 230), and left it open as to whether these capacities are parapsychological or not. There are many alternative explanations, such as suggestion, imagination, exaggerated reporting, or a temporary extension of one's sensory and motor skills under unusual circumstances (e.g., physical and emotional arousal, ingestion of mind-altering substances, high levels of motivation). Nonetheless, the literature demonstrates that unusual phenomena can be linked to shamanic calling, to shamanic training, and to shamanic practice (e.g., DuBois, 2009; Winkelman, 2010, pp. 117–118).

In our opinion, it is likely that many if not most accounts of shamans' unusual behaviours and experiences have ordinary explanations. One's reputation becomes enhanced as tales are told and retold over the years, becoming embellished in the process. In addition, coincidence can be magnified by practitioners who point out the significance of an unexpected rainstorm, the sudden appearance of a "power animal", or an event that seems to conform to someone's dream of the previous night. It also must be recalled that, in the shamanic worldview, one's imagination and dreams are as "real" as public events, and those who listen to a shaman's stories might not be able to separate the two.

In addition, shamans were the first magicians as well as the first healers. They realised the value of drama, of shock, and of surprise in mobilising a client's self-healing capacities, and provided these elements through theatrical means. Murphy (1964), in her work among Eskimo shamans on Canada's St. Lawrence Island, discovered that instructions in ventriloquism and legerdemain were part of shamanic training. Reichbart (1978) suggested that deliberate sleight-of-hand can be used by shamans to create a psychological environment conducive to the manifestation of actual parapsychological events.

Kelly and Locke (1982) suspected that parapsychological investigations in shamanic settings will become more fruitful to the degree that investigators succeed in penetrating sympathetically, and in depth, the details of training settings and work environment. A promising example was the work of Boshier among shamans in southern Africa, but his untimely death cut short these contributions. However, Van de Castle (1974) was able to break through some of the customary reserve of Cuna Indian practitioners in Panama by bringing along a British psychic claimant, who was so successful in demonstrating his skills in diagnosis and healing that villagers began requesting his services.

In regard to the scientific status of parapsychology, Irwin (1999) has taken a position that is frequently heard among contemporary parapsychologists:

> In the final analysis, what fairly can be said of parapsychology? As far as spontaneous cases are concerned it seems likely that there are numerous instances of self-deception, delusion, and even fraud. Some of the empirical literature likewise might be attributable to shoddy experimental procedures and to fraudulent manipulation of data. Be this as it may, there is sound phenomenological evidence of parapsychological experiences and possibly even experimental evidence of anomalous events too, and behavioral [sic] scientists ethically are obliged to encourage the investigation of these phenomena rather than dismissing them out of hand. If all of the phenomena do prove to be explicable within conventional principles of mainstream psychology surely that is something worth knowing, especially in relation to counseling [sic] practice; and if just one of the phenomena should be found to demand a revision or an expansion of contemporary psychological principles, how enriched behavioral science would be. (p. 319)

The study of shamanism by parapsychologists and other scientists affords a unique opportunity to meet these goals. This opportunity has been bypassed for many decades, but the current interest in shamanism affords a chance for parapsychologists, with their unique training and perspective, to join this investigation. Anthropologists, ethnologists, psychologists, and other investigators of shamanic behaviour and experience dare not ignore this aspect of a shaman's repertoire if they are to gain an in-depth understanding of shamanic phenomena. (Storm & Rock, 2011)

Conclusion

Many psychic experiences associated with shamanism are explainable by trickery, sleight-of-hand, expectancy, coincidence, suggestion, and so on. But some are not. Parapsychologists have already made a modest beginning in attempting to demystify those phenomena that resist conventional explanation. This chapter contributes to the demystification of shamanism by outlining specific research strategies that may be used to investigate the relationship between shamanism and psychic experiences. If any psychic events are discovered, this will provide a bonus. If not, an important dimension of shamanism will be more fully understood.

Chapter Ten

Shamanism and the Demystification Journey

In this chapter we provide a brief survey of the Western encounter with shamanism. Within that context, we revisit each of the preceding nine chapters, pointing out their points of congruence with other investigators who have attempted to demystify shamans and shamanism. We emphasise the work of psychologists, because this approach reflects our background and training, but we have included material from anthropology, sociology, and the neurosciences when it was appropriate to do so.

The Western academic and scholarly encounter with shamanism took place over several centuries, entering into mainstream discourses in the 1700s (Flaherty, 1992). The earliest concepts of shamanism derived from a Christian perspective, labelling shamans misguided at best and diabolical at worst. In Europe, the Enlightenment produced a profound shift in attitudes; shamanism was no longer demonised by academia but was seen as riddled with superstition and irrational beliefs and practices. With the emergence of psychoanalysis, shamans were re-cast once again, this time as hysterics or schizophrenics. Hence, the Western discovery and description of shamanism is rooted in the religious and social history of Western scholarship (DuBois, 2009).

Current concepts of shamanism were stimulated by developments in several fields. One critical development in scholarship on shamanism was Mircea Eliade's (1989) classic work, *Shamanism: Archaic Techniques of Ecstasy*. In preparation for this venture, the multi-lingual Eliade was determined to read every existing publication on the topic (Sullivan, 2004). His book challenged the view that shamanism was a mental disorder; rather, he interpreted the dramatic rituals, visions, and behaviours as signs of life-transforming spiritual experiences with a wide range of consequences beneficial to shamans and their societies (p. ix).

Shamans appear to have emerged as distinct practitioners by Upper Palaeolithic times, as evidenced by cave paintings that portray such shamanic themes as birdmen, wounded men, soul flights, and animal spirit allies (Winkelman, 2010), although this attribution is not without controversy. However, between 30,000 and 60,000 YBP (years before the present), cave paintings not only flourished but were accompanied by figures, jewellery, and decorations that demonstrated what Winkelman referred to as "a new mentality", an "integrated functioning" that was "a key feature of the modern mind and its cognitive fluidity" (p. 76). Mind-altering substances were not used in every shamanic tradition, but—contrary to Eliade—were present from the beginning serving as "psychointegrators" that disinhibited the brain stem and limbic structures "resulting in enhanced informational inflow, emotional lability, increased visual experiences, and synchronous brain discharges" (p. 144).

In our opinion, Winkelman's 2000 book and its expanded 2010 revision has supplanted Eliade's volume as the major academic sourcebook on the topic of shamanism. Not only has he provided additional material, but he has given considerable space to such topics as evolutionary biology, the neurosciences, spirituality, and cross-cultural studies.

As mentioned earlier, one of Winkelman's (1992) major contributions has been his cross-cultural study of 47 societies in which he focused on magico-religious practitioners, that is, those individuals who occupy a socially recognised role that has as its basis an interaction with the non-ordinary, non-consensual dimensions of existence. This interaction involves special knowledge of purported spiritual entities and how to relate to them, as well as alleged powers that allow these practitioners to influence the course of nature or human affairs in ways not ordinarily possible. Winkelman coded each type of practitioner separately on such characteristics as the type of magical or religious activities performed, the techniques employed, the procedures used to produce shifts in consciousness, the practitioner's mythological worldview, psychological characteristics, perceived power, socioeconomic status, and political role. Statistical analysis provided a division into four groups:

1.   *the shaman complex* (shamans, shaman-healers, and healers)

2.   *priests and priestesses*

3.   *diviners, seers, and mediums*

4.   *malevolent practitioners* (witches and sorcerers)

The shaman appeared to be most often present in hunting/gathering and fishing societies. The introduction of horticulture and agriculture gave rise to the priest. Shamanic oral traditions, which differ from the body of sacred scripture as maintained by an organised priesthood, remain flexible and adaptive, with each situation seen as unique. Political differentiation of the society led to a further division of labour into those of healers, mediums, and malevolent practitioners. Any given society may have one or more magical-religious practitioners. Among the South African !Kung, for example, the majority of males are magical-religious practitioners, along with a sizeable minority of females (R. Katz, 1982).

Using Winkelman's terminology, the shaman-healer specialises in healing practices, while the healer typically works without the dramatic alterations of consciousness that characterise the shaman and, to a lesser extent, the shaman-healer. Diviners (as well as seers and mediums) act on a client's request to heal or to prophesy after they have "incorporated" spirits. These practitioners typically report that they are conduits for the spirits' power, without claiming to exercise personal volition once they "incorporate" (or are "possessed by") the spirits. Shamans, on the other hand, frequently interact with the spirits and sometimes "incorporate" them, but remain in control of the process, suspending volition only temporarily.

For example, volition is surrendered during some Native American ritual dances when there is an intense "flooding". Nevertheless, the shamans purportedly know how to enter and exit this type of intense experience. Malevolent practitioners are thought to have control over some of the "lower" spirits along with access to "power" through rituals. Typically, they do not see their mission as empowering society as a whole (as do the shamans). Rather, they are employed by members of their community to bring harm to enemies (inside or outside the community) or to seek favour from the deities for specific individuals through sorcery, witchcraft, "hexes", and "spells".

The more complex a society, the more likely it is to have representatives of each type of practitioner, except for the prototypical shaman. It should be kept in mind, of course, that categories are never absolute; some practitioners are difficult to classify, and others switch roles according to the occasion (Heinze, 1988). Furthermore, in some societies, (e.g., Diné, Lakota, Yanomami) the line between sorcerers and shamans is quite thin (Jokiæ, 2006).

Although shamanism is not and never has been an institutionalised religion (Pratt, 2007, p. 393), shamans have been dubbed *magico-religious practitioners* by Winkelman. One could make the claim that shamans appear to have been humankind's first psychotherapists, first physicians, first magicians, first performing artists, first storytellers, and first weather forecasters. They were originally active in hunting/gathering and fishing tribes and still exist there in their most unadulterated form; however, shamanic practitioners also appear in nomadic-pastoral, horticultural, agricultural, and even urban societies today. The word "shaman" is a social construct that originated in Siberia and was later applied to a diverse range of practitioners in many parts of the world. Some scholars (e.g., Hutton, 2001) doubt that the term should be used cross-culturally, because it is a Eurocentric concept. Winkelman (2002) has rejected this assertion, emphasising cross-cultural studies and evolutionary models. Positing the shaman as "a cross cultural phenomenon" (p. 69), he has demolished arguments to the contrary on several grounds, including the shamans' organisation of communal healing and divination rituals, their high social status, their leadership roles, and their ability to deliberately undertake "vision quests" and "soul flights" on behalf of their community. These latter activities involve accessing what Winkelman refers to as a transcendent, "integrative mode of consciousness", that differs from ordinary wakefulness as well as from dreaming and non-dreaming sleep (p. 22).

Winkelman's work has opened a new chapter of discourse for scholars interested in shamanism, as it is based on empirical studies as well as data from the neurosciences, the social sciences, and the behavioural sciences. It is in the spirit of Winkelman's high regard for shamanism, coupled with his attempts to demystify an important human phenomenon, with which we have undertaken the investigations presented in this book. Winkelman's writings are rooted in anthropology and there are a dozen other disciplines that have made substantial input into contemporary knowledge about shamanism. Consequently, our modest contributions are far from the last word on any of the topics we have investigated.

Chapter One

With the advent of modern science, shamanic practices were denounced as fraud, trickery, and delusion; psychiatrists depicted shamanic practices as pathological manifestations of disordered affect and cognition. It was assumed that shamanic practices would disappear with the spread of modern rationality. But this obituary was premature. Winkelman (2010) commented, "Just as it seemed shamanism might slip into its final demise within modern rational consciousness, its practices re-emerged in modern societies" (p. 2). In Chapter 1, we traced Western perspectives on shamanism and how they have changed. We also presented a psychological definition of "shaman".

The term "shamanism" was used by DuBois (2009) "to describe traditions of spiritual travel characterised by various culturally recognised and defined trance states and undertaken for a range of reasons including healing, divination, and the management of luck" (p. 25). However, such phrases as "spiritual travel" and "trance states" do not enjoy standard referents; the former is metaphysical in nature, and the latter is open to multiple interpretations. Walter (2004) has pointed out that definitions take two major trends: some definitions are very broad, while others are more circumscribed. Those writers in the latter category tend to delimit the term to past and present Siberian and Arctic practitioners; Kehoe (2000) stated that "it is confusing and misleading to use a simple blanket word, lifted from an unfamiliar Asian language, for a variety of culturally recognised distinct practices and practitioners" (p. 53). However, Winkelman's research permitted an empirical determination of shamanism as a cross-cultural phenomenon; moreover, Winkelman (2010) found Kehoe's criticism of Eliade's failure to use systematic cross-cultural research legitimate—and answered it.

Definitions that take the broader perspective generally refer to shamanic interaction with discarnate entities referred to in English as "spirits". Lewis's (1984) description of shamans includes their "power to control the spirits" (p. 9); Shirokogoroff (1935) referred to a shaman as a master of spirits; Townsend (1997) provided a definition that included the phrase "a shaman is one who has direct communication with spirits" (2001, p. 1); Walsh (2007) described shamans as "voluntarily entering altered states of consciousness in which they experience themselves or their spirit interacting with other entities ...; Bockman and Hultkrantz (1978) stated that the two most important components of shamanism are the practitioners' ability to be in contact with the supernatural world and their ability to act on behalf of their communities in a way based on their extraordinary ecstatic experiences, achieved with the aid of their "helping spirits" (p. 11). The latter authors (as well as Walsh) have included mention of shamans' services to their communities, an essential but often overlooked aspect of shamanism, as well as their interaction with spirits. We suggest that "spirits" be treated as a social construct, a stance that will permit researchers to explore and discuss this aspect of shamanism without becoming embroiled in veridicality issues.

Walsh (2007) has presented a sophisticated postmodern account of the problems that arise when differing worldviews regarding spirits are compared. In addition to our designation of spirits as social constructs, Walsh suggested that they might be Jungian archetypes, creatures of the imagination, or entities dwelling at the limen or border of ordinary and non-ordinary reality. He concluded that "we may be unable to determine the precise nature ... of something [because] the available data may be interpreted in many ways ... and we have no absolute method by which to decide which interpretations are best" (p. 148). Nonetheless, Harner (2010) astutely noted that acknowledging the reality of spirits is "fundamental to success in shamanic work" (p. 2).

Given this background, one can understand the rationale for Krippner's (2005) definition of shamanism as cited in Chapter 1: "From a psychological perspective, shamans can be described as community-sanctioned spiritual practitioners who claim to deliberately modify their attention in an attempt to access information not ordinarily available to members of their social group" (p. 204). First, shamans are granted privileged status by the community they serve. Second, shamans take an active stance in changing or shifting their attentional states, or what we have called "patterns of phenomenal properties". Third, this shift is attempted in order to access information not ordi-

narily available to others. A child might report a dream that is meaningful for the tribe, a warrior might have a premonition of approaching
enemies, a hunter might have a vision of where game can be found —
but these are rare and spontaneous occurrences, whereas shamans
need to be able to obtain this knowledge at will. Shamans are required
to have the discipline to seek counsel and power from spirits, from animal allies, from ancestors, or from any number of other sources.
Finally, shamans are "spiritual practitioners", a term equivalent to
Winkelman's "magico-religious practitioner". Krippner (e.g., 2005)
has defined "spirituality" as "an awareness of a broader life meaning
that goes beyond the immediacy of everyday expediency and material
concerns" (p. 204), a definition that bypasses the dogmas of organised
religions and provides opportunities for measurement through content analysis, questionnaires, or other qualitative or quantitative
instruments.

Chapter Two

In Chapter 2 we suggested that *Homo sapiens* were probably unique
among early humans in their ability to symbolise, mythologize, and,
eventually, to shamanize. This topic also has been dealt with by
Winkelman (2010), who has provided more depth to our discussion of
the neurobiological capacities for knowing of the species. Such common shamanic practices as journeying, accessing imagery, and assuming an animal identity "are not strictly cultural but are structured by
underlying biologically inherent structures" (p. 38). These
"neurognostic structures" predispose and mediate the organisation of
experience. "Universal shamanic characteristics reflect these
neurognostic structures, such as those of archetypes, the primordial
organisation of the collective unconscious" (p. 38). *Homo sapiens'* eventual domination may have been due to use of these neurognostic structures to produce explanations of daily experience that assisted human
survival.

One of Eliade's greatest flaws was to label the use of mind-altering substances as "degenerate" and of fairly recent origin. However, archaeologists have discovered evidence of the prehistoric use of mind-altering plants in the Indus Valley, ancient Greece, the Americas, and several other locations. The Greek historian Herodotus provided a detailed description of Scythian funerary rites in which a community participated in a cannabis-enhanced sweat lodge. DuBois (2009) has interpreted this passage as describing a communal shamanic cleansing ritual, rather than one in which a singular shaman presided. Similar community functions have been described by Berman (2000), who also saw the origins of shamanism as group-oriented rather than dependent on a designated practitioner.

The substances that Winkelman (2010) referred to as "psycho-integrators" permeate the shamanic record. He arrived at this term because the patterns of effects revealed by cross-cultural research are similar, and because neurobiological research has demonstrated that they release the inhibitory effects of serotonin in the brain. One of the oldest traditions involves the use of an Amazonian brew concocted from plants found in the rain forest. Variously known as yagé, hoasca, and ayahuasca, the effects of this substance have been studied by Shanon (2002) through the lens of cognitive psychology. Ayahuasca typically produces colourful visions coupled with personal insights, metaphysical ideations, and powerful spiritual experiences. The brew contains juice from the *Banisteriopsis caapi* vine (which contains harmine and other harmala alkaloids in its stems), usually combined with *Psychotria viridis*, a shrub that produces N-N-dimethyltryptamine (Labate & MacRae, 2010).

Shanon (2010) asked his informants what types of knowledge were obtained through ingesting ayahuasca. The most common type mentioned was factual knowledge about themselves, their peers and family members, and even other civilisations. Shanon doubted that all of this information was veridical, especially information referring to other civilisations. The second type was psychological knowledge such as personal insights, solutions to interpersonal problems, and the meaning of one's life. A third type of knowledge was that related to Nature; for instance, transformation into one's animal helper is reported by both shamans and non-shamans. Another type is the collection of philosophical and metaphysical insights; frequent comments reported by Shanon were "It all has meaning" and "There is a great story behind it all" (p. 269). Other types of insights cited by Shanon include well-being, artistic creativity, and specialised knowledge; thus Shanon's theory of consciousness emerged from several of his own ayahuasca sessions. The cognitive factors he identified included mental lucidity, intuition, empathy, creativity, meaningfulness, and inspiration.

Contrary to some other writers' coupling of shamanic visions and Jungian archetypes (e.g., Ryan, 2002), Shanon insisted that ayahuasca visions need not be conceived and modelled in terms of depth psychology or any other form of symbolic representation. It would be more appropriate, he noted, to view them as works of art that need to be appreciated and admired rather than deciphered. One does not have to interpret a painting or a musical composition; the proper manner in which ayahuasca visions are to be studied is comparable to hermeneutics applied to the arts. Indeed, Eliade's methodology has been described as "a hermeneutical study" by Walter (2004, p. xix). In hermeneutic investigations, the meaning of what is being studied gradually unfolds, a process that is descriptive of how both Eliade and Shanon arrived at their insights.

Hubbard (2002c, 2003), another cognitive psychologist, has found similarities between concepts in shamanism and ideas in cognitive psychology. For example, the "web of life", as described in many shamanic traditions, emphasises the interdependence and interconnectedness of all living forms. Different species are seen as different nodes in a larger web, and these nodes are connected by linkages that reflect how the actions of any given species impact the actions of members of other species. This entire web is immersed in meaning (Capra, 1996;

Eliade, 1989) and can be considered an immense signal system (Laughlin, McManus, & d'Aquili, 1990; Kalweit, 1992). To Hubbard, this imagery resembles the network models of semantic memory in cognitive science, specifically memory for facts and descriptions consisting of general, abstract, and conceptual knowledge. Information is not stored locally but is distributed across the entire neural network (Anderson, 1995). These connections are not limited to the brain but place meaning out into the world (Hardy, 1998); this extension of meaning is consistent with the shamanic view that both living and non-living aspects of Nature have beliefs, desires, and other mental states. Visual imagery and other mental representations can be accommodated by network models, and the interplay between image and environment is apparent in many shamanic rituals (Hubbard, 2003). The flow of information and influence between organism and environment might be more bi-directional than expected, and may serve to facilitate shamanic healing.

In psychology, the term "locus of control" refers to an individual's tendency to believe that either external or internal forces control his or her life. In general, an internal locus of control is felt to be more adaptive than an external locus (Lefcourt, 1976). However, the shamanic worldview attributes considerable causation to spirits, ancestors, deities, and other external agents. This stance may help an individual, family, or clan cope more easily with life's challenges and difficulties (Hubbard, 2002c, p. 35). The Western emphasis on individual volition may not be pertinent when collective societies face emergencies; an internal locus of control might be adaptive in an individualistic society, but a perceived external locus of control might be more appropriate in certain other cultures.

A final example of Hubbard's (2003) comparisons involves shamanic masks and costumes. When shamans don a mask or costume, they are entering a sacred space that is not ordinarily accessible. The masks and costumes become vehicles for a journey into other worlds, which Hubbard equates with the unconscious. The mask and costume provide powerful images for capturing and encoding elements of the experience, making the implicit (something of which the shaman is unaware) more explicit. This confrontation could lead to personal growth, as the new images and experiences are assimilated in a form that can be retrieved for the shaman's work as a healer, mediator, or counsellor. Hubbard concludes his presentation by noting that the many similarities between cognitive science and shamanism at a basic cognitive level make a strong case that numerous aspects of shamanic cognition may not be fundamentally different from non-shamanic cognition. Not only have Hubbard's analyses demystified many aspects of shamanism, but they have identified shamanism as a resource worthy of serious study by psychologists and their colleagues.

Chapter Three

Harner (1980) has described a "shamanic state of consciousness" that typifies "core shamanism". Other writers have used the plural term, writing of "shamanic states", but the phrase occurs throughout the literature. Dowson (1999) argued that three elements embrace intercultural similarity and community specificity: shamans continuously alter their consciousness; these altered states are accepted as important ritual practices by the shaman's community; and knowledge concerning these altered states is controlled so that socially sanctioned practices are carried out. However, in Chapter 3 we argued that affixing the qualifier "shamanic states" to consciousness results in a confusion of consciousness with the content of consciousness. We further argued that this "consciousness/content fallacy" could be avoided if the term "shamanic patterns of phenomenal properties" (an extrapolation of the term "phenomenal field") were used. For us, the pattern of phenomenal properties that constitute shamanic experience and the pattern of phenomenal properties that comprise ordinary waking (non-shamanic) experience might not differ fundamentally.

A similar position has been taken by Berman (2000), who has taken issue with the facile use of the term "altered state" to describe shamanic consciousness. He considered shamanic experience to be a heightened state of awareness and attention within ordinary waking consciousness, rather than a quality that is "altered". If such a heightened state of awareness or attention increased the scope of what was in awareness but did not significantly influence subjective experience, it would not constitute an "altered state". This heightened state need not be limited to transcendental stimuli, but would be useful in practical tasks such as finding game animals, locating and using medicinal plants, harvesting crops, and other matters of daily survival (Krippner, 2000). Hubbard (2003) added that, during the course of the shaman's apprenticeship, he or she acquires expertise that allows for improved performance in these tasks, leading to a facilitation of pattern recognition and retrieval.

Winkelman (2010) also noted the problematic nature of the phrase "altered state of consciousness", preferring to explore "altered consciousness within the broader frameworks of the biological and epistemological foundations of consciousness in general" (p. 21). He has called for a conceptualisation of consciousness in relationship to its biological means of operation, and also for understanding waking, altered, and integrative consciousness in terms of the body's and the culture's propensities for knowing. Winkelman called this a "neurophenomenological approach", and we see our term "patterns of phenomenal properties" as congruent with this perspective.

Chapters Four and Five

In these two chapters, we presented several models that could be useful in describing and differentiating shamanic systems of healing and dreaming. We observed that Harner (2010) has enumerated ten "principles" that shamanic systems of dreaming have in common, but the model we presented is helpful for noting nuances that differentiate the systems. We might also recommend Walsh's (2007) model for mapping "states of consciousness" (pp. 238–239), as it clearly deserves wider application.

Winkelman (2010) has delineated several "shamanistic therapies", identifying the physiological processes that underlie the three major therapeutic bases: a "special state" of consciousness, a belief in spirits, and community rituals (p. 183). The Foundation for Shamanic Studies offers training workshops and certificates in shamanic counselling. The Foundation has a mission — namely, the preservation, study, and transmission of ancient shamanic knowledge. Its faculty code of ethics sets out four guidelines: strive to work in harmony with and for each other; teach for positive use, as a healing force in the world; refrain from taking advantage of students; treat each other with care, patience, tolerance, and compassion. The Foundation's activities involve not only training, but the revival of shamanism in various parts of the world where its survival is threatened. It has also engaged in research projects, among them a study that found that shamanic journeying, aided by percussive drumming, bolstered the human immune system. The effect was stronger in journeys to the "upper world" than to the "lower world", and when the purpose of the journey was specifically geared to increase salivary immunoglobulin type A (S. Harner, 2003; Harner & Tyron, 1992, 1996).

In commenting on the Foundation and so-called contemporary "neo-shamanisms", Winkelman (2004) observed, "Some of the modern borrowings have attempted to maintain a focus upon the classic aspects of shamanic practice; these aspects are emphasised in the concept of Core Shamanism developed by Michael Harner (1990) and in the activities of the Foundation for Shamanic Studies.... Many other modern adaptations, however, were not based upon the primordial hunter-gatherer patterns of shamanism, resulting in the extension of the term *shaman* to a bewildering variety of practitioners, some of which have little relationship to original forms of shamanism" (p. 69).

A popular magazine, *Shaman's Drum*, regularly features field reports of shamanic healing (e.g., Carpenter & Krippner, 1989). In addition, it carries advertisements from purported shamans offering a variety of services to the periodical's readers. The Society for Shamanic Practitioners publishes a somewhat different periodical, *The Journal of Shamanic Practice,* which also carries a bevy of advertisements regarding purported shamanic practices and services. The articles in the journal focus on the application of shamanism (e.g., Krippner, 2009). Articles for both publications are peer reviewed, and both boast a distinguished editorial board. The Society describes itself as "an international alliance of people dedicated to the re-emergence of shamanic practices in modern society, especially those that promote healthy individuals and viable communities" (p. 3).

In psychological therapy, the term "evidence-based practice" refers to psychotherapies that have demonstrated their effectiveness in controlled studies. But what is considered "effective" in Western psychotherapy may be very different from criteria used by shamanic practitioners. Even so, Torrey's (1986) cross-cultural observations led him to conclude that indigenous healers and Western psychiatrists were about equally effective in the treatment of clients with mental disorders, even though diagnostic criteria differed from culture to culture. However, Torrey distilled four components of successful treatment by both groups of practitioners: a shared worldview that makes the "naming process" possible; personal characteristics of the practitioner that promote success; positive client expectations; and therapeutic techniques that empower the client.

DuBois (2009) noted that "more so than virtually any other aspect of shamanism, the issue of healing challenges Western presuppositions regarding veracity and interpretive objectivity" (p. 133). A course of therapy that treats elements of a "stolen soul" or damaged relations with invisible entities has no facile counterparts in Western medicine. Sometimes the therapy can be considered a "success" even when the client dies, a sign of failure in Western medicine (p. 134). The model we have presented allows for the description of shamanic healing practices in their own terms, without the use of a Procrustean bed to shoehorn descriptions of shamanic practices into Western terms.

In contrast to shamanic therapies, the use of dreams in Western psychological therapy has a promising track record. A "cognitive-experiential" method for integrating dreamwork into psychotherapeutic sessions received positive ratings from clients in terms of satisfaction. In comparison with psychotherapy sessions that ignored dreams, clients using the cognitive-experiential method made more gains in insight, in behaviour change, and in problem-solving (Hill & Rochlen, 2009). This method involves three stages: exploration, insight, and action, combining client-centred, phenomenological, Freudian, Jungian, Gestalt, and cognitive-behavioural approaches. Once an integral part of psychological therapy, dreamwork virtually disappeared, but began to revive alongside what is known as the "grassroots dreamwork movement" (Hillman, 2009).

This movement coincided with the interest in shamanism, and both emerged with the rediscovery of consciousness studies in the 1960s. There were many triggers for this development, among them the experimental and informal use of psychedelic drugs, the influx of Eastern philosophy and meditation, research involving the placebo effect, and the decline of behaviourism as the dominant paradigm in psychology as cognitive psychology became more popular. Walsh (2007) added humanistic, transpersonal, and Jungian psychologies to the mix. The advent of the periodical *Dream Network* in 1982 and the founding a year later of the International Association for the Study of Dreams, combined with a variety of workshops, classes, and dream groups, gave impetus to the movement. Many of the latter groups utilised the Ullman-Zimmerman (1979) "experiential dream group" method, which does not require a psychotherapist's presence but which does have built-in safeguards to protect the person whose dream is the focus for the group activity.

Ullman (1999) appreciated the role that the grassroots dream movement could make to society, observing that "cultural anthropologists have long viewed dreams as useful instruments for studying the mores and value systems of [other] cultures. Logically, they should be as useful in the examination of our own society" (p. 259). Taking a perspective reminiscent of shamanic practice, Ullman continued, "Our dream imagery has an intrinsic bidirectional [nature] that points inwardly to the innermost and often hidden aspects of our personal being and outwardly to the source of their origin and to their possible connection to prevailing social realities that otherwise tend to be obscured from view" (p. 259).

The grassroots dream movement is not confined to the United States. The International Association for the Study of Dreams holds annual conferences in various parts of the world and publishes a respected journal, *Dreaming*. Each of these conferences features at least one panel or presentation on shamanic dreamwork. The application of shamanic healing and shamanic dream models for cross-cultural research can prevent Western hegemony from diluting or co-opting practices that indigenous people have found of value over the millennia.

Chapters Six, Seven, and Eight

In Chapter 6 we raised questions about the fundamental nature of shamanic journeying images, and how the origin of a shamanic journeying image might be found. In Chapter 7 we proposed criteria for a visual mental image to qualify as a shamanic journeying image. The aim of Chapter 8 was to examine the relationship between the shaman's conscious experiences and the purported non-physical worlds.

Because shamans claim to access information from non-ordinary, non-consensual reality (i.e., the "spirit world"), these are crucial issues not only for research but for practice. These three chapters are especially useful in addressing the implications of Winkelman's "integrative mode of consciousness" in shamanism. This biological potential can be brought into play by ritually induced modifications of patterns of phenomenal properties that push psychological functions beyond their limits, by sensory overload or deprivation, or focusing or withdrawing attention, all of which involve disrupting and destabilising waking consciousness in ways that permit the emergence of symbolic and cognitive processes that are ordinarily repressed. Ironically, the shaman's "normal" equilibrium must be thrown out of balance for integration to occur. The resulting integrative processes are epitomised in the visionary experiences that are one of shamanism's signature features.

Symbolic images such as flights of ascent or descent, death and rebirth, and communication with spirit and animal allies reflect the shaman's developing identity and its maintenance over the years. The visionary experiences of shamans play an important role in adapting to both the shaman's inner and outer environments. Visual symbolism predates language, and shamanic rituals preserve its access to intuition, mythology, creativity, and other functions that were adaptive in human evolution. Shanon (2002) noted that ayahuasca imagery is not exclusively visual, and that synesthesia—a blending of the senses— was commonly reported. In whatever form they take, they imbue the experiencer with a remarkable impression of reality, so much so that participants often find themselves interacting with the entities and situations that are evoked.

Chapter Nine

Anomalies in dream reports have become a topic of study using both experimental and non-experimental research methods. At one point in time, researchers would have doubted that something as elusive as a dream could be studied in a laboratory setting, but there is now a robust literature on the topic (e.g., Roe & Sherwood, 2009). Much the same can be said of anomalous experiences in shamanism, but Chapter 9 presents a variety of methods that have been developed to study these reported phenomena.

There is considerable controversy regarding the veridicality of these reports. Krippner and Friedman (2010) have used the terms "advocates" and "counter-advocates" to describe those who are either positively or negatively inclined toward the reality of these reports. In shamanic studies, Turner (1992) would represent the advocate position; during a healing ritual in Zambia, she observed a shaman extract a harmful spirit from a sick woman's back. She reported seeing a large gray "blob" emerge from the woman's back. The "blob" appeared to have both form and definition, and to be negative in nature. Turner did not feel that what she saw could be interpreted as a metaphor or a symbol; at that moment she knew that it was "spirit stuff".

Shanon (2010) represents the counter-advocate position. While interviewing participants in ayahuasca sessions, he found that "drinkers may experience visions of ... ancient Egypt and with this conclude that various specific things are shown to them and they are led to believe that what they see is/was actually the case" (p. 267). However, he added, "Personally, I do not believe in ayahuasca providing or enabling any such non-ordinary factual knowledge" (p. 267). For Shanon, it is "crucial to distinguish between experiences in which a person feels telepathic and actual occurrences of such paranormal information transfer" (p. 267), a stance that would be taken by most advocates as well. He concluded, "Rather than say that ayahuasca involves paranormality, I would say that it involves the same challenge, both personal and intellectual, nay mystery, that is presented by the genius of artistic creation" (p. 277). We would respond that it is exactly this mystery that we are attempting to unravel, whether or not it is found to involve any "paranormal" anomaly. Among their other roles, shamans are "tricksters", and investigators of shamanic phenomena need to bear this in mind; things are not always what they seem to be when one enters the shaman's world.

Finally, it should be noted that Shanon did not resolve the conundrum posed by Narby (1998) regarding ayahuasca that was cited earlier in this book:

> Here are people without electron microscopes who choose, among 80,000 Amazonian plant species, the leaves of a bush containing a ... brain hormone, which they combine with a vine containing substances that inactivate an enzyme of the digestive tract, which would otherwise block the effect. And they do

this to modify their consciousness. It is as if they knew about the molecular properties of plants and the art of combining them, and when one asks them how they knew these things, they say their knowledge comes directly from [the] plants". (p. 11)

It is puzzles of this nature that need to be addressed, not only for an understanding of shamanism but for a fuller comprehension of the human species and its potential. We hope that, as a reader of this book, you have gained an appreciation of shamanic epistemology and technology as well as bewilderment that Western science has degraded or belittled them far too long. Sometimes ignorance is bred from fear, and in this case perhaps the fear was of humanity's unplumbed nature. However, if the human species is to survive, it will need all the resources it can muster, and shamanic ways of being, ways of knowing, and ways of healing are too vital to be ignored.

References

Achterberg, J. (1985). *Imagery in healing: Shamanism and modern medicine.* Boston: Shambhala.

Achterberg, J. (1987). The shaman: Master healer in the imaginary realm. In S. Nicholson (Ed.), *Shamanism: An expanded view of reality* (pp. 103-124). Wheaton, IL: The Theosophical Publishing House.

Alexander, R.D. (1979). *Darwinism and human affairs.* Seattle: University of Washington Press.

Almond, P. (1982). *Mystical experience and religious doctrine.* New York: Mouton Publishers.

Alvear, J. (1998). *A short spiritist doctrine: The history, beliefs, and healing practices of the spiritist healers of the Philippines* (H. Martin, Trans.). Savannah, GA: Metamind. (Original work published 1907)

American Psychiatric Association. (1994). *DSM-IV.* Arlington, VA: American Psychiatric Association.

Anderson, J.A. (1995). *An introduction to neural networks.* Cambridge, MA: MIT Press.

Anisimov, A.F. (1963). The shaman's tent of the Evenks and the origin of the shamanistic rite (E. Dunn & S. Dunn, Trans.). In H.N. Michael (Ed.), *Studies in Siberian shamanism* (pp. 84-207). Toronto: Arctic Institute of North America, University of Toronto.

Austin, J. (1998). *Zen and the brain: Toward an understanding of meditation and consciousness.* Cambridge, MA: MIT Press.

Baars, B.J. (1997). *In the theater of consciousness: The workspace of the mind*. New York: Oxford University Press.

Babcock-Abrahams, B. (1975). A tolerated margin of mess: The trickster and his tales reconsidered. *Journal of the Folklore Institute, 11,* 147-186.

Basilov, V. (1997). Shamans and their religious practices from shamanism among the Turkic peoples of Siberia. In M. M. Balzar (Ed.), *Shamanic worlds: Rituals and lore of Siberia and Central Asia* (pp. 3-48). Armonk, NY: North Castle Books.

Benedict, R.F. (1923). *The concept of the guardian spirit in North America* (American Anthropological Association memoirs no. 29). Menasha, WI: Banta.

Benjafield, J. (1992). *Cognition*. Englewood Cliffs, NJ: Prentice-Hall International.

Berman, M. (2000). *Wandering god: A study in nomadic spirituality*. Albany: State University of New York Press.

Bernstein, D.M., Belicki, K., & Gonzalez, D. (1995). Trait personality and its relationship to two different measures of dream content. *Sleep Research, 24,* 139.

Best, J. (1995). *Cognitive psychology* (4th ed.). New York: West.

Biet, A. (2001). Evoking the devil: Fasting with tobacco to learn how to cure. In J. Narby & F. Huxley (Eds.), *Shamans through time: 500 years on the path of knowledge* (pp. 16-17). New York: Jeremy P. Tarcher/Putnam. (Original work published 1664)

Bittman, B.B., Berk, L.S., Felten, D.L., Westengard, J., Simonton, O.C., Pappas, J., et al. (2001). Composite effects of group drumming music therapy on modulation of neuroendocrine-immune parameters in normal subjects. *Alternative Therapies, 7,* 38-47.

Blackburn, S. (1996). *The Oxford dictionary of philosophy*. Oxford, UK: Oxford University Press.

Block, N. (1995). On a confusion about a function of consciousness. *Behavioural and Brain Sciences, 18,* 227-247.

Block, N. (2002). Concepts of consciousness. In D. Chalmers (Ed.), *Philosophy of mind: Classical and contemporary readings* (pp. 206-218). New York: Oxford University Press.

Boaz, N.T. (1997). *Eco homo: How the human being emerged from the cataclysmic history of the earth*. New York: Basic Books.

Bockman, L., & Hultkrantz, A. (1978). *Studies in Lapp shamanism*. Stockholm: Almquist and Wiksell.

Bogoras, V. (1904-1909). *The Chuckchee: The Jessup North Pacific expedition*. New York: American Museum of Natural History.

Boshier, A. (1974). African apprenticeship. *Parapsychology Review, 5*(4), 1-3, 25-27.

Boshier, A., & Costello, D. (1975). *Witchdoctor*. Johannesburg: Museum of Man and Science.

Bourguignon, E. (1976). *Possession*. San Francisco: Chandler and Sharp.

Bourguignon, E. (1979). *Psychological anthropology: An introduction to human nature and cultural differences*. New York: Holt.

Bourguignon, E., & Evascu, T. (1977). Altered states of consciousness within a general evolutionary perspective: A holocultural analysis. *Behavior Science Research, 12,* 199 - 216.

Boyer, L. B., Klopfer, B., Brawer, F. B., & Kawai, H. (1964). Comparisons of the shamans and pseudoshamans of the Apaches of the Mescalero Indian reservation: A Rorschach study. *Journal of Projective Techniques, 28,* 173-180.

Breasure, J. (1996, March). The mind, body and soul connection. *Counseling Today,* p. 5.

Brown, D. P., & Engler, J. (1986). The stages of mindfulness meditation: A validation study (Parts I and II). In K. Wilber, J. Engler, & D. P. Brown, *Transformations of consciousness* (pp. 161-218). Boston: Shambhala/New Science Library.

Brown, M.F. (1989). Dark side of the shaman. *Natural History, 11,* pp. 8-10.

Bruce, R.D. (1975). *Lacandon dream symbolism. Vol. 1. Dream symbolism and interpretation among the Lacandon Mayas of Chiapas, Mexico*. Mexico City: Euroamericanas.

Bruchac, J. (1993, Summer). Respecting the sacredness of sweat lodges. *Shaman's Drum,* p.20.

Bucknell, R. (1989a). Buddhist *jhana* as mystical experience. In G. Zollschan, J. Schumaker & G. Walsh (Eds.), *Exploring the paranormal: Perspectives on belief and experience* (pp. 131-149). Bridport: Prism Press.

Bucknell, R. (1989b). Buddhist meditation and mystical experience. Paper presented at *The 14th Annual Conference of the Australian Association for the Study of Religions*, Perth, Australia.

Campbell, J. (1993). *The hero with a thousand faces* (3rd ed.). London: Fontana.

Capra, F. (1996). *The web of life*. New York: Harper Collins.

Cardeña, E., Lynn, S.J., & Krippner, S. (Eds.).(2000). *Varieties of anomalous experience: Examining the scientific evidence*. Washington, DC: American Psychological Association.

Carpenter, B., & Krippner, S. (1989, Fall). Spice island shaman: A Torajan healer in Sulawesi. *Shaman's Drum, 644*, 47-52.

Casanowicz, I.M. (1924). *Shamanism of the natives of Siberia*. Washington, DC: Annual Report to the Smithsonian Institution.

Cavalli-Sforza, L.L., & Cavalli-Sforza, F. (1995). *The great human diasporas: The history of diversity and evolution* (S. Thorne, Trans.). New York: Addison-Wesley.

Chadwick, N. (1942). *Poetry and prophecy*. Cambridge: Cambridge University Press.

Chalmers, D.J. (1996). *The conscious mind: In search of a fundamental theory*. New York: Oxford University Press.

Chalmers, A. (1999). *What is this thing called science?* (3rd ed.). St. Lucia, Australia: University of Queensland Press.

Chapple, C. (1990). The unseen seer and the field: Consciousness in Samkhya and yoga. In R. Forman (Ed.), *The problem of pure consciousness* (pp. 53-70). Oxford, UK: Oxford University Press.

Chari, C.T.K. (1960). Parapsychological studies and literature in India. *International Journal of Parapsychology, 2*, 24-36.

Clottes, J., & Lewis-Williams, D. (1998). *The shamans of prehistory: Trance and magic in the painted caves* (S. Hawkes, Trans.). New York: Harry N. Abrams. (Original work published 1996)

Coan, R.W. (1987). *Human consciousness and its evolution: A multidimensional view*. New York: Greenwood Press.

Collins Concise Dictionary (1999). *Definitions* (pp. 854, 1507). Pymble, Australia: HarperCollins.

Combs, A., & Krippner, S. (2003). Process, structure, and form: An evolutionary transpersonal psychology of consciousness. *International Journal of Transpersonal Studies, 22*, 47-60.

Corballis, M.C. (1991). *The lopsided ape: Evolution of the generative mind*. New York: Oxford University Press.

Cushman, P. (1995). *Constructing the self, constructing America*. Reading, MA: Addison-Wesley.

D'Andrade, R.G. (1990). Some propositions about the relations between cultural and human cognition. In J.W Stigler, R.A. Shweder, & G. Herdt (Eds.), *Cultural psychology: Essays on comparative human development* (pp. 65-129). New York: Cambridge University Press. (Original work published 1961)

Degarrod, L. N. (1989). *Dream interpretation among the Mapuche Indians of Chile*. Unpublished doctoral dissertation, University of California, Los Angeles.

Degarrod, L. N. (2004). Dreams and visions. In M.N. Walter & E.J.N. Fridman (Eds.), *Shamanism: An encyclopedia of world beliefs, practices, and cultures* (pp. 89-95). Santa Barbara, CA: ABC-CLIO.

Delluc, B., Delluc, G., & Delvert, R. (1990). *Discovering Lascaux*. Lucon: Sud Ouest.

DeMause, L. (1998). The history of child abuse. *Journal of Psychohistory, 25*, 216-236.

DeMause, L. (2002). The evolution of psyche and society. *Journal of Psychohistory, 29*, 238-285.

Dennett, D. (2006). *Breaking the spell: Religion as a natural phenomenon*. New York: Viking.

de Oviedo, G. F. (2001). Devil worship: Consuming tobacco to receive messages from nature. In J. Narby & F. Huxley (Eds.), *Shamans through time: 500 years on the path of knowledge* (pp. 11-12). New York: Jeremy P. Tarcher/Putnam. (Original work published 1535)

Desjarlais, R. (1989). Healing through images: The magical flight and healing geography of Nepali shamans. *Ethos, 17,* 289-307.

Devereux, G. (1951). *Dream and reality: The psychotherapy of a Plains Indian.* Albany, NY: New York University Press.

Devereux, G. (1961). Shamans as neurotics. *American Anthropologist, 63,* 1080-1090.

Devereux, P. (1997). *The long trip: A prehistory of psychedelia.* New York: Penguin/Arkana.

Diamond, J. (1997). *Guns, germs, and steel: The fates of human societies.* New York: Norton.

Diderot, D. (2001). Shamans are imposters who claim they consult the devil—and who are sometimes close to the mark. In J. Narby & F. Huxley (Eds.), *Shamans through time: 500 years on the path of knowledge* (pp. 355-358). New York: Jeremy P. Tarcher/Putnam. (Original work published 1765)

Diderot, D., & associates. (1965). *Encyclopédie. English. Selections.* (N.S. Hoyt & T. Cassirer, Eds. & Trans.). Indianapolis: Bobbs-Merrill. (Original work published 1784)

Dobkin de Rios, M. (1984). *Hallucinogens: Cross-cultural perspectives.* Albuquerque: University of New Mexico Press.

Dobkin de Rios, M., & Winkelman, M. (1989). Shamanism and altered states of consciousness: An introduction. *Journal of Psychoactive Drugs, 21,* 1-7.

Domhoff, G.W. (2003). *The scientific study of dreams: Neural networks, cognitive development, and content analysis.* Washington, DC: American Psychological Association.

Donald, M. (1991). *Origins of the modern mind: Three stages in the evolution of culture and cognition.* Cambridge, MA: Harvard University Press.

Dow, J. (1986). *The shaman's touch: Otomi Indian symbolic healing.* Salt Lake City: University of Utah Press.

Dowson, T.A. (1999). Rock art and shamanism: A methodological impasse. In A. Rozwadowski, M.M. Kosko, & T.A. Dowson (Eds.), *Rock art, shamanism, and Central Asia: Discussions of relations* (pp. 39-56). Warsaw: Wyadawnicrwo Academickie.

Drury, N. (1987). *The shaman and the magician: Journeys between the worlds* (2nd ed.). London: Arkana.

DuBois, T.A. (2009). *An introduction to shamanism.* New York: Cambridge University Press.

Durkheim, E. (1995). *The elementary forms of religious life.* (K.E. Fields, Trans.). New York: Free Press. (Original work published 1912)

Eacker, J. N. (1972). On some elementary philosophical problems of psychology. *American Psychologist, 27*(6), 553-565.

Eggan, D. (1949). The significance of dreams for anthropological research. *American Anthropologist, 51*, 177-198.

Eggan, D. (1952). The personal use of myth in dreams. *Journal of American Folklore, 68*, 67-75.

Eggan, D. (1966). The Hopi dream in cultural perspective. In G.E. von Grunebaum & R. Caillois (Eds.), *The dream and human societies* (pp. 237-263). Berkeley: University of California Press.

Eliade, M. (1959). *The sacred and the profane: The nature of religion.* Orlando, FL: Harcourt Brace Jovanovich.

Eliade, M. (1989). *Shamanism: Archaic techniques of ecstasy* (W. R. Trask, Trans.). Princeton, NJ: Princeton University Press. (Original work published 1951)

Ellwood, R. (1987). Shamanism and theosophy. In S. Nicholson (Ed.), *Shamanism: An expanded view of reality* (pp. 253-64). Wheaton, IL: The Theosophical Publishing House.

Erdoes, R. (1972). *Lame Deer, seeker of visions.* New York: Simon & Schuster.

Estrada, A. (Ed.). (1981). *María Sabina: Her life and chants.* Santa Barbara, CA: Ross-Erickson.

Evans, D. (1989). Can philosophers limit what mystics can do? A critique of Steven Katz. *Religious Studies, 25*, 53-60.

Fabrega, H., Jr., & Silver, D.B. (1973). *Illness and shamanistic curing in Zinacantan: An ethnomedical analysis.* Stanford, CA: Stanford University Press.

Fagan, B.M. (1990). *The journey from Eden: The peopling of our world.* London: Thames & Hudson.

Faron, L. (1968). *The Mapuche of Chile*. New York: Holt, Rinehart and Winston.

Farthing, G. W. (1992). *The psychology of consciousness*. Englewood Cliffs, NJ: Prentice-Hall.

Feinberg, T. (2001). *Altered egos: How the brain creates the self*. New York: Oxford University Press.

Feinstein, D., & Krippner, S. (1988). *Personal mythology*. Los Angeles: Tarcher.

Feinstein, D., & Krippner, S. (2008). *Personal mythology: Using ritual, dreams, and imagination to discover your inner story* (3rd ed.). Santa Rosa, CA: Energy Psychology Press/Elite Books.

Fischer, R. (1980). State-bound knowledge: "I can't remember what I said last night, but it must have been good." In R. Woods (Ed.), *Understanding mysticism* (pp. 306-311). London: Athlone.

Flaherty, G. (1992). *Shamanism and the eighteenth century*. Princeton, NJ: Princeton University Press.

Forde, C.D. (1931). *Ethnography of the Yuma Indians*. Berkeley: University of California Publications in Archaeology and Ethnography.

Forman, R. (1990a) Introduction: Mysticism, constructivism, and forgetting. In R. Forman (Ed.), *The problem of pure consciousness* (pp. 53-70). Oxford, UK: Oxford University Press.

Forman, R. (1990b). Eckhart, gezucken, and the ground of the soul. In R. Forman (Ed.), *The problem of pure consciousness* (pp. 98-120). Oxford, UK: Oxford University Press.

Forman, R. K. C. (1996). *What does mysticism have to teach us about consciousness?* Revised version of a paper delivered at "Towards a Science of Consciousness 1996" (Tucson II), April 1996.

Fox, R. (1988). *Energy and the evolution of life*. New York: Freeman.

Frank, J.D., & Frank, J.B. (1991). *Persuasion and healing* (3rd ed.). Baltimore: Johns Hopkins University Press.

Franklin, R. (1990). Experience and interpretation in mysticism. In R. Forman (Ed.), *The problem of pure consciousness* (pp. 288-304). Oxford, UK: Oxford University Press.

Garcia, F.O. (1990). The concept of dissociation and conversion in the new edition of the International Classification of Disease (ICD-10). *Dissociation, 3*, 204-208.

Gazzaniga, M.S. (1994). *Nature's mind*. New York: Basic Books.

Gergen, K. (1992). *The saturated self.* New York: Basic Books.

Gergen, K. (2001). Psychological science in a postmodern context. *American Psychologist, 56*, 803-813.

Giesler, P.V. (1984). Parapsychological anthropology: Multi-method approaches to the study of psi in the field setting. *Journal of the American Society of Psychical Research, 78*, 289-330.

Giesler, P.V. (1986). GESP testing of shamanic cultists. *Journal of Parapsychology, 50*, 123-153.

Gill, J.H. (1984). Mysticism and mediation. *Faith and Philosophy, 1*, 111-121.

Gimello, R. (1978). Mysticism and meditation. In S.T. Katz (Ed.), *Mysticism and philosophical analysis* (pp. 170-199). London: Sheldon Press.

Gimello, R. (1983). Mysticism in its contexts. In S.T. Katz (Ed.), *Mysticism and religious traditions* (pp. 61-88). New York: Oxford University Press.

Globus, G. (1995). *The postmodern brain*. Philadelphia: John Benjamins.

Gmelin, J.G. (2001). Shamans deserve perpetual labor for their hocus-pocus. In J. Narby & F. Huxley (Eds.), *Shamans through time: 500 years on the path of knowledge* (pp. 27-28). New York: Jeremy P. Tarcher/Putnam. (Original work published 1751)

Goldman, A.I. (2000). Can science know when you're conscious? Epistemological foundations of consciousness research. *Journal of Consciousness Studies, 7*, 3-22.

Goldstein, M., & Goldstein, I.E. (1978). *How we know: An exploration of the scientific process*. New York: Plenum Press.

Goodman, F. (1992). *Ecstasy, ritual, and alternate reality*. Bloomington, ID: Indiana University Press.

Gore, R. (1997, September). The dawn of humans. *National Geographic*, pp. 92-99.

Gore, R. (2000, January). People like us. *National Geographic*, pp. 90-117.

Graham, L.R. (1995). *Performing dreams: Discourse of immortality among the Xavante of Central Brazil*. Austin: University of Texas Press.

Greenfield, S. (1987). The return of Dr. Fritz: Spiritist healing and patronage networks in urban, industrial Brazil. *Social Science and Medicine, 24*, 1095-1106.

Griffiths, P. (1990). Pure consciousness and Indian Buddhism. In R. Forman (Ed.), *The problem of pure consciousness* (pp. 71-97). Oxford, UK: Oxford University Press.

Grim, J.A. (1983). *The shaman: Patterns of Siberian healing*. Norman: University of Oklahoma Press.

Grof, S., & Grof, C. (1989). *Spiritual emergency*. Los Angeles: Tarcher.

Gross, P. R., & Levitt, N. (1998). *Higher superstition: The academic left and its quarrels with science* (2nd ed.). Baltimore, MD: Johns Hopkins University Press.

Guryev, D. (1990). *The riddle of the origin of consciousness* (A. Lehto, Trans.). Moscow: Progress Publishers.

Haberlandt, K. (1994). *Cognitive psychology*. Boston: Allyn and Bacon.

Hacking, I. (1983). *Representing and intervening*. Cambridge: Cambridge University Press.

Halifax, J. (1979). *Shamanic voices*. New York: E. P. Dutton.

Halifax, J. (1982). *Shaman: The wounded healer*. New York: Crossroad.

Hallowell, A.I. (1966). The role of dreams in Ojibwa culture. In G.E. von Grunebaum & R. Caillois (Eds.), *The dream and human societies* (pp. 269-289). Berkeley: University of California Press.

Hallowell, A.I. (1971). *The role of conjuring in Salteaux society* New York: Octagon Books.

Hamayon, R.N. (1996). Shamanism in Siberia: From partnership in supernature to counter-power in society. In N. Thomas & C. Humphrey (Eds.), *Shamanism, history, and the state* (pp. 76-89). Ann Arbor: University of Michigan Press.

Hansen, G.P. (2001). *The trickster and the paranormal*. New York: Xlibris.

Hardy, C. (1998). *Networks of meaning*. Westport, CT: Praeger.

Harner, M. (1980). *The way of the shaman: A guide to power and healing*. San Francisco: Harper & Row.

Harner, M. (1987). The ancient wisdom in shamanic cultures. In S. Nicholson (Ed.), *Shamanism: An expanded view of reality* (pp. 3-16). Wheaton, IL: Theosophical Publishing House.

Harner, M. (1988). Shamanic counseling. In G. Doore (Ed.), *Shaman's path* (pp. 179-187). Boston: Shambhala.

Harner, M. (1990). *The way of the shaman* (3rd ed.). San Francisco: Harper & Row.

Harner, M. (2010, December). A core shamanic theory of dreams. *Shamanism: The Journal of the Foundation for Shamanic Studies*, pp. 2-4.

Harner, S. (2003, Fall-Winter). Shamanic journeying and immune response hypothesis testing. *Shamanism: The Journal of the Foundation for Shamanic Studies*, pp. 9-14.

Harner, S., & Tyron, W. (1992). Effects of shamanic drumming on salivary immunoglobulin A, salivary immunoglobulin M, anxiety, and well-being. In J. Pentikainen & M. Hoppal (Eds.), *Proceedings of the International Association of Historians of Religion* (pp. 196-204). Helsinki: Finnish Literature Society.

Harner, S., & Tyron, W. (1996). Psychological and immunological responses to shamanic journeying with drumming. *Shaman*, 4(1-2), 89-97.

Hawk Wing, P. (1997). Lakota teachings: Inipi, Humbleciya, and Yuwipi ceremonies. In D. F. Sandner & S. H. Wong (Eds.), *The sacred heritage: The influence of shamanism on analytical psychology* (pp. 193-202). New York: Routledge.

Heil, J. (1998). *Philosophy of mind*. London: Routledge.

Heinze, R.I. (1991). *Shamans of the 20th century*. New York: Irvington.

Herder, J. G. (2001). Misled imposters and the power of imagination. In J. Narby & F. Huxley (Eds.), *Shamans through time: 500 years on the path of knowledge* (pp. 36-37). New York: Jeremy P. Tarcher/Putnam. (Original work published 1785)

Hick, J. (1989). *An interpretation of religion: Human response to the transcendent*. London: Macmillan Press.

Hick, J. (1993). *Disputed questions in theology and the philosophy of religion.* New Haven, CT: Yale University Press.

Hill, C.E., & Rochlen, A.B. (2009). Working with dreams: A cognitive-experiential model. In S. Krippner & D.J. Ellis (Eds.), *Perchance to dream: The frontiers of dream psychology* (pp. 71-77). New York: Nova.

Hillman, D. (1990). The emergence of the grassroots dream movement. In S. Krippner (Ed.), *Dreamtime and dream work: Decoding the language of the night* (pp. 13-20). New York: Jeremy P. Tarcher/Putnam.

Hillman, D. (2009). The emergence of the grasswork dream movement in the United States. In S. Krippner & D.J. Ellis (Eds.), *Perchance to dream: The frontiers of dream psychology* (pp. 13-20). New York: Nova.

Hobson, J.A. (1988). *The dreaming brain.* New York: Basic Books.

Hobson, J.A. (2002). *Dreaming: An introduction to the science of sleep.* Oxford, UK: Oxford University Press.

Hoppal, M. (1987). Shamanism: An archaic and/or recent belief system. In S. Nicholson (Ed.), *Shamanism: An expanded view of reality* (pp. 76-100). Wheaton, IL: Quest.

Houran, J., Lange, R., & Crist-Houran, M. (1997). An assessment of contextual mediation in trance states of shamanic journeys. *Perceptual and Motor Skills, 85,* 59-65.

Hubbard, T.L. (2002a). Some cognitive aspects of shamanism. In A. Kaszniak (Ed.), *Tucson 2002: Toward a science of consciousness, conference research abstracts* (pp. 135-136). Tucson: Center for Consciousness Studies, University of Arizona.

Hubbard, T.L. (2002b). Cognitive science and shamanism I: Webs of life and neural nets. *Shamanism, 15,* 4-10.

Hubbard, T.L. (2002c). Some correspondences and similarities of shamanism and cognitive science: Interconnectedness, extension of meaning, and attribution of mental states. *Anthropology of Consciousness, 13,* 26-45.

Hubbard, T.L. (2003). Further correspondences and similarities of shamanism and cognitive structures. *Anthropology of Consciousness, 14,* 40-74.

Hufford, D. (1995). Cultural and social perspectives on alternative medicine: Background and assumptions. *Alternative Therapies in Health and Medicine, 1*(1), 53-61.

Hughes, R. (2000, September 11). The real Australia. *TIME*, pp. 99-100, 102, 104, 106-107, 110-111.

Hugh-Jones, S. (1996). Shamans, prophets, priests and pastors. In N. Thomas & C. Humphrey (Eds.), *Shamanism, history, and the state* (pp. 32-75). Ann Arbor: University of Michigan Press.

Hurdle, D.E. (2002). Native Hawaiian traditional healing: Culturally based interventions for social work practice. *Social Work, 47*, 183-192.

Hutchins, E. (1995). *Cognition in the wild*. Cambridge, MA: MIT Press.

Hyman, R. (1977). "Cold reading": How to convince strangers that you know all about them. *Skeptical Inquirer, 2*, 18-37.

Irwin, H. (1985). *Flight of mind: A psychological study of the out-of-body experience*. Metuchen, NJ: Scarecrow.

Irwin, H.J. (1999). *An introduction to parapsychology* (3rd ed.). Jefferson, NC: McFarland.

Irwin, L. (1990). The bridge of dreams: Myth dreams and visions in native North America. Unpublished doctoral dissertation, Indiana University. *Dissertation Abstracts International, 51*(3), 895A.

Irwin, L. (1994). *The dream seekers: Native American visionary traditions of the Great Plains*. Norman: University of Oklahoma Press.

James, W. (1890). *Principles of psychology* (2 vols). New York: Dover.

Jecupé, K.W. (1998). *A terra dos mil povos* [The land of a thousand people]. São Paulo, Brazil: Editora Petrópolis.

Jensen, A.E. (1963). *Myth and cult among primitive people*. Chicago: University of Chicago Press.

Jerison, H. (1990). Paleoneurology and the evolution of mind. In R.R. Llinas (Ed.), *The workings of the brain: Development, memory, and perception* (pp. 3-16). New York: W.H. Freeman.

Jilek, W. (1982). *Indian healing*. Blaine, WA: Hancock House.

Jokiæ, Z. (2006). Cosmo-genesis or transformation of the human body into a cosmic body in Yanomami shamanistic initiation. *Shaman, 14*, 19-39.

Kalweit, H. (1988). *Dreamtime and innerspace: The world of the shaman*. Boston: Shambhala.

Kalweit, H. (1992). *Shamans, healers, and medicine men*. Boston: Shambhala. (Original work published 1987)

Kant, I. (1781/1933). *The critique of pure reason* (2nd ed.). London: Macmillan Press.

Kaplan, S. (2000). Human nature and environmentally responsible behaviour. *Journal of Social Issues, 58*, 491-508.

Kardec, A. (1971). *The medium's book*. London: Psychic Press.

Katz, R. (1982). *Boiling energy: Community healing among the Kalahari Kung*. Cambridge, MA: Harvard University Press.

Katz, S. T. (1978). Language, epistemology, and mysticism. In S.T. Katz (Ed.), *Mysticism and philosophical analysis* (pp. 22-74). London: Sheldon Press.

Katz, S. T. (1983). The 'conservative' character of mystical experience. In S.T. Katz (Ed.), *Mysticism and religious traditions* (pp. 3-60). New York: Oxford University Press.

Kehoe, A. (2000). *Shamans and religion: An anthropological exploration in critical thinking*. Prospect Heights, IL: Waveland Press.

Kelly, E.F., & Locke, R.G. (1982, May/June) Pre-literature societies. *Parapsychology Review*, pp. 1-7.

Kessler, G., & Prigge, N. (1982). Is mystical experience everywhere the same? *Sophia, 21*, 39-55.

Kilbourne, B. (1990). Ancient and native people's dreams. In S. Krippner (Ed.), *Dreamtime and dreamwork: Decoding the language of the night* (pp. 194-203). Los Angeles: Tarcher/Putnam.

Kim, U., & Berry, J.W. (1993). *Indigenous psychologies: Research and experience in cultural context*. Los Angeles: Sage.

Kingdon, J. (1993). *Self-made man: Human evolution from Eden to extinction*. New York: John Wiley & Sons.

Klein, D.B. (1984). *The concept of consciousness: A survey*. Lincoln: University of Nebraska Press.

Kleinman, A. (1980). *Patients and healers in the context of culture: An exploration of the borderland between anthropology, medicine, and psychiatry.* Berkeley: University of California Press.

Klopfer, B., & Boyer, L.B. (1961). Notes on the personality structure of a North American Indian shaman: Rorschach interpretation. *Projective Techniques and Personality Assessment, 25,* 170-178.

Kracke, W.H. (1987). "Everyone who dreams has a bit of shaman": Cultural and personal meanings of dreams — evidence from the Amazon. *Psychiatric Journal of the University of Ottawa, 12,* 65-71.

Kracke, W. (1991). Languages of dreaming: Anthropological approaches to the study of dreaming in other cultures. In J. Gackenbach & A.A. Sheikh (Eds.), *Dream images: A call to mental arms* (pp. 203-224). Amityville, NY: Baywood.

Kramer, M. (2007). *The dream experience: A systematic exploration.* New York: Routledge/Taylor & Francis Group.

Krasheninnikov, S. P. (2001). Blinded by superstition. In J. Narby & F. Huxley (Eds.), *Shamans through time: 500 years on the path of knowledge* (pp. 29-31). New York: Jeremy P. Tarcher/Putnam. (Original work published 1755)

Kremer, J.W. (1996). The shadow of evolutionary thinking. *ReVision, 19*(1), 41-48.

Kremer, J.W. (2002). Radical presence. *ReVision, 24*(3), 11-20.

Kremer, J.W. (2003). *Trance als multisensuelle Kreativitätstechnik.* In P. Luckner (Ed.), *Multisensuelles Design. Eine Anthologie* (pp. 591-620). Halle, Germany: University Press of Burg Giebichenstein – Hochschule für Kunst und Design.

Kremer, J.W. (2004). Ethnoautobiography as practice of radical presence - storying the self in participatory visions. *ReVision, 26*(2), 5-13.

Kremer, J., & Krippner, S. (1994). Trance postures. *ReVision, 16,* 173-182.

Krippner, S. (1972). Altered states of consciousness. In J. White (Ed.), *The highest state of consciousness* (pp. 1-5). Garden City, NJ: Doubleday.

Krippner, S. (1976). Psychic healing in the Philippines. *Journal of Humanistic Psychology, 16*(4), 3-31.

Krippner, S. (1990a). Native healing. In J.K. Zeig & Munion, W.M. (Eds.), *What is psychotherapy? Contemporary perspectives* (pp. 179-185). San Francisco: Jossey-Bass.

Krippner, S. (1990b). Tribal shamans and their travels into dreamtime. In S. Krippner (Ed.), *Dreamtime and dreamwork* (pp. 185-193). Los Angeles: Jeremy P. Tarcher.

Krippner, S. (1992,Winter). The shaman as healer and psychotherapist. *Voices*, pp. 12-23.

Krippner, S. (1993). Cross-cultural perspectives on hypnotic-like procedures used by native healing practitioners. In J.W. Rhue, S.J. Lynn, & I. Kirsch (Eds.), *Handbook of clinical hypnosis* (pp. 691-717). Washington, DC: American Psychological Association.

Krippner, S. (1994). 10-facet model of dreaming for use in cross-cultural studies. *Dream Network Journal, 13*(1), 9-11.

Krippner, S. (1995a). A cross-cultural comparison of four healing models. *Alternative Therapies in Health and Medicine, 1*, 21-29.

Krippner, S. (1995b). A model of dreaming derived from the Mapuche tradition in Chile. In R.I. Heinze (Ed.), *Proceedings of the 12th International Conference on the Study of Shamanism and Alternate Modes of Healing* (pp. 97-106). Berkeley, CA: Independent Scholars of Asia.

Krippner, S. (1995c). Psychical research in the postmodern world. *Journal of the American Society for Psychical Research, 89*, 1-18.

Krippner, S. (1998/1999). Transcultural and psychotherapeutic aspects of a Candomble' practice in Recife, Brazil. In S. Krippner & H. Kalweit (Eds.), *Yearbook of cross-cultural medicine and psychotherapy: Mythology, medicine, and healing: Transcultural perspectives* (pp. 67-86). Berlin: Verlag fur Wissenschaft und Bildung.

Krippner, S. (2000). The epistemology and technologies of shamanic states of consciousness. *Journal of Consciousness Studies, 7*, 93-118.

Krippner, S. (2002a). The Kallawaya healing system of the Andes. In C.E. Gottschalk-Batschkus & J.C. Green (Eds.), *Handbook of ethnotherapies* (pp. 437-442). Munich: Institut fur Ethnomedizine.

Krippner, S. (2002b). Conflicting perspectives on shamans and shamanism: Points and counterpoints. *American Psychologist, 57*(11), 962-977.

Krippner, S. (2005). Spirituality across cultures, religions, and ethnicities. In R.H. Cox, B. Ervin-Cox, & L. Hoffman (Eds.), *Spirituality & psychological health* (pp. 204-240). Colorado Springs: Colorado School of Professional Psychology Press.

Krippner, S. (2009). Anyone who dreams partakes of shamanism. *Journal of Shamanic Practice, 2* (2), 33-40.

Krippner, S., Budden, A., Bova, M. & Galante, R. (2010). The indigenous spiritual healing tradition in Calabria, Italy. In A. Husain (Ed.), *Explorations in human spirituality* (pp. 295-324). New Delhi: Global Vision Publishing House.

Krippner, S., & Combs, A. (2007, Winter). Dreams are patterned: An argument for continuity. *Dream Network,* 17-46.

Krippner, S., & Dillard, J. (1988). *Dreamworking.* Buffalo, NY: Bearly.

Krippner, S., & Friedman, H.L. (Eds.).(2010). *Debating psychic experience: Human potential or human illusion?* Santa Barbara, CA: Praeger/ABC-CLIO.

Krippner, S. & Kremer, J.W. (2010). Hypnotic-like procedures in indigenous shamanism and mediumship. In D. Barrett (Ed.), *Hypnosis and hypnotherapy: Vol. 1: Neuroscience, personality, and cultural factors* (pp. 97-124). Santa Barbara, CA: Praeger.

Krippner, S., & Meacham, W. (1968). Consciousness and the creative process. *The Gifted Child Quarterly, 12,* 141-157.

Krippner, S., & Taubold, S. (2005). Constructing a model of *Espiritista* healing in the Philippines. *Anthropology of Consciousness, 15,* 42-51.

Krippner, S., & Thompson, A. (1996). A 10-facet model of dreaming applied to dream practices of sixteen Native American cultural groups. *Dreaming, 6,* 71-96.

Krippner, S., & Welch, P. (1992). *Spiritual dimensions of healing: From tribal shamanism to contemporary health care.* New York: Irvington.

Labate, B.C., & MacRae, E. (Eds.).(2010). *Ayahuasca, ritual and religion in Brazil.* London: Equinox.

Lafitau, J. F. (2001). The savages esteem their jugglers. In J. Narby & F. Huxley (Eds.), *Shamans through time: 500 years on the path of knowledge* (pp.

23-26). New York: Jeremy P. Tarcher/Putnam. (Original work published 1724)

Langdon, E.J.M. (1992). Introduction: Shamanism and anthropology. In E.J.M. Langdon & G. Baer (Eds.), *Portals of power: Shamanism in South America* (pp. 1-21). Albuquerque: University of New Mexico Press.

Larsen, S. (1976). *The shaman's doorway: Opening the mythic imagination to contemporary consciousness.* New York: Harper & Row.

Laubscher, B. (1938). *Sex, custom and psychopathology: A study of South African Pagan Natives.* New York: McBride.

Lauden, L. (1996). A confutation of convergent realism. In D. Papineau (Ed.), *The philosophy of science* (pp. 107-138). Oxford, UK: Oxford University Press.

Laughlin, C., McManus, J., & d'Aquili, E. (1990). *Brain, symbol, and experience: Toward a neurophenomenology of consciousness.* Boston: Shambhala.

Lee, R.L.M. (1989). Self-presentation in Malaysian spirit séances: A dramaturgical perspective on altered states of consciousness in healing ceremonies. In C.A. Ward (Ed.), *Altered states of consciousness and mental health: A cross-cultural perspective* (pp. 251-266). Los Angeles: Sage.

Lefcourt, H.M. (1976). *Locus of control: Current trends in theory and research.* Hillsdale, NY: Erlbaum.

Leon, C.A. (1975). El duende and other incubi. *Archives of General Psychiatry, 32*, 155-162.

Lepore, S.J. (1994). Social support. In V. S. Ramachandran (Ed.), *Encyclopedia of human behaviour* (pp. 247-262). San Diego, CA: Academic Press.

Lepp, T. (2004). Psychopomp. In M.N. Walter & E.J.N. Fridman (Eds.), *Shamanism: An encyclopedia of world beliefs, practices, and culture* (Vol. 1, pp. 217-218). Santa Barbara, CA: ABC-CLIO.

Lerche, P. (2000, September). Quest for the lost tombs of the Peruvian cloud people. *National Geographic*, pp. 64-81.

Lewis, I.M. (1984). What is a shaman? In M. Hoppal (Ed.), Shamanism *in Eurasia* (pp. 3-11). Gottingen: Edition Herodot.

Lewis, I. (1990). Shamanism: Ethnopsychiatry. *Self and Society, 18*, 10-21.

Lewis-Fernandez, R., & Kleinman, N. (1995). Cultural psychiatry: Theoretical, clinical, and research issues. *Cultural Psychiatry, 18*, 433-448.

Lewis-Williams, D.J. (1998). The mind in the cave — the cave in the mind: Altered consciousness in the Upper Paleolithic. *Anthropology of Consciousness, 9*, 13-21.

Lincoln, J.S. (1935). *The dream in primitive cultures.* Baltimore: Williams and Wilkins.

Lormand, E. (1996). Nonphenomenal consciousness. *Nous, 30*, 242-261.

Loux, M. (1998). *Metaphysics: A contemporary introduction.* London: Routledge.

Lubinski, D., & Thompson, T. (1993). Species and individual differences in communication based on private states. *Behaviour and Brain Sciences, 16*, 627-680.

Ludwig, A.M. (1992). Culture and creativity. *American Journal of Psychotherapy, 46*, 454-469.

Lukoff, D., Lu, F., & Turner, R. (1998). From spiritual emergency to spiritual problem: The transpersonal roots of the new *DSM-IV* category. *Journal of Humanistic Psychology, 38*(2), 21-50.

Luna, L.E., & White, S.F. (2000). Introduction. In L.E. Luna & S.F. White (Eds.), *Ayahuasca reader: Encounters with the Amazon's sacred vine* (pp. 1-17). Santa Fe, NM: Synergetic Press.

Mahler, H. (1977, November). The staff of Aesculapius. *World Health,* p. 3.

Mahoney, M., & Albert, C.J. (1997). Worlds of words. *Constructivism in the Human Sciences, 1*(3/4), 22-26.

Malcolm, N. (1981). Wittgenstein's philosophical investigations. In V. C. Chappell (Ed.), *The philosophy of mind* (pp. 74-100). New York: Dover.

Malinowski, B. (1954). *Magic, science and religion, and other essays.* Garden City, NY: Doubleday/Anchor Books.

Mandell, A. (1980). Toward a psychobiology of transcendence: God in the brain. In J.M. Davidson & R.J. Davidson (Eds.), *The psychobiology of consciousness* (pp. 379-464). New York: Plenum.

Mandelstam Balzer, M. (1996). Flights of the sacred. *American Anthropologist, 98*(2), 305-318.

Mandler, H. (1988). How to build a baby: On the development of an accessible representational system. *Cognitive Development, 3*(2), 113-136.

Matlin, M. (1998). *Cognition* (4th ed.). Fort Worth, TX: Harcourt Brace.

Matt, D. (1990). *Ayin*: The concept of nothingness in Jewish mysticism. In R. Forman (Ed.), *The problem of pure consciousness* (pp. 121-59). Oxford, UK: Oxford University Press.

Maxfield, M. (1994). The journey of the drum. *ReVision, 16,* 157-163.

McClenon, J. (1997). Shamanic healing, human evolution, and the origin of religion. *Journal for the Scientific Study of Religion, 36,* 345-354.

McDowall, D. (1996). *Healing: Doorway to the spiritual world.* Shepparton, Australia: Cosmos.

Medin, D., Ross, B., & Markman, A. (2001). *Cognitive psychology* (3rd ed.). Fort Worth, TX: Harcourt.

Mercante, M.S. (2010). *Images of healing: Spontaneous mental imagery and healing process of the Barquinha, a Brazilian ayahuasca religious system.* Saarbrücken, Germany: Lambert Academic Publishing.

Merkur, D. (1998). *The ecstatic imagination: Psychedelic experiences and the psychoanalysis of self-actualization.* Albany: State University of New York Press.

Metzner, R. (1999). *Green psychology: Transforming our relationship with the earth.* Rochester, VT: Park Street Press.

Mithen, S. (1996). *The prehistory of the mind.* New York: Thames and Hudson.

Moffit, A., Kramer, M., & Hoffman, R. (1993). *The functions of dreaming.* Albany: State University of New York Press.

Morgan, W. (1932). Navajo dreams. *American Anthropologist, 33,* 390-404.

Moss, R. (1992, Summer). Black robes and dreamers: Jesuit reports on the shamanic dream practices of the Northern Iroquoians. *Shaman's Drum,* pp. 30-39.

Moss, R. (2005). *Dreamways of the Iroquois: Honoring the secret wishes of the soul.* Rochester, VT: Destiny Books.

Murphy, J.M. (1964). Psychotherapeutic aspects of shamanism on St. Lawrence Island, Alaska. In A. Kiev (Ed.) *Magic, faith, and healing* (pp. 53-83). New York: Free Press.

Nairne, J. (1997). *Psychology: The adaptive mind*. Pacific Grove, CA: Brooks/Cole.

Narby, J. (1998). *The cosmic serpent: DNA and the origins of knowledge*. New York: Jeremy P. Tarcher/Putnam.

Narby, J., & Huxley, F. (2001). Introduction. In J. Narby & F. Huxley (Eds.), *Shamans through time: 500 years on the path to knowledge* (pp. 1-8). New York: Jeremy P. Tarcher/Putnam.

Natsoulas, T. (1978). Consciousness. *American Psychologist, 33*, 906-914.

Negro, P.J., Jr., Palladino-Negro, P., & Louza, M.R. (2002). Do religious mediumship dissociative experiences conform to the sociocognitive theory of dissociation? *Journal of Trauma and Dissociation, 3*, 51-73.

Neher, A. (1961). Auditory driving observed with scalp electrodes in normal subjects. *Electroencephalography and Neuropsychology, 13*, 449-451.

Nesse, R.N., & Berridge, K.C. (1997). Psychoactive drug use in evolutionary perspective. *Science, 278*, 63-66.

Newberg, A., d'Aquili, E., & Rause, V. (2001). *Why God won't go away: Brain science and the biology of belief*. New York: Ballantine.

Newton, N. (1996). *Foundations of understanding*. Philadelphia: John Benjamins.

Nielsen, T., & Lara-Carrasco, J. (2007). Nightmares, dreaming, and emotional regulation: A review. In D. Barrett & P. McNamara (Eds.), *The new science of dreaming: Content, recall, and personality correlates* (pp. 253-284). Westport, CT: Praeger.

Noel, D.C. (1997). *The soul of shamanism: Western fantasies, imaginal realities*. New York: Continuum.

Nolen, W.A. (1974). *Healing: A doctor in search of a miracle*. New York: Random House.

Noll, R. (1983). Shamanism and schizophrenia: A state-specific approach to the "schizophrenia metaphor" of shamanic states. *American Ethnologist, 10*, 433-459.

Noll, R. (1985). Mental imagery cultivation as a cultural phenomenon: The role of visions in shamanism. *Current Anthropology, 26*, 443-461.

Noll, R. (1987). The presence of spirits in magic and madness. In S. Nicholson (Ed.), *Shamanism: An expanded view of reality* (pp. 47-61). Wheaton, IL: Quest.

Nowak, B., & Dentan, R.K. (1983). Problems and tactics in the Transcultural study of intelligence: An archival report. *Behavioral Science Research, 18,* 45-99.

O'Brien, G., & Opie, J. (1997). Cognitive science and phenomenal consciousness: A dilemma, and how to avoid it. *Philosophical Psychology, 10,* 269-286.

O'Conner, B.B., Calabrese, C., Cardeña, E., Eisenberg, D., Fincher, J., Hufford, D.J., Jonas, W.B., Kaptchuck, T., Martin, S.C., Scott, A.W., & Zhang, X. (1997). Defining and describing complementary and alternative medicine. *Alternative Therapies in Health and Medicine, 3*(2), 49-57.

O'Nell, C.W. (1976). *Dreams, culture and the individual.* San Francisco: Chandler and Sharp.

Opler, M.E. (1936). Some points of comparison and contrast between the treatment of functional disorders by Apache shamans and modern psychiatric practice. *American Journal of Psychiatry, 92,* 1371-1387.

Ornstein, R., & Carstenson, L. (1991). *Psychology: The study of human experience* (2nd ed.). San Diego, CA: Harcourt Brace Jovanovich.

Pekala, R. J. (1991). *Quantifying consciousness: An empirical approach.* New York: Plenum Press.

Perovich, A. (1990). Does the philosophy of mysticism rest on a mistake? In R. Forman (Ed.), *The problem of pure consciousness* (pp. 237-253). Oxford, UK: Oxford University Press.

Perrin, M. (1992). The body of the Guajiro shaman: Symptoms or symbols? In E.J.M. Langdon & G. Baer (Eds.), *Portals of power: Shamanism in South America* (pp. 103-125). Albuquerque: University of New Mexico Press.

Persinger, M.A. (1993). Vectorial cerebral hemisphericity as differential sources for the sensed presence, mystical experiences and religious conversions. *Perceptual and Motor Skills, 76,* 915-930.

Peters, L. (1981). An experiential study of Nepalese shamanism. *The Journal of Transpersonal Psychology, 13,* 1-26.

Peters, L. (1982). Trance, initiation, and psychotherapy in Tamang shamanism. *American Ethnologist, 9,* 21-46.

Peters, L. (1989). Shamanism: Phenomenology of a spiritual discipline. *The Journal of Transpersonal Psychology, 21,* 115-137.

Peters, L. (1990). Mystical experience in Tamang shamanism. *ReVision, 13*(2), 71-85.

Peters, L.G., & Price-Williams, D. (1980). Towards an experiential analysis of shamanism. *American Ethnologist, 7,* 397-418.

Petrovich, A. (2001). The shaman: A villain of a magician who calls demons. In J. Narby & F. Huxley (Eds.), *Shamans through time: 500 years on the path of knowledge* (pp. 18-20). New York: Jeremy P. Tarcher/Putnam. (Original work published 1672)

Pinker, S. (1997). *How the mind works.* New York: W.W. Norton.

Povinelli, D.J. (1993). Reconstructing the evolution of mind. *American Psychologist, 48,* 493-509.

Pratt, C. (2007). *An encyclopedia of shamanism* (Vol. 2). New York: Rosen.

Pressman, T.E. (1992). The therapeutic potential of nonordinary states of consciousness, as explored in the work of Stanislav Grof. *Journal of Humanistic Psychology, 32,* 8-27.

Pribram, K.H. (1991). *Brain and perception.* Hillsdale, NJ: Lawrence Erlbaum.

Prigge, N., & Kessler, G. (1990). Is mystical experience everywhere the same? In R. Forman (Ed.), *The problem of pure consciousness* (pp. 269-287). Oxford, UK: Oxford University Press.

Quartz, S.R., & Sejnowski, T.J. (1997). The neural basis of cognitive development: A constructivist manifesto. *Behavioural and Brain Sciences, 20,* 537-596.

Reber, A.S., & Reber, E. (2001). *The Penguin dictionary of psychology* (3rd ed.). London: Penguin.

Reed, S. (1992). *Cognition* (3rd ed.). Pacific Grove, CA: Brooks/Cole.

Reichbart, R. (1978). Magic and psi: Some speculations on their relationship. *Journal of the American Society for Psychical Research, 72,* 153-175.

Reichel-Dolmatoff, G. (2001). *The shaman and the jaguar: A study of narcotic drugs among the Indians of Colombia.* Philadelphia: Temple University Press. (Original work published 1975)

Reichenbach, H. (1951). *The rise of scientific philosophy.* Berkeley: University of California Press.

Rey, G. (1981). Introduction: What are mental images? In N. Block (Ed.), *Readings in philosophy of psychology* (vol. 2, pp. 117-127). London: Methuen.

Richardson, A. (1969). *Mental imagery.* New York: Springer.

Ripinsky-Naxon, M. (1993). *The nature of shamanism.* Albany: State University of New York Press.

Robinson-Riegler, G., & Robinson-Riegler, B. (2004). *Cognitive psychology.* Boston: Pearson.

Rock, A.J. (2006). Phenomenological analysis of experimentally induced visual mental imagery associated with shamanic journeying to the lower world. *International Journal of Transpersonal Studies, 25,* 45-55.

Rock, A.J., & Baynes, P.B. (2005). Shamanic journeying imagery, constructivism and the affect bridge technique. *Anthropology of Consciousness, 16*(2), 50-71.

Rock, A. J., & Baynes, P.B. (2007). What are the origins of shamanic journeying imagery? The modification of a hypnoanalytic technique to address an enduring methodological problem. *Humanistic Psychologist, 35*(4), 349-361.

Rock, A.J., Casey, P.J., & Baynes, P.B. (2006). Experimental study of ostensibly shamanic journeying imagery in naïve participants II: Phenomenological mapping and modified affect bridge. *Anthropology of Consciousness, 17*(1), 65-83.

Rock, A.J., & Krippner, S. (2007a). Does the concept of 'altered states of consciousness' rest on a mistake? *International Journal of Transpersonal Studies, 26,* 33-40.

Rock, A.J., & Krippner, S. (2007b). Shamanism and the confusion of consciousness with phenomenological content. *North American Journal of Psychology, 9*(3), 485-500.

Rock, A. J., & Krippner, S. (2008). Proposed criteria for the necessary conditions for shamanic journeying imagery. *Journal of Scientific Exploration, 22*(2), 215-226.

Roe, C.R., & Sherwood, S.J. (2009). Evidence for extrasensory perception in dream content: A review of experimental studies. In S. Krippner & D.J. Ellis (Eds.), *Perchance to dream: The frontiers of dream psychology* (pp. 211-238). New York: Nova.

Rogers, S. L. (1982). *The shaman: His symbols and his healing power.* Springfield, IL: Charles C Thomas.

Rogo, D. S. (1987). Shamanism, ESP, and the paranormal. In S. Nicholson (Ed.), *Shamanism: An expanded view of reality* (pp. 133-144). Wheaton, IL: Theosophical Publishing.

Rose, R. (1956). *Living magic.* New York: Rand McNally.

Rosenberg, D. (2000). *The philosophy of science: A contemporary introduction.* London: Routledge.

Roszak, T. (1992). *The voice of the earth.* New York: Simon & Schuster.

Rothberg, D. (1990). Contemporary epistemology and the study of mysticism. In R. Forman (Ed.), *The problem of pure consciousness* (pp. 163-210). Oxford, UK: Oxford University Press.

Rothenberg, J. (1981). Preface. In A. Estrada (Ed.), *María Sabina: Her life and chants* (pp. 13-20). Santa Barbara, CA: Ross-Erikson.

Ruhlen, M. (1994). *The origin of language: Tracing the evolution of the mother tongue.* New York: John Wiley & Sons.

Ryan, R. (2002). *Shamanism and the psychology of C. J. Jung.* New York: Vega Books.

Rychlak, J.F. (1997). *In defense of human consciousness.* Washington, DC: American Psychological Association.

Saklani, A. (1988). Preliminary tests for psi - ability in shamans of Garhwal Himalaya. *Journal of the Society for Psychical Research, 55*, 60-70.

Sandner, D.F. (1979). *Navajo symbols of healing.* New York: Harcourt Brace Jovanovich.

Sandner, D.F. (1997). Introduction: Analytical psychology and shamanism. In D.F. Sandner & S.H. Wong (Eds.), *The sacred heritage: The influence of shamanism on analytical psychology* (pp. 3-11). New York: Routledge.

Sansonese, J.N. (1994). *The body of myth: Mythology, shamanic trance, and the sacred geography of the body*. Rochester, VT: Inner Traditions International.

Sartre, J-P. (1958). *Being and nothingness: An essay on phenomenological ontology*. New York: Philosophical Library.

Savary, L.M. (1990). Dreams for personal and spiritual growth. In S. Krippner (Ed.), *Dreamtime and dreamwork: Decoding the language of the night* (pp. 6-12). Los Angeles: Tarcher/Putnam.

Schwartz, S. (2009, Spring). The mist wolf. *Parabola,* pp. 6-11.

Shanon, B. (2002). *The antipodes of the mind: Charting the phenomenology of the ayahuasca experience.* Oxford, UK: Oxford University Press.

Shanon, B. (2010). The epistemics of ayahuasca visions. *Phenomenological Cognitive Science, 9,* 263-280.

Shaw, C. (1995, July/August). A theft of the spirit. *New Age Journal,* pp.84-89, 92.

Sherman, H. (1967). *"Wonder" healers of the Philippines.* Los Angeles: DeVoss.

Shirokogoroff, S. (1935). *Psychomental complex of the Tungus.* London: Kegan Paul.

Shweder, R. (1972). Aspects of cognition in Zinacanteco shamans: Experimental results. In W. Lessa & E.Z. Vogt (Eds.), *Reader in comparative religion: An anthropological approach* (3rd ed., pp. 407-412). New York: Harper & Row.

Shweder, R.A. (1979). Aspects of cognition in Zinacanteco shamans: Experimental results. In W.A. Lessa & E.Z. Vogt (Eds.), *Reader in comparative religion: An anthropological approach* (4th ed., pp. 327-331). New York: Harper & Row.

Shweder, R.A. (1990). Cultural psychology: What is it? In J.W. Stigler, R.A. Shweder, & G. Herdt (Eds.), *Cultural psychology: Comparative essays on human development* (pp. 1-43). New York: Cambridge University Press.

Shweder, R.A., & Bourne, E.J. (1986). Does the concept of the person vary cross-culturally? In R.A. Shweder & R.A. Le Vine (Eds.), *Culture theory:*

Essays on mind, self, and emotion (pp. 158-199). Cambridge, England: Cambridge University Press.

Siegel, J.M. (1997). Monotremes and the evolution of REM sleep. *Sleep Research Society Bulletin, 4*, 31-32.

Siegler, M., & Osmond, H. (1974). *Models of madness, models of medicine.* New York: Macmillan.

Silby, B. (1998). On a distinction between access and phenomenal consciousness. Retrieved January 11, 2006, from http://www.deflogic.com/articles/silby011.html

Silverman, J. (1967). Shamans and acute schizophrenia. *American Anthropologist, 69,* 21-31.

Solso, R. (2001). *Cognitive psychology* (5th ed.). Boston: Allyn and Bacon.

Some, M.P. (1994). *Of water and the spirit: Ritual, magic, and initiation in the life of an African shaman.* New York: Tarcher/Putnam.

Spier, L. (1970). *Yuman tribes of the Gila River.* New York: Cooper Square Publishers.

Spindler, G., & Spindler, L. (1971). *Dreamers without power: The Menomini Indians.* New York: Holt, Rinehart and Winston.

Sprafkin, R.P. (1994). Social skills training. In R.J. Corsini (Ed.), *Encyclopedia of psychology* (2nd ed., pp. 442-444). New York: Wiley-Interscience.

Stein, M. (Ed.).(1942). *Jungian analysis.* LaSalle, IL: Open Court.

Sternberg, R. (2003). *Cognitive psychology* (3rd ed.). South Melbourne, Australia: Thomson Wadsworth.

Stevens, A. (1982). *Archetypes.* New York: William Morrow.

Stoeber, M. (1991). Constructivist epistemologies of mysticism: A critique and a revision. *Religious Studies, 28,* 107-116.

Storm, L., & Rock, A. (2011). *Shamanism and psi: Imagery cultivation as an alternative to the Ganzfeld protocol.* Gladesville, Australia: Australian Institute of Parapsychological Research.

Strassman, R.J. (2001). *DMT: The spirit molecule.* Rochester, VT: Park Street Press.

Stringer, C., & McKie, R. (1996). *African exodus: The origins of modern humanity.* New York: Henry Holt.

Sullivan, L.E. (2004). Foreword. In M.N. Walter & E.J.N. Fridman (Eds.), *Shamanism: An encyclopedia of world beliefs, practices, and culture* (Vol. 1; pp. ix-x). Santa Barbara, CA: ABC-CLIO.

Swami, S., & Yeats, W. (1970). *The ten principal Upanishads.* London: Faber.

Tart, C.T. (1969). Introduction. In C.T. Tart (Ed.), *Altered states of consciousness* (pp. 1-7). New York: Wiley.

Tart, C.T. (1975). *States of consciousness.* New York: Dutton.

Tart, C.T. (1987). On the scientific study of other worlds. In D. Weiner and R. Nelson (Eds.), *Research in parapsychology* (pp. 145-146). Metuchen, NJ: Scarecrow Press.

Tattersall, I. (1998). *Becoming human: Evolution and human uniqueness.* New York: Harcourt Brace.

Taubold, S. (2003). The system of healing used by the Filipino *Espiritistas*: An archival study. Unpublished doctoral dissertation, Saybrook Graduate School, San Francisco, CA.

Taussig, M. (1987). *Shamanism, colonialism, and the wild man: A study in terror and healing.* Chicago: University of Chicago Press.

Taussig, M. (1989). The nervous system: Homesickness and Dada. *Stanford Humanities Review, 1,* 44-81.

Taylor, E., & Piedilato, J. (2002). Shamanism and the American psychotherapeutic counter-culture. *Journal of Ritual Studies, 16,* 129-139.

Taylor, J.G. (2002). Paying attention to consciousness. *Trends in Cognitive Science, 6,* 206-210.

Tedlock, B. (1987). Zuni and Quiche' dream sharing and interpreting. In B. Tedlock (Ed.), *Dreaming: Anthropological and psychological interpretations* (pp. 105-131). New York: Cambridge University Press.

Tedlock, B. (1991). The new anthropology of dreaming. *Dreaming, 1,* 161-174.

Tedlock, B. (1992). *The beautiful and the dangerous: Encounters with Zuni Indians.* New York: Viking.

Thevet, A. (2001). Ministers of the devil who learn about the secrets of nature. In J. Narby & F. Huxley (Eds.), *Shamans through time: 500 years on the path of knowledge* (pp. 13-16). New York: Tarcher/Putnam. (Original work published 1557)

Torrey, E. F. (1986). *Witch doctors and psychiatrists*. San Francisco: Harper & Row.

Townsend, J.B. (2001). Modern non-traditional and invented shamanism. In J. Pentikainen (Ed.), *Shamanhood: Symbolism and epic* (pp. 257-264). Budapest: Akademiai Kiado.

Townsley, G. (2001). "Twisted language," a technique for knowing. In J. Narby & F. Huxley (Eds.), *Shamans through time: 500 years on the path of knowledge* (pp. 263-271). New York: Tarcher/Putnam. (Original work published 1993)

Traditional Medical Practitioners: Pros and Cons. (1980, May 3). *The Lancet, 315*(8175), 963-964. DOI: 10.1016/S0140-6736(80)91410-5

Triandis, H.C. (1980). Introduction. In H.C. Triandis & W.W. Lambert (Eds.), *Handbook of cross-cultural psychology* (Vol.1, pp. 1-14). Boston: Allyn & Bacon.

Turner, E. (1992). The reality of spirits. *ReVision, 15*(1), 28-32.

Turner, V. (1968). *The drums of affliction: A study of religious processes among the Ndembu of Zambia*. Oxford, UK: Clarendon.

Ulin, R.C. (1984). *Understanding cultures: Perspectives in anthropology and social theory*. Austin: University of Texas Press.

Ullman, M. (1960). The social roots of the dream. *American Journal of Psychoanalysis, 20*, 180-196.

Ullman, M. (1987). Dreams and society. In M. Ullman & C. Limmer (Eds.), *The variety of dream experience* (pp. 279-294). New York: Continuum.

Ullman, M. (1999). Dreams and society. In M. Ullman & C. Limmer (Eds.), *The varieties of dream experience* (2nd ed., pp. 255-274). Albany: State University of New York Press.

Ullman, M., & Zimmerman, N. (1979). *Working with dreams*. Los Angeles: Tarcher.

Vajnstejn, S.I. (1968). The Tuvan (Soyot) shaman's drum and the ceremony of its 'enlivening.' In V. Dioszegi (Ed.), *Popular beliefs and folklore tradition in Siberia* (pp. 331-338). Bloomington: Indiana University Press.

Valsiner, J. (1995). Editorial introduction. *Culture and Psychology, 1,* 163-165.

Vanaria, T. (1997, March). Creation theory. *Ambassador,* pp. 20-25, 40.

Van de Castle, R.L. (1974). Anthropology and psychic research. In J. White & E.D. Mitchell (Eds.), *Psychic exploration: A challenge for science* (pp. 269-287). New York: G.P. Putnam's Sons.

Van de Castle, R.L. (1977). Parapsychology and anthropology. In B.B. Wolman (Ed.), *Handbook of parapsychology* (pp. 667-686). New York: Van Nostrand Reinhold.

Vandervert, L.R. (1996). From idiot-savants to Albert Einstein: A brain-algorithmic explanation of savant and everyday performance. *New Ideas in Psychology, 14,* 81-92.

Vandervert, L.R. (1997). The evolution of Mandler's conceptual primitives (image-schemas) as neural mechanisms for space-time simulation structures. *New Ideas in Psychology, 15,* 105-123.

Van Ommeren, M., Komproe, I., Cardeña, E., Thapa, S.B., Prasain, D., de Jong, J.T.V.M., et al. (2002, April). *Psychological profile of Bhutanese shamans.* Paper presented at the annual conference of the Society for the Anthropology of Consciousness, Tucson, AZ.

Vasu, R. (1979). *The vedanta sutras of Badarayana with the commentary of Baladeva* (2nd ed.). New Delhi, India: Oriental Books Reprint Corporation.

Vaux, A. (1988). *Social support: Theory, research, and intervention.* New York: Praeger.

Vitebsky, P. (2001). *Shamanism.* Norman: University of Oklahoma Press.

Wade, J. (1996). *Changes of mind: A holonomic theory of the evolution of consciousness.* Albany: State University of New York Press.

Waldman, C. (1998). *Encyclopedia of Native American tribes.* New York: Checkmark.

Wallace, A.F.C. (1958). Dreams and the wishes of the soul: A type of psychoanalytic theory among the seventeenth century Iroquois. *American Anthropologist, 60,* 234 - 248.

Walsh, R. (1989a). What is a shaman? Definition, origin and distribution. *Journal of Transpersonal Psychology, 21,* 1-11.

Walsh, R. (1989b). The shamanic journey: Experiences, origins, and analogues. *Revision, 12*, 25-32.

Walsh, R. (1990a). *The spirit of shamanism*. New York: Tarcher/Putnam.

Walsh, R. (1990b). Shamanic cosmology: A psychological examination of the shaman's worldview. *ReVision, 13*(2), 86-100.

Walsh, R. (1993a). Mapping and comparing states. In R. Walsh and F. Vaughan (Eds.), *Paths beyond ego: The transpersonal vision* (pp. 38-46). New York: Penguin Putnam.

Walsh, R. (1993b). Phenomenological mapping and comparisons of shamanic, Buddhist, yogic, and schizophrenic experiences. *Journal of the American Academy of Religion, 61*, 739-769.

Walsh, R. (1994). The making of a shaman: Calling, training, and culmination. *Journal of Humanistic Psychology, 34*, 7-30.

Walsh, R. (1995). Phenomenological mapping: A method for describing and comparing states of consciousness. *Journal of Transpersonal Psychology, 27*, 25-56.

Walsh, R. (2001). Shamanic experiences: A developmental analysis. *Journal of Humanistic Psychology, 41*(3), 31-52.

Walsh, R. (2007). *The world of shamanism: New views of an ancient tradition*. Woodbury, MA: Llewellyn.

Walter, M.N. (2004). Introduction. In M.N. Walter & E.J.N, Fridman (Eds.), *Shamanism: An encyclopedia of world beliefs, practices, and culture* (Vol. 1, pp. xv-xxviii). Santa Barbara, CA: ABC-CLIO.

Ward, C.A. (1989). Possession and exorcism: Psychopathology and psychotherapy in a magico - religious context. In C.A. Ward (Ed.), *Altered states of consciousness and mental health: A cross-cultural perspective* (pp. 125-137). Los Angeles: Sage.

Warner, R. (1980). Deception and self-deception in shamanism and psychiatry. *International Journal of Social Psychiatry, 26*, 41-52.

Wasson, R.G. (1981). A retrospective essay. In A. Estrada (Ed.), *María Sabina: Her life and chants* (pp. 7-11). Santa Barbara, CA: Ross-Erikson.

Wasson, R.G., Cowan, G., Cowan, F., & Rhodes, W. (1974). *Maria Sabina and her Mazatec mushroom velada*. New York: Harcourt Brace Jovanovich.

Watkins, J.G. (1971). The affect bridge: A hypnoanalytic technique. *The International Journal of Clinical and Experimental Hypnosis, 19*(1), 21-27.

Watson, L. (1985). *Lightning Bird: The story of one man's journey into Africa's past.* New York: Simon and Schuster/Fireside.

Westen, D. (1999). *Psychology: Mind, brain, & culture* (2nd ed.). New York: Wiley.

Whitehead, A.N. (1946). *Science and the modern world* (2nd ed.). London: Cambridge University Press.

Whitley, D.S. (1998). Cognitive neuroscience, shamanism and the rock art of native California. *Anthropology of Consciousness, 9,* 22-37.

Whitley, D.S. (2009). *Cave paintings and the human spirit.* Amherst, NY: Prometheus Books.

Wiercinski, A. (1989). On the origin of shamanism. In M. Hoppal & O.J. von Sadovskzy (Eds.), *Shamanism: Past and present* (pp. 19-23). Los Angeles: International Society for Trans-Oceanic Research.

Wilber, K. (1981). *Up from Eden: A transpersonal view of human evolution.* Garden City, NY: Doubleday.

Wilber, K. (1993). *The spectrum of consciousness* (2nd ed.). Wheaton, IL: Quest.

Wilson, S., & Barber, T.X. (1981). Vivid fantasy and hallucinatory abilities in the life histories of excellent hypnotic subjects ("somnambules"): Preliminary report with female subjects. In E. Klinger (Ed.), *Imagery: Concepts, results, and applications* (pp. 133-149). New York: Plenum Press.

Wilson, S.C., & Barber, T.X. (1983). The fantasy-prone personality: Implications for understanding imagery, hypnosis, and parapsychological phenomena. In A.A. Sheikh (Ed.), *Imagery: Current theory, research, and application* (pp. 340-387). New York: John Wiley & Sons.

Winkelman, M.J. (1982). Magic: A theoretical assessment. *Current Anthropology, 23,* 37-66.

Winkelman, M.J. (1986). Trance states: A theoretical model and cross-cultural analysis. *Ethos, 14*(2), 174-203.

Winkelman, M. (1992). *Shamans, priests, and witches: A cross-cultural study of magico-religious practitioners.* Tempe: Anthropological Research Papers, Arizona State University.

Winkelman, M. (1993). The evolution of consciousness. *Anthropology of Consciousness, 4*(3), 3-9.

Winkelman, M. (1997). Altered states of consciousness and religious behaviour. In S. Glazier (Ed.), *Anthropology of religion: A handbook of method and theory* (pp. 393-428). Westport, CT: Greenwood.

Winkelman, M. (2000). *Shamanism: A neural ecology of consciousness and healing.* London: Bergin and Garvey.

Winkelman, M. (2004). Cross-cultural perspectives in shamanism. In M.N. Walter & E.J.N. Fridman (Eds.), *Shamanism: An encyclopedia of world beliefs, practices, and culture* (Vol. 1, pp. 61-70). Santa Barbara, CA: ABC-CLIO.

Winkelman, M. (2010). *Shamanism* (2nd ed.). Santa Barbara, CA: Praeger.

Winkler, M., & Krippner, S. (1994). Persuasion. In V.S. Ramachandran (Ed.), *Encyclopedia of human behaviour* (pp. 481-488). San Diego, CA: Academic Press.

Wiseman, R., & Morris, R.L. (1995). *Guidelines for testing psychic claimants.* Amherst, NY: Prometheus Books.

Wittgenstein, L. (1958). *Philosophical investigations* (3rd ed.). Oxford, UK: Basil Blackwell.

Woodhouse, M. (1990). On the possibility of pure consciousness. In R. Forman (Ed.), *The problem of pure consciousness* (pp. 254-268). Oxford, UK: Oxford University Press.

World Health Organisation. (1992). *The international statistical classification of diseases and related health problemss.* Geneva: Author.

Worrall, J. (1996). Structural realism: The best of both worlds. In D. Papineau (Ed.), *The philosophy of science* (pp. 139-165). Oxford, UK: Oxford University Press.

Znamenski, A.A. (2007). *The beauty of the primitive.* New York: Oxford University Press

Zung, O. (1985). *Reliving the past: The worlds of social history.* Chapel Hill: University of North Carolina Press.

Zusne, L. (1989). Altered states of consciousness, magical thinking and psychopathology: The case of Ludwig Staudenmaier. In C.A. Ward (Ed.), *Altered states of consciousness and mental health: A cross-cultural perspective* (pp. 233-250). Los Angeles: Sage.

Index of Names

Achterberg, Jeanne 91
Alvear, Juan 103
Antonio, Don 11
Aristotle 35, 119

Baars, BJ 59
Baba, Solomon 186, 187
Baladeva 82
Balzer, Mandelstam 15-16
Basilov, V 18
Benedict, Ruth 122-3
Benjafield, J 79, 80
Berman, M 23, 54, 60, 62-3, 64, 203, 206-7
Biet, Father Antoine 10
Blackburn, S 167-8
Blackfoot Indians 124
Block, N, on consciousness 78-9, 80, 86, 87
Bockman, L and A Hultkrantz 200-1
Bogoras, V 185-6, 187
Boshier, A 184, 186-7, 193
Bourguignon, E 9, 54, 117, 123
Boyer, LB 19, 25
Brown, DP and J Engler 25
Brown, MF 28-9
Bruchac, J 123

Candomblé (Brazilian folk healer) 96
Carpenter, B and S Krippner 181
Chadwick, Nora 21
Chalmers, D 73-4, 151
Chapple, C 79n
Chari, CTK 187
Clottes, J and D Lewis-Williams 62, 64
Coan, RW 26, 68, 70
Combs, A and S Krippner 165
Corballis, MC 58

Costello, Miss 186, 187

D'Andrade, RG 119, 123
De Mause, L 15
de Rios, Dobkin 55, 56
Degarrod, LN 119, 128, 132, 134
Dennett, D 92
Devereux, George 14-15
Devi, Yashoda 188-9
Diderot, Denis 12
Donald, M 57
Dow, J 11, 31
Dowson, TA 206
DuBois, TA 142, 200, 203, 209
Durkheim, E 56-7, 59

Eckhart, Meister 79n
Einstein, Albert ix
Eliade, Mircea x, 20-1, 22, 24-5, 26, 49, 60,
    68, 156, 158, 160, 196, 200, 203, 204
Ellwood, R 156
Erdoes, R 183

Fabrega, H and DB Silver 19
Farthing, GW 145-6
Fernández de Ovieda, Gonzalo 10
Flaherty, G 12
Forman, R 78, 79n
Frank, JD and JB Frank 20, 111
Frank, Jerome D 91
Freud, Sigmund 115-17, 122, 135

Gergen, K 27
Giesler, PV 188, 189
Gimello, R 173, 174
Globus, G 63

Gmelin, Johann 12-13
Griffiths, P 79n
Gross, PR and N Levitt 29-30

Halifax, J 181
Hallowell, AI 183
Hamayon, RN 28
Hansen, George 14, 27, 28, 29, 110
Harner, Michael 11, 141, 145, 156, 165, 201, 206, 207, 208
Harner, S and W Tryon 21
Heinze, RI x-xi, 21
Herodotus 203
Hick, J 174
Hobson, JA 67, 114
Houran, J, R Lange and M Crist-Houran 141
Hubbard, TL xi, 30, 33, 204, 205-6, 207
Hughes 61
Husserl 79
Hyman, R 185

Irwin, L 137-8, 193

James, W 151
Jensen, AE 192
Jerison, H 58
Jung, Carl 46, 72, 115-17, 135

Kalweit, H 157
Kant, Immanuel 82, 156, 173, 174
Kardec, Allen 101, 103, 104-5, 110
Katz, ST 174
Kehoe, A 200
Kelly, EF and RG Locke 192-3
Kilbourne, B 114
Klein, DB 151
Kleinman, A 36-7, 38-9
Klopfer, B and LBBoyer 25
Kramer, M 7, 42-3, 113
Krasheninnikov, Stepan 13
Krippner, Stanley 43, 50, 60, 71, 88, 92-3, 95ff, 114-15, 120, 121, 124ff, 128, 134, 137, 201, 202
   and Combs 114-5, 165
   and Friedman 212
   and Meacham 88n
   and María Sabina 43, 50
   and Rolling Thunder 71
   and April Thompson 114-15, 121, 124, 125-6, 127

Lafitau, Father Joseph SJ 12
Langdon, Jean 30-1

Laubscher, B 186, 187
Lauden, L 167
Lee, RLM 118
Leon, CA 39
Ler, Rohanna 181-2
Lerche, P 45
Lewis, I 200
Lewis-Fernandez, R and N Kleinman 37-8
Lewis-Williams, DJ 62
Lincoln, JS 136
Lubinski, D and T Thompson 66
Ludwig, AM 62

Maxfield, M 21
McClenon, J 34-5, 47
Mercante, MS 145-6
Merkur, D 66
Metzner, R 39
Mithen, S 59, 62, 65
Moss, R 125
Murphy, JM 182, 192

Narby, J 71, 213-14
Narby, J and F Huxley ix
Natsoulas, T 80
Ndaleni (witchdoctor) 186-7
Negro, PJ, P Palladino-Negro, and MR Louza 35
Neher, A 21
Nesse, RN and KC Berridge 56
Newton, N 57, 59
Nielsen T and J Lara-Carrasco 118
Noel, DC 165
Noll, R 19, 83-4, 165
Nowak, B and RK Dentan 120

O'Brien, G and J Opie 86
Opler, ME 36

Pekala, RJ 82, 87n, 151
Persinger, Michael 33
Peters, LG and D Price-Williams 22, 83, 165
Peters, L 84, 141, 156
Petrovitch, Avvakum 10-11
Pinker, S 47
Popper, Karl 167

Reber, AS and E Reber 86
Reichbart, R 191, 192
Reichel-Dolmatoff, G 27
Reichenbach, H 150
Ripinsky-Naxon, M 20, 21, 26
Rock, AJ, PJ Casey and PB Baynes 144, 145

Rock, AJ and Baynes 143, 144
  Rock, AJ 144-5
Rolling Thunder (medicine man and
  shaman) 71, 184, 185
Rose, R 188
Rosenberg, D 148
Roszak, T 39
Rothenberg, J 74

Sabina, María (Doña María) 41, 42, 43-5, 48,
  50, 54-5, 69, 70, 74, 158-9, 177
Saklani, A 188, 189
Sandner, DF 18-19, 136
Sansonese 58, 64, 65
Sartre, Jean-Paul 79, 80
Schopenhauer, Arthur 85-6
Schwartz, S 184, 185
Semyonov, Semyon 159-60
Shanon, B 203-4, 212, 212, 213
Sharanahua Indians (Peru) 119
Sherman, Harold 104
Shirokogoroff 17, 157, 200
Shweder, R 23, 43
Silverman, Julian 15, 83
Somé, Malidoma Patrice 190-1
Spindler, G and L Spindler 138
Sternberg, R 169
Stevenson, Robert Lewis 74n
Strassman, RJ 146-7, 156, 173-4

Tart, CT 88, 150, 166
Tattersall, I 60-1
Taubold, Scott 96
Taussig, M 66
Taylor, John 33
Tedlock, B 124, 134, 136, 140
Thevet, Andre 10

Torrey, E Fuller 20, 35, 91, 209
Townsend, JB 200
Townsley, G 29
Triandis, HC 117
Trilles, Father 183
Turner, V 212-13

Ullman, Montague 114-17, 122, 135, 210-11

Vajnstein, SI 15
Valsiner, J 140
Van de Castle, RL 193
Vandervert, LR 58, 72-3
Vitebsky, P 42

Wade, J 54
Walsh, Roger 4-5, 17, 25, 32, 68, 83, 84-5, 89,
  111, 157, 158, 159, 170, 200, 201, 207, 210
Walter, MN 200, 204
Ward, CA 118
Wasson, R Gordon 44, 50
Watkins, JG 144
Weiant, CW 180-1
Whitehead, AN 150-1
Whitley, DS 16, 55
Wilber, Ken 24-5, 26, 67, 68-9, 70, 82
Wilson S and TX Barber 20
Wing, Pansy Hawk 31
Winkelman, MJ xi, 8-9, 21, 28, 32, 34, 45,
  50-1, 52-3, 54, 61-2, 91, 113, 196-8, 199,
  200, 202, 203, 207, 208, 211
Wiseman R and RL Morris 187
Wittgenstein, Ludwig 149, 150, 151-2

Zimmerman, Nan 115
Znamenski, AA 16, 21

Index of Subjects

abisua (shaman) 8
aborigines, Australian 61, 68, 188
  shamans 170, 188
advocates and counter-advocates 212, 213
'Affect Bridge' 144
  Modified Affect Bridge 144, 145
Africa, Western, shamans 36
Afro-Brazilian 'shamanic cultists' 188
Aguaruna society (Peru) 28-9
Ainu shamanism 68
Akimel O'odham see Pima Indians
Alaskan Eskimos shamanism 68, dreams
  124
albystar (Tuvan shamanic disease) 14, 15
allopathic biomedicine 95-6, 97, 106, 100-1,
  108-10, 209
  allopathic biomedical model 100
  biomedicine 2
  compared to indigenous usage of plants 92
  diagnosis 100
  etiology 100
  function of institution 101
  patients and treatment 100, 101
  and non-Western medicine 35, 209
  role of patients in 101, 111
  prognosis 100-1
  views of espiritistas 108
Altaic shaman 158
Altamira cave 61, 62
altered states of consciousness (ASC) 21, 24,
  42, 53-6, 66, 83, 88, 207
  and dreaming 139
  as heightened awareness 23
  induction of 24
  integrative mode of consciousness 21-2
  shamanism and 21-3, 32, 54, 55-6, 77, 83,
    106, 200-1, 206-7
  see also shamanic states of consciousness
Amazon region, shamanic practices in 71
American Psychiatric Association 18, 37-8
Americas:
  shamanism in xi, 3, 9
  see also Native Americans, individual
    tribes and countries
animals 26, 59, 64, 71, 163
  animal allies 71, 196, 202, 204, 212
  animal spirits 39
  animal totems 48, 55
  behaviour of 41
  cave art 60, 61
  in dreams 119
  power animals 40, 56, 182, 192
  in shamanism x, 25, 61, 157, 170
anthropology:
  and dreams 114, 125, 136, 210
  and folk healers 110
  and misreading subjects 182-3
  and parapsychology 181, 192, 193
  shamanic journeying 153
  and shamanic trickery 14, 97
  and shamanism 4, 40, 97, 124, 135. 138,
    140, 199
anti-realism 166, 171
Apache shamans 19, 25, 36
archetype 46, 72-3, 117, 135, 201, 202, 204
  see also Jung
Arctic, shamanism in 200
aswang (witches, Philippines) 102
Australia
  rock paintings 61
  shamanism in 68, 157-8, 170

telepathic experiments 188
totemism 56
awareness, sense of 49
ayahuasca 29, 38, 71, 89, 145, 163, 203-4, 212,
    213
Aztecs 52

banal (Philippines) 103
barang (practice, Philippines) 103
bear and shamanism 26
Bhutanese shamans 19-20
biomedicine. Western 2, 96, 104, 108, 110
bisa ('vital energy', Philippines) 103
Blackfoot Indians 124
Block, N, on consciousness 78-9, 80, 86, 87
Bomvu Ridge, South Africa 62
boundaries, blurring of 28-9
Brazil, mediumship in 35
    Afro-Brazilian 'shamanic cultists' 188
Brihadaranyaka-Upanishad 82
Buddhism 68, 51, 68, 79n, 84
    Buddhist shamans 31

Candomblé (folk healing, Brazil) 96
Calabria (Italy) 96
call to shamanize 9, 92
Candomblé (Brazilian folk healer) 96
cave art 60-1
'central axis' 156, 157
ceremony 47
Chachapoya ('Cloud People'), Peru 45
chants 8, 54, 55
charlatan model 11-14
Chauvet Cave 62
chiefs 129
Christianity 68, 79n
    and shamans 8, 10-11, 96, 195
    Christian shamans 31, 110
    syncreticism 11, 50, 104
    see also Filipino Christian Spiritism
Christian Spiritualists of the Philippines
    104
Chuckchee, Siberia 185-6
client-practitioner relationship 2
cognitive neuroscience/psychology 32-4
'cognitive-experimental' method 210
Colombia, spirit possession in 39
colonialism and shamanism 16, 24, 111
complementary and alternative medicine
    (CAM) 93-5
conjuring 81ff, 187
consciousness studies 210
consciousness 49, 73-4
    defined 77ff

access-consciousness (a-consciousness)
    78-9
change of consciousness 54
as 'cognisor' of objects 78
consciousness awareness process 81
consciousness and the content of
    consciousness 80
construct 33
as having an object 79
mapping 89
modes of consciousness 113
monitoring consciousness
    (m-consciousness) 79
and phenomenological content 78-80
phenomenal conscience (p-conscience)
    78, 79, 80
self-consciousness (s-consciousness) 79
self-regarding 81-2
    see also altered states of consciousness,
    shamanic states of consciousness
consciousness/content fallacy 2, 75, 77-8,
    81-2, 85, 87-8, 89-90, 206
    see also shamanic states of consciousness
constructivism 168, 173, 174, 175
    see also deconstructionism
core shamanism 206, 208
    see also shamanic states of consciousness
cosmology of shamanic worlds 153, 156
Creek tribe and shamans 51
cross-cultural investigations 91, 92, 117-18,
    209
    archival data methods 123-6
    cross cultural healing 91
    possibilities for cross-cultural
    misinterpretation 118
Crow Indians
    and dreams 124, 136
    and shamans 51
cultural competence 37
cultural myths 37
Cuna Indians (Panama) 8, 68, 193
curanderismo (Mexican-American folk
    healing) 43, 96
curses 105

Dagara shamanism 190
Dakota Sioux 124
death and rebirth, symbolic 15, 30, 157, 162,
    170, 212
Decadent and Crude Technology Model
    24-6
deconstructionism 40, 63, 69
    deconstructionist model 1, 27-31
deer and shamanism 26

delusion and shamanism 199
demonic model of shamans 10-11
devil 10, 11-12, 24
    Western perceptions of shamanism and
        the devil 10, 11
*Diagnostic and Statistical Manual of Mental
    Disorders* (APA) 18, 19, 37
Diegueno and shamans 55
dimethyltryptamine-induced experiences
    146, 156, 173-4, 203
Diné 198
directionality and shamanism 55
'distance healing', and 'distant surgery'
    106, 108
diviners 9, 52, 53, 129, 197, 198
    as conduits for spirits 9
    divination 45, 54
dreams 2-3, 66-7, 113ff, 185, 202, 211
    analysis of functions of dreams 118-19
    anomalous dreams 117, 120-1, 128, 132,
        212
    comparing dream systems 114ff
    cross cultural work on 117
    as cultural texts 138
    directed daydreaming 84
    discussing dreams 129
    Dream Circles 122
    dream cultures 117, 127-8, 137, 139
    dream living 125
    dream meanings 55, 127, 202
    dreams and non-western culture 30,
        119ff, 210
    dream language 119-20
    dream societies 127, 137
    European dreamers 113
    function of the dream 67, 115-17, 118-19,
        125, 126-8
    interpretation of dreams 9, 38, 55, 85, 91,
        128, 130, 135
    levels of analysis 128ff
    linkage with waking life 114, 119, 125,
        139, 189, 192
    lucid dreams 55, 84, 88-9, 119, 136
    measuring dreams 113
    Native American 113-14, 121, 122-3, 124
        126ff, 135, 136, 137, 139
    non Western dream models 138
    plasticity of dreams 137
    Revised 10-Facet Ullman-Zimmerman
        Model 3, 115-17, 126-8, 128, 140
    Shakespeare's view 114
    shamanic dreams 3, 8, 30, 42, 55, 84,
        113ff, 140, 163, 172, 179, 189, 199, 207
    sources of dreams 119

    and spirit world 104, 126, 129
    synthesis of dream systems 126-8
    types of dreams 136
    use of dreams in shamanic and Western
        systems compared 114ff, 121, 125, 136,
        210
    uses of dreams 118-19
    visionary 117, 120-1, 122, 123, 130, 132-4,
        136, 139
    Western interpretations 115-7, 119, 120,
        121, 125, 134, 135, 137, 138-9, 140
    see also dreamwork, Freud, Mapuche,
        postmodernism, shaman,
        Ullman-Zimmerman model
Dream Network (journal) 210
dreamers 66, 126, 129
    tribal dreamers 129
    official dreamers 129
Dreaming (journal) 211
dreamwork 114, 115-17, 119-20, 121, 123,
    124, 125, 127, 131, 140, 210
    'grassroots dreamwork movement'
        210-11
    models of dreamwork 135-6
    role of dreamworkers 127, 135
    see also shamans

Ecological Psychology/ecopsychology
    39-40
ecological unconscious 39
ecstasy, shamans and x, 20-1, 22, 83, 123
    and narcotics 25, 66
ecstatic journeying x, 21, 22
Eliade, Mircea x, 20-1, 22, 24-5, 26, 49, 60,
    68, 158, 196, 200, 203
    and 'central axis' 156
    methodology 204
    and 'ritual death and resurrection' 160
emic and etic models of accounts 135
enkantos (malevolent spirits, Philippines)
    103, 104
Enlightenment, Western, and shamanism
    11-13
entities 156, 168, 171, 191, 203, 209, 212
    as archetypes 201
    and consciousness 78, 79, 86
    discarnate x, 102, 200
    and dualism 104
    exosomatic 172, 173-4, 175-6
    and reification 150-1, 156, 167, 174
    shamanic interacting with spirit entities
        8, 9, 11, 30, 43, 53, 74, 146, 152, 172,
        173-4, 175-6, 197, 200, 212
    spirit 1, 30, 43, 53, 74, 102, 192, 197, 200,

209, 212
malevolent 9, 89, 152, 165
epistemology 3, 29, Chapter 2, 94, 103,
    Chapter 6, 150, 152, 168, 175, 176, 207
    postmodernist 63
    shamanic 1, 2, 63-7, 142, 149, 152, 214
Eskimo shamanism: 157
    Alaskan 68, 124
    Labrador 158, 170
    St Lawrence Island 182, 192
espiritistas (Philippines) 101, 102, 104, 106ff
    and Christianity 106-7, 110
    as serving the population 107
    domain of 107ff
    accessibility 106
    theories 104-5
    see also barang, Christian Spiritists of the
        Philippines, Philippine Healers' Circle
        Inc, Union of Espiritistas of the
        Philippines
ethics, shamanic 11, 68
ethnographic negative interpretations of
    shamanism 10-17, 25, 26, 28
ethnomycology 44
etteten yald'ar (shamanic sickness) 15-16
exosomatic entities 174-5, 176

faith healers 105, 111
    see also shamanic healers
fallacy of misplaced concreteness 151
fallacy of reification 150-2
fantasy-prone personalities 20, 46-7, 54
Filipino Christian Spiritism 101ff
    and allopathic biomedical system 103,
        108-10
    attributions of success in 105
    benefits and barriers 108ff
    concepts and theories 103-5, 108
    extent 108
    goals of spiritism 104-5
    goals 103, 105
    influences on 104, 110
    measure of success 102-3,105
    methods used 106-7
    responsibilities of participants 107-8
    social organization in 105-6
    spiritism 103
    and trickery 105, 106, 110-11
    views of suffering and death 105, 109
    see also magnetic healing, psychic surgery,
        Roman Catholicism
Filipino Espiritista system 96
folk healing and medicine 96, 110
    and Western medicine 110

Foundation for Shamanic Studies, The 208
fraud, possibilities for 180, 192, 199
Freud, Sigmund 122
    and dreams 115-17, 135
    Freudianism 3, 125, 135, 210

Garhwal, India 188
gayuma (witchcraft, Philippines) 102, 103
Gestalt approach 210
'global workspace' 59
God 11, 79n, 103, 105, 107, 109
Great Spirit 68, 100, 158
Guarani Indians (Brazil) 122

Halifax, J 181
hallucinogens and shamanic techniques 26
hand tremblers (Navajo) 54
hataalii (Navajo) 19, 54
healers 52, 197-8
    see also shamanic healers
healing systems, comparison of 2
'healing the planet' 39
herbs, sacred 70
hermeneutics 138, 204
hexes 52, 53, 105, 198
Hiaux cave 61
higher states of consciousness 24, 25, 26,
    67-71
Higher Superstition: The Academic Left and Its
    Quarrels with Science 30
Hinduism 68
hoasca 203
Holy Spirit 102, 103, 105, 106, 107, 110
Homo sapiens and other species of human
    1-2, 34, 47, 48-9, 59, 65-6, 202
Hopi 124, 135
    shamans 38
Hubbard, TL xi, 30, 33, 204, 205-6, 207
human development 59-60, 67-8
    behaviour 12
Hurons 12, 122

Ibo tribe, west Africa 51
'images of achievement' 58
image-schemas 72-3, 74
inaduledi shaman 8
incorporation of spirits, by shamans   x
individuals and shamans 28-9, 37
initiation, shamanic see under shamans
inner heat ix, 48, 59
Inquisition 12
International Association for the Study of
    Dreams 210, 211

*International Statistical Classification of
Diseases and Related Health Problems* 38
Iroquois 12, 122, 135, 139
    dreamwork 125

Japanese Buddhists 51
Jesuits 55, 122
Jivaro people, South America 51
Journal of Shamanic Practice, The 209
journeying imagery, shamanic *see under*
    shamanic journeys
Jung, Carl 46, 72, 115-17, 135
    and dreams 115-17, 135
    Jungian interpretations 3, 46, 125, 135, 210
    see also archetypes

kaivalyam 79n
kalusugan ('good health', Philippines) 103
Kazakhs 52
Kehoe, A 200
Kimen tribe and shaman 51
knowledge, obtaining of 49
Krippner, Stanley 43, 50, 60, 71, 95, 128,
    201, 202
    and Combs 114-5, 165
    comparison of healing systems 95ff
    and consciousness 88
    dreamworking and systems 114-15, 124ff.
        134
    and Friedman 212
    Lascaux cave 60
    and Mapuche shaman 128
    and Meacham 88n
    and María Sabina 43, 50
    and Native American and their dreams 134
    NIH model 95-6
    and postmodernism 50
    and Rolling Thunder 71
    Siegler-Osmond model 92-3, 95
    on spirituality 202
    and April Thompson 114-15, 121, 124,
        125-6, 127
    on dreams 124ff, 137
    and Ullman-Zimmerman model 115, 120,
        121, 128
    10-faceted Ullman-Zimmermand Model
        115, 126-8, 129
    see also shamans
!Kung people, Africa, and shamanism 46,
    197
Kurd Dervish priests 51
Kwakiutl Indians 124, 135

Lakota tribe 31, 198

Land of the Dead 170
landscape of shamanic journeying 154, 155
language 56-7, 58, 59
    and shamans 74
    and symbolic images 59, 72
Lascaux caves 60-1, 62
legerdemain 192
Les Trois Frères 64
likas and *di-kilala*, (natural and un-natural
    ailments, Philippines) 103
'locus of control' 205
lonco (chiefs) 129
lost objects, shamanic location of 129, 180
lower worlds (underworld) x, xi, 1, 4, 53,
    56, 141-2, 156-7, 159, 168, 170, 208
    geography of 157
    journeying to 21, 22, 48, 144-5, 146, 155,
        156, 158, 160-1, 163, 165, 169, 212
    obstacles in 158, 170
    as place of test 158, 170
    see also middle world, upper world
lucid dreams *see under* dreams
Luiseno Indians and shamans 55

machi (shamans) 129
magic 27, 37, 50, 54, 62, 83-4, 100, 191
    shamans as magicians 12, 31, 35, 49, 183,
        192, 197, 202
magico-religious practitioners 8, 34-5, 49,
    50-1, 197, 198, 202
'magnetic healing' 102, 106
Magyar shamans 155, 170
malevolent practitioners 9, 52, 53, 197, 198
Mandan Indians 124, 136
mangkukulam (sorcerers, Philippines) 102
Mapuche Dream System 128-34, 137
    function of 129
    interpretation of dreams 129-31
    Mapuche and dreamers 129
    reanalysis of dreams 132, 133
    role of dreams 132
    role of the dreamworker 131-2
    techniques of analysis used 130-1
    views of anomalous and visionary
        dreams 132ff
'marginalised other' 28, 31
Maricopa Indians 124
masks and costumes 205-6
'materialisations' 106
Mazatec (Mexico) 43-4, 158, 159
    shaman 181
    shamanism 43, 48
    see also María Sabina, velata
meditation 24, 25, 32, 79n, 163, 210

mediums 9, 52, 197, 198
    in Philippines 102, 103, 104-5, 108, 109
memory 41, 58, 145-6, 150, 175, 205
    altered states of consciousness and
        memory 22, 83, 144
    as component of consciousness construct
        33, 78,
    false memory 149, 150, 180, 191
    and learning 72
    shamanic journeying 142, 144, 145, 172,
        174
Menominee Indians 124, 136, 138-9
mental health model of shamans 14-17,
    18-19, 195, 196
mental imagery 17, 58, 72, 145, 169-70
    shamanic aspects of 3, 67, 84-5, 86, 141ff,
        147-9, 151
metaphysical entity, autonomous existence
    of 14
    construction of 168
Mexico, shamanism in 11, 19
middle world (reality) 1, 4, 53, 125, 141,
    156, 169
    barrier with non-ordinary world 61
    see also lower world, upper world
mind altering plants and substances 38, 43,
    54-5, 88, 131, 192, 196
    and boundaries 29, 55
    Eliade's views on 25, 26, 68, 196, 203
    mind altering procedures 8
    as psychointegrators 196
mind, evolving 56, 59, 63-4
mindfulness meditation 25
miraçâo 145
missionaries 11, 12, 24, 183
Models of Madness, Models of Medicine 92
modernity 63
Mohawks 135
Mojave Indians 124, 135, 136, 139
Mongol shamans 170
Moso shamans 170
multi-layered universe 3-4, 141
    see also lower world, middle world, upper
        world
mushrooms, psychotropic 43, 50, 54-5, 159
    psilocybin 43, 44
Muslim shamans 31
mythology 47, 66
    development of myths 65-6
    myth of ecstasy 22
    myth and the human body 58
    mythmaking and human evolution 57-8
    mythological worldviews 49
    myths and dreams 122, 137

Na-hki shamans 170
naïve participants and shamanic journeying
    144-5
National Institute of Health Model (NIH,
    US) 93, 96
Native American 38, 121, 122, 125ff
    attempts to divert dream-predictions 135
    and dreams 113, 122-3, 124, 125, 134-5,
        137-8, 139
    dream societies 137, 139
    dream system 123, 136
    dreaming and Ullman-Zimmerman
        model 121, 126-8, 136
    ritual dances 9, 198
    and shamans 51, 113-14
    spiritual-earthly boundary 125, 134
    vision quest 165
    worldview 33, 38, 140
    see also under individual tribes
Navajo 54, 124, 135, 136, 139
    ceremonies 43
    dreams 139
    dream interpretation 136
    sand paintings 56
    and shamanism 19, 43, 54, 55
Neanderthals 65
nele shaman 8
neo-shamanism xii, 142, 152, 166, 208
nervous system, development of 73
neuro-epistemological framework and
    images of reality 72
neurognostic potentials and structures 45-6,
    47, 57, 61-2, 73, 202
neurophenomenological approach 207
neuropsychology 57
'new mysterians' 57
Niaux cave 61
niempin 129
nightmares 118, 136
non-consensual reality see spirit world
nonphysical worlds (NPWs) 4, 166, 168-9,
    171-7
    multiple shamanic access 175,
    as artefact 172
North American shamanic tradition 9, 33,
    68, 113ff, 170
    vision quest 165
    see also under individual tribes
Northern Iroquois 124, 135, 136, 139
noumenal/phenomenal distinction 156, 174

Office of Alternative Medicine (OAM, US)
    93
Ojibwa 124, 136

Ojibway Indians 55
Ononharoia (midwinter ceremony, Iroquois) 135
ontology 142
orenda 125
Otomi Indians 11
ouiruame shaman 8
out-of-body journeying 21, 22

Pacific Northwest, spirit dances 43
pajé 10
Pangasinan (Philippines) 105-6
panggagaway (sorcery, Philippines) 102, 103
Parapsychological Association 183
parapsychological research and shamans 13-14, 27, 179, 180, 181, 192-3, 194
'participant-observation' method 136
pelon (diviners) 129
perceptual flooding 9
perispirit 104-5
personal mythology 32
Perubian Chachapoya (Cloud People) 43
peuma (dreams, Mapuche) 129, 131, *wesa peuma* 130
peumafe (tribal dreamers, Mapuche) 129
peyote 38
phenomenal field 2, 86, 206
    phenomenal experience 86, 87n, 89-90
    phenomenal properties 82ff, stages of 88-9
    see also shamanic states of consciousness
Phenomenology of Consciousness Inventory 151
Philippines 101ff
    Christianity in 107, 109, 110
    spiritual tradition in 103-4
    see also espiritas, Filipino Christian Spiritism
Philippine Healers' Circle, Inc 104
Philippine Medical Association 109
piayes 10-11
Piltzintecuhtli (the 'Noble Infant') 50
Pima Indians (*Akimel O'odham*) and shamanism 96-100
    anthropological study of 97
    client's behaviour 98
    clients and shamans 99
    etiology 98
    and Europeans 98
    goals of healing 100
    illness and treatment: diagnosis 97
    prognosis 99
    rights and duties of tribespeople 99-100

treatment of illness 98-9
    types of illness 98-9
placebo response 2, 14, 92, 107
Plains Indians 56
plants 50, 57, 59, 71, 72, 92, 157, 170, 188, 207, 213
    see also mind altering substances
Poetry and Prophecy 21
possession of shamans x
post trance memory 83
postmodernism 27, 29-30, 31, 63, 70
    attitudes to language 72, 133
    denunciations of 29
    and dreams 138
    and epistemologies 50, 63
    and non-Western modes of thought 29-30
    and the 'other' 136
    postmodern paradigm 140
    postmodern perspectives 138
    and shamanism 31, 50, 201
    worldviews 50, 201
    see also deconstructionist model
poulli 129
power animal 40, 58, 163, 182, 192, 204, 212
power objects 28, 45, 58, 182
power places 28, 58
prayer 32
priests and priestesses 9, 48, 51, 53, 54, 197
private language argument 3, 143, 149-50, 151, 152
privileged observer 149-50
pseudo-shamans 19
psychic claimants, testing 187, 188, 189
psychic phenomena 179
psychic surgery 102, 103, 105-6, 110, 111
psychointegrators 203
psychokinesis 179, 180, 188
psychological interpretations of shamanism 77ff
    cross-cultural psychology 117-18, 138
    cultural psychology 138, 209
    'pop psychologists' 123
Psychological therapy and shamanism 36-9
psychological therapy/psychotherapy 36-9, 113
Psychomental Complex of the Tungans 17
psychopathology model 118
psychotropic agents and drugs 66-7, 89, 203-4
pudak 158
pure consciousness event (PCE) 33, 79n

Quetzalcoatl 50

Rappahannock shamans 92
Rarimuri Indians (Mexico) 8
realism 171-2, 174, 176
   shamans as realists 3, 4, 165, 166, 168, 176
   and shamanic journeying 165ff
   realist interpretation of shamanism 166,
      167, 168,
   types of realism 167-8
'reductionists' 57
reification 3
   fallacy of 150-2
religion, organised 51, 166, 202
   epistemological investigations into 142-3
   and shamans 25, 31, 68-9, 70, 195, 198
   shamanism as religion 68
   trances 42
   see also Filipino Christian Spiritism,
      magico-religious practitioners, Roman
      Catholicism
religious pluralism 174
religious-related dissociative experiences
   35
   spiritual emergence or emergency 18, 37
research into shamanism 182-3
   into native healing traditions 96-7
Rhetoric 35
ritual ix, x, 8, 23, 38, 41ff, 47, 60, 120, 126,
   127, 208
   cleansing ritual 203
   dances 9, 24, 55-6, 198
   healing ritual 38, 43, 46, 98, 99, 213
   and mythology 41, 51, 75, 139
   ritual behaviour 18, 21, 31, 41, 56-7, 131
   ritual objects 42, 45
   ritualised shamanic performance 2, 8, 9,
      28, 34, 41, 46, 48, 55, 60, 70, 179, 189,
      184, 196, 198, 199, 205, 206, 211, 212
   smoke blowing 56
   ritual magic 83
ritual leaders 129
River People see Pima
role-playing 63-4
Roman Catholicism 8, 43, 55, 133, 159
   in Philippines 101, 104, 107, 110
   see also Filipino Christian Spiritism
Rorschach Inkblot tests and shamans 19, 25
Rouffignac cave 61

sabía 43
Sakha (Yakut), shamanism in 15-16
sakit (illness, Philippines) 103
sala (Philippines) 103
Salteaux Indians, Canada 183
samadhi 79n

sand painting 38, 56, 98
Sansonese 58, 64, 65
saweame (chanter) 8
scenario-building 57
schizophrenia model and shamanism 15,
   18, 19, 83, 84
seers 9, 197, 198
'sexual possession' 129
shaman 129, 139-40, 197
   origin of term ix-x, 7, 10, 58-9, 199
   definition of term 12
   term as a construct 7, 10-11, 12, 58-9, 69
   activities 11, 22, 31-2, 73-4
   accessing information 7, 24
   as active seekers of information 201-2
   animal spirit allies x, 196, 202, 204, 212
   as artists 61, 62
   as biologically derived human
      specialisation 45
   as birdman 196
   capabilities x, 13
   and cave art 61
   capacity to shamanize 9, 92, 202
   and Christianity 10, 31, 68, 96, 195
   see also Filipino Christian Spiritism
      claims 7
   cold reading of clients 185
   and colonial authority 31, 111
   and community service x-xi, 9, 10, 24,
      25-6, 28, 30-1, 35-6, 40, 48-9, 51, 53, 73,
      92, 95, 119, 122, 133, 163, 198, 199, 201,
      206, 208
   as conduits of spirit's power x, 9, 30-1,
      198
   conflict between shamans 11
   cosmology 158, 165, 168
   deconstructionist 27-8, 31
   and dreams 8, 67, 113, 119ff, 127, 128,
      129, 139
   as dreamworker 117, 120, 127, 134, 135,
      136, 139, 140
   emotional states 22-3
   empowering clients 14, 35, 36, 54, 98, 99,
      105ff, 111, 192
   epistemology of 1, 2, 46, 57, 63ff, 71, 74,
      142-3, 144
   ethical system of 11
   and fantasy proneness 20, 23, 46-7, 54
   functions x
   geographical spread of 8, 40
   as healers 35, 36, 38-40, 51-2
   heightened awareness 23
   and 'Higher States' 67
   imaginative capacity 20, 23, 46, 47, 49, 74,

92, 163, 182
incorporation of spirits x, xi, 22, 42, 198
initiation x, 42, 68, 190-1
internal states 23-4
language use 29
limitations on x
as magico-religious practitioners 192,
    198, 202
as mediator between worlds xi, 27, 30-1,
    201
and medical diagnosis 97-8, 192,
methodology 39
neurognostic potentials 45-6, 47, 62
and NPWs 4, 166, 168, 172, 173, 171ff
occurrence x, 197, 198-9
ontological aspects 4, 84, 142, 143, 144,
    145, 146, 147, 148, 151, 152, 156, 166,
    167, 169, 171n, 176, 177
as operating on *limens*/boundaries x, 14,
    27
perception of environment 47
personality structure 42
phenomenal field 2
physical deconstruction 30
and power x, 30-1
predictions 185ff
privileged observer 149-50
as psychologists xii
and psychopathology 84
and psi/psychic phenomena 179ff, 192
as realists 4, 165, 166, 167ff
relationship with society 2, 7, 11, 12, 14,
    25-6, 30-1, 49, 51, 52-364, 198
relationship with clients 14, 22, 35-6, 37,
    96, 97, 98, 102ff, 139, 185, 209
and relationship with the world 24
and religion see under religion
and ritual x, 42, 43
roles 8, 27, 52
and schizophrenia 83
selection and training 3, 9-10, 11, 20, 26,
    84, 162, 181-2, 190-1, 192, 207
skills of 9-10, 31, and sorcerers 28-9, 52
and spirit world 3, 8, 9, 12, 18, 20, 52, 62,
    71, 102, 200
status in society 28
surrendering volition 9
symbolic death and rebirth x, 59, 157,
    160, 162, 170
syncreticism 50
as 'technicians of ecstasy' x, 20-1
trance x, 21, 22, 59
treatment of illness 97-9
as trickster xi, 4, 12-13, 14, 27, 31, 107, 213

types of 8-9, 26
use of imagery xi, 3, 4, 17, 67, 84, 85, 86,
    116, 142ff, 151ff, 160, 161, 202
use of mind-altering substances 8, 25, 26,
    29, 43, 54-5, 68, 131n 192, 196, 203
as visualiser 141
and visions 56, 83
ways of knowing 53
as 'wounded healers' 15, 20, 196
see also altered states of consciousness,
    dreams, higher states of consciousness,
    lower world, mind altering drugs,
    nonphysical worlds, out-of-body
    journeying, María Sabina, shamanic
    journeying, dreams, shamanic states of
    consciousness, soul flight, spirit world,
    upper world, Western views of
    shamanism
shamanism:
  adaptive symbolisms 65
  analysing experience 88
  and boundaries between waking life and
      dream life 189-90, 192
  breaking down of categories 27, 52
  adaptive symbolisms 65
  analysing experience 88
  and boundaries between waking life and
      dream life 189-90, 192
  breaking down of categories 27, 52
  character of 7, 59
  culmination of wisdom 26
  deconstruction 27
  dynamic aspects of 53
  and ecstatic state x, 83
  functions of x-xi, 14
  impact upon human evolution xi, 47-8,
      65-6, 73, 196
  initiation x, 17, 42, 51, 68, 160, 190-1
  initiatory crisis 15, 17, 42
  involuntary/possession x, 9
  and mental illness 14-17, 18, 19, 28, 38,
      195, 199
  as mediated process 175
  and mental imagery 141
  and myths 1-2, 65, 71
  mystery of ix
  as an oral tradition 25-6
  origins of ix-x, 7, 34-5, 60, 196-7
  and psychology 5, 77
  and psychotherapy xii, 1, 20
  as a religion 68-9
  rituals 8, 205, 212
  shamanism as biologically derived
      specialisation 45

shamanic construct 34
shamanic crisis 26, 42
shamanic knowledge 41ff
shamanic modification of attentional
    states 23-4
shamanic mythology 71
shamanic power 30-1
shamanic technologies 1-2, 8, 24-6, 33,
    41ff, 68, 72, 74-5, 111
shamanic ways of knowing 53
and spirit world x, 20, 71, 92
status of 28
symbolism 26
trance 42
universal shamanic characteristics 202
use of term 200
voluntary x, 9
and Western science 30
Western worldview and 12-13, 16, 26
interaction with Western worldview 30
worldviews 33, 34, 50, 71, 205
see also private language argument,
    shamanic journeys, ritual
shaman ancestor 160, 161
Shamanism: Archaic Techniques of Ecstasy
    24-5, 68, 196
shaman complex 9, 53, 197
shamanic cosmology, three 'worlds' of 62,
    74, 84-5, 143, 153, 154, 156, 157, 159, 160,
    163, 168, 169, 183
Shaman's Drum 208
shaman-healers xi, 9, 38, 39-40, 45, 51, 52,
    91, 197-8
'shamanic illness'/initiatory crisis 14-18,
    26, 42
shamanic journeys xi, 3, 4, 39, 84-5, 27, 39,
    64, 131, 142, 143ff, 151, 152, 153ff, 165ff.
    206
    absence of modality 154
    criteria for identifying and mapping
        journeys 153ff
    deductive and inductive models of 147ff
    defining 160-3
    and exosomatic entities 174-5, 176
    and imagery systems 3, 1, 4, 41, 116, 124,
        128, 146, 161, 163, 172
    influences of cultural imagery 143
    integration 212
    issue of realism 165ff, ontology of 166
    journeying imagery 143ff, 162-3, 171ff, 211
    lack of boundary between dream world
        and reality 139, 189-90, 192, 211
    locating lost objects 180
    and memory 146

    as mental image 174
    multidimensional mapping of shamanic
        journeying 84, 141-2
    necessary conditions for integrated
        journeying 153ff
    ontology of shamanism 142, 143, 145, 149
    and psychic phenomena 179ff
    privileged and non- privileged observers
        149-50
    shamanic dream system 113ff
    typology of shamanic journeying 145, 146
    use of imagery 153ff, 158-9
    visual aspects 154ff
    as visualiser 141ff
    see also nonphysical worlds, sleight of
        hand, shamanic journeying, Maria
        Sabina
shamanic medicine 36, 92
shamanic nonphysical worlds 4
shamanic patterns of phenomenal
    properties 2, 142
shamanic practices 33, 142
Shamanism: Archaic Techniques of Ecstasy
    24-5, 68, 196
shamanic patterns of phenomenal
    properties 2, 142
shamanic practices and therapeutic strategy
    142
shamanic states of consciousness (SSCs) 1, 2, 9,
    21, 22, 23-4, 32, 42, 46-7, 53-5, 61-2, 63-4,
    66, 70, 77ff, 87, 171, 206-7
    as heightened awareness 23
    image-schemas of 73
    ayahuasca use 29, 71
    image-schemas of 73
    as pattern of phenomenal properties 77,
        82ff
    and ritual 42, 206
    shamanic allies x, 61, 71, 196, 202, 212
    shamanic dream systems 3, 119
    shamanic journeying image 3, 4
    shamanic objects of consciousness 85
    shamanic society and ritual 21, 41, 46, 55
    stages of shamanic consciousness 64
    theories of SSCs 82ff
    see also altered states of consciousness,
        soul flight, trance
Sharanahua Indians (Peru) 119
Short Spiritist Doctrine, A 103
Shweder 23, 43
si'paaame shaman 8
Siberia, shamanism in ix, xi, 11, 12-13,
    16-17, 18-19, 160-1, 170, 185-6, 200

Siegler-Osmond Model 92-3, 96
  Krippner modification of 93
signal system 1
Sioux and shamanism 183
sleight-of-hand and shamanism 4, 14, 107,
  111, 182, 183, 187, 192, 194, 211
snake, mythic 170
social modelling 35
social psychology and shamanism 34-6
Society for Shamanic Practitioners 208-9
society 37, 53, 56, 92, 93, 94, 101, 205, 209,
  210, 211
  development of 26, 51-2, 53, 68
  faith healers and 110, and magic 191
  and malevolent practitioners 198
  shamans and 14, 16, 26, 27, 28, 30, 51, 54,
    127, 197
Sora practitioner, 42
sorcerers 8, 9, 10, 28, 52, 102, 197
  sorcery 102, 198
soul flight (shamanic trance) 1, 21, 22, 23,
  42, 175, 196, 199
Soul Flight Model 20-4
soul retrieval 38
soul-travel 126
South American shamans 113
  and dreams 134
  native society's world views 121
Soviet views of shamanism 16-17
Spanish inquisition and veladas 43, 48
spells, casting of 51, 52, 53, 198
spirit world/realm 3, 18, 20, 29, 40, 44, 52,
  53, 62, 71, 102, 109, 176, 198, 210, 211
  and dreams 126, 129, 132
  incorporation of x, xi, 9, 11, 22, 42, 52, 89,
    188, 198
  ontological status of spirit worlds 176
  spirit helper and allies 168, 196
  'spiritual injections' 106, 108
  spiritual travel 200
  spirit dances 43
  spirit entity 9
  spirit possession 118
  evil spirits 108
  spirit visitations 138
spiritism see Filipino Christian Spiritism
spiritual development (Philippines) 103
spiritual emergence/emergency 18
spiritual energy 102
spiritual practitioners 202
  categories of 50-3
  access to spiritual entities 50-1
spirituality 202
spirtual possession 118

state of consciousness (SoC) 81, 82, 83, 150
sukuruame (sorcerer) 8
supernatural (Mapuche) 132
symbolic death and rebirth see under
  shamanism
symbolic manipulation and shamanic
  rituals 55-6
  symbolism 60
  symbolic images 212
syncretisation, shamanic 11, 50, 68, 104, 107

Tamang
  cosmology 156-7
  shaman 162, 170
tang-ki (Taiwanese shamanic) healing 39
Taoism 68
'technologies of the sacred' 23-4, 49
  see also shamanic technology
telepathy and related phenomena 121, 179,
  180, 188, 213
Tibetan Buddhism 68
tobacco 10
Tongarsoak (Great Spirit) 158
totenism, Australian 56
Townsend, JB 200
Townsley, G 29
traditions 84
trance state x, 9, 21, 38
  dissociative 37
  and mind-altering substances 25
  predisposition to 64, 124
  shamanic 15, 21, 22, 42, 59, 83, 92, 118,
    189, 200
Transcultural Psychosocial Organization of
  Amsterdam 19-20
transpersonal experience 84
  transpersonal sources 147-9
Triandis, HC 117
trickery, allegations of against shamanism
  4, 12-13, 105, 110, 199
  practices 14, 31, 97, 186, 187, 194
tricksters and shamanism xi, 4, 14, 27,
  111-12, 213
  and Philippine espiritista 107, 110-11
Tukano, South America 64
Tungus reindeer herders (Siberia) ix, 7, 17,
  15
Tuva, shamans in 15

Ullman, Montague 114-17, 122, 210-11
  dreams 115-17, 135
  on cultural roots of dreaming 122
Ullman-Zimmerman model 114-17, 118,
  128, 210

distinguishing function and motive 118
Krippner and 120, 121
Krippner and Thompson on 15ff
underworld see lower world
Union of *Espiritistas* of the Philippines 102,
   104
   canonical body of knowledge 103,
universe, multi-level 3-4, 169
upper worlds x, xi, 1, 3, 40, 53, 56, 141, 156,
   157, 168, 170, 208
   journeying to 21, 22, 48, 162, 169, 212

Vedanta-sutras of Badarayana 82
veladas 42-3, 50, 69-70
ventriloquism 182, 185, 187, 192
visions 8, 22, 56, 124, 128, 202
   dreams 117, 120-1, 122, 123, 130, 132-4,
      136, 139
   and mind-altering plants 25, 55, 203, 204
   shamanic 20, 30, 45, 64, 65, 83-4, 139, 196,
      204
   visionary experiences 212
   vision quests 56, 165, 199
   visionary states, shamanic and other
      83-4, 121-2
   Western and shamanic interpretations of
      visions 165

wabeno (Ojibway) 55
Walsh, Roger 4-5, 17, 25, 32, 68, 111, 157,
   158, 170, 200, 201, 210
   controlled visionary states functioning 83
   mapping states of consciousness 89, 207
   phenomenological research into
      shamanism 84-5
   on use of images 159
waniame shaman 8
'Waters of Death' 158
'web of life' 204-5
West African shamans 36
Western Europe, human development in 60
Western allopathic medicine *see* under
   allopathic biomedicine
Western interpretations of shamanism xi,
   xii, 1, 4, 28, 30, 31-2, 40, 72, 165-6, 195-6,
   199-200, 209, 210, 214
   and anomalous phenomenon 120
   assumptions about the self 42
   and ayahuasca 71
   compared with non-Western cultures 18
   compatibility with shamanism 30
   concepts of consciousness 56, 119-20
   concept of the unconscious 119
   and dreams 115-7, 119, 120, 121, 125, 134,

135, 137,138-9, 140
   emphasis on individual volition 205
   and mental health 15, 18, 20, 38, 91, 92
   models of shamanism 1, 10-31, 72, 199
   modernity and human culture 71-2
   and native people 58-9, 96-7, 124
   negative attitudes towards shamanism
      10ff, 28, 30, 53, 70, 91, 110, 195
   neo-shamanism xii
   and non-western belief systems 29-30, 37,
      38, 42, 92, 126, 134, 135, 137
   psychotherapy 165, 166, 209
   psychodynamic models 139
   and shamanism 4, 7, 31-2, 37, 114-15, 166,
      195ff
   and shamanic healing system 91ff, 111,
      209, 210
   and shamanism as fraud 199-200
   and spiritual emergence 18, 30
   traditions 83-4
   Western dream models 3, 139
   western dreamworking 115, 135
   Western modernity and universal culture
      71-2
   Western psychological perspectives 7
   Western science 30, 70-1
   worldview 40, 165, 205
   see also deconstructionism, dreams,
      dreamworker, espiritista
Winkelman, MJ
   and altered states of consciousness   21,
      199, 203, 207
   and dreams 113
   'modes of consciousness ' 113, 211
   on neo-shamanism 208
   neurophenomenological framework 32,
      34, 61-2, 207
   on psychointegrators 203
   on shamans xi, 28, 32, 34, 45, 51, 62, 198,
      199, 200, 207, 208
   shaman complex 52-3, 54, 91, 113, 196-8,
      202
   study of magico-religious practitioners
      8-9, 21, 34, 50-1, 196-7, 198, 200, 202, 203
witches 9, 10, 52, 102, 197
   witchcraft 102, 104, 109, 198
Wonder Healers of the Philippines 102
World Health Organisation 10
   study of traditional systems of medicine
      95
world hypothesis/personal mythology 32
World Tree/pillar 56, 170
worldviews 28, 32, 110, 119, 139, 201, 209
   and interpretation of problems 37

mythological 49, 50, 57-8, 197
  shamanic 9, 25, 33, 34, 44, 50, 68, 111, 205
  shared 35, 41, 48, 50, 121
  Western 119, 165, 180
'wounded healers', shamans as 15, 20

Xavante Indians (Brazil) 121-2

yagé 203
Yaminahua (Peruvian Amazon), shamans
  29

'Yankush' (shaman) 28-9
Yanomami tribe 198
Yuma Indians 124, 136, 139
Yuwipi ceremony 31

Zambia, healing ritual in 213
Zinacanteco shamans, Mexico 19 23, 46
Zuni Indians 68, 124, 136